Transformational Conversion

by

Wilson Awasu

ISBN: 1-4033-0312-6 (E-book)
ISBN: 1-4033-0313-4 (Paperback)
ISBN: 1-4033-0314-2 (Hardcover)
ISBN: 1-4033-0315-0 (RocketBook)

This book is printed on acid free paper.

1stBooks - rev. 07/09/02

Contents

Illustration

Disciplers

Illustration

1

Ripple transformational conversions

If someone told me one sermon would convert people within 20-mile radius, I would doubt it. But it happened. Who won't be astounded?

I was a teenager. I had organized a 10-day evangelistic outreach to a town in Kedame in Ghana. Ten of us formed the team.

The five churches there had struggled for survival against constant harassment, intimidation and terrorism at the hands of three powerful legendary spiritists. Think of those churches as king Saul and the Israeli soldiers. Then think of the spiritists as Goliath of Gath.

For years the spiritists dared the churches. "Let any of you cross us. And we will finish you one by one as our ancestors did the missionaries whose tombs you whitewash constantly." The ancestors of those spiritists used spiritual means to kill the first missionaries who went there in the early 19th century. And since then, the town had languished in the shadow of spiritism.

I heard the story at an adult's prayer meeting I chanced to attend. The story angered me to pray. As I prayed, my anger turned into a burden. I checked out the facts from Bill Zottey, a colleague of mine who comes from there. He confirmed them. He took me there to see it and feel it for myself. Firsthand experience crushed me.

My initial burden developed into a growing sense of an invitation from God to go preach Jesus Christ there. I was excited. But I was also afraid. I didn't know what to expect, or exactly what to do.

Anyhow, I prayerfully put a team together. I negotiated and had the support of all the churches there. The traditional rulers of the town skeptically approved. What hope was there for a teenager battling centuries of occult domination? Comparatively, there was more hope for David against Goliath. I didn't need to be persuaded about that. I knew it.

Therefore I fasted ten days to prepare myself spiritually for the outreach. I developed laryngitis, and so Bill took our first night open-air meeting. We cancelled the second because it rained all day all night.

Moments before I mounted the open air pulpit the third night, a good-doer alerted me. "The spiritists are here tonight. They came prepared to oppose you. If you cross them, they'll kill you. Therefore be careful what you say. We don't want you to die."

My heart sank. I trembled. I prayed silently. But I felt pulled within to challenge the spiritists as Elijah did the prophets of Baal. What? I reasoned. Elijah was a man of God. And he was a grown up man. I was only a teenager and not a man of God. How could I? What if...?

Lost in mental wanderings, I neither heard the joint choir sing nor the Emcee when he introduced me and invited me to the pulpit. Someone sitting by jolted me, "You're on, preacher!" On, indeed! Who? Me? How?

I staggered to the pulpit still trembling. I panned the audience, gripping the lectern for support lest I dropped to the platform. I prayed. Then I especially welcomed the spiritists to the meeting, letting them know that we knew they were in attendance.

Starting with the tombs of the missionaries, I recounted some marvels that they were reputed for. In a very weak voice, I said, "Everybody knows that you could spiritually deposit needles in people's lungs and watch them suffer and choke helplessly to death. You kill with a curse, a hex, and a spell. I want to give you a feat to perform tonight. I give myself to you. Kill me in ten minutes by any means you choose. If you succeed in killing me, then everybody would know that your powers are supreme. But if you fail, then, let everybody know that the God I preach, he is God."

A deafening silence chilled the place. Ten minutes passed, I was still alive. I gave them five extra minutes. I pushed them hard to react ruthlessly. The extra time also left me alive.

So then, I invited them to take the whole night. "Right now," I said, "I am closing the meeting. Take the whole night and use it to try and kill me. If you succeed then you are indeed the greatest. But if I come back here to preach tomorrow night, then, you and everybody should know that the God I preach, he is God."

We closed.

On our way back to our lodging, some of my teammates faulted me, "You didn't preach a sermon. Why?"

"I thought I did!" I vaguely protested.

"No, you didn't," another one retorted.

I felt I had disappointed them. And perhaps I had let God down as well. O boy! Several thoughts raced through my mind all at once. What if God didn't ask me to do what I just did? Was I prepared to die? My whole life lay ahead of me. What was I thinking, to do what I did, outraging merciless and powerful spiritists?

5

Endless reasoning invaded me temporarily. Half-confused and half-disappointed at myself for letting everybody down, including God, I slept with my shoes, clothes and glasses on.

Four o'clock the next morning, there was a rough knock on my door. This is it, I said to myself half-asleep. The spiritists have come to get me. They would skin me alive. I expected the worst.

Slowly, I turned the knob to open the door while planning how to skip back, jump through the window and away from outraged and bloodthirsty spiritists. However, instead of them, two young men greeted me. They urgently invited me to the spiritists.

"What for?" I asked.

"Quick, quick! Don't ask questions! Come with us at once. You'll know when you meet them," the messengers pressed impatiently.

Quickly I thought. Perhaps the spiritists would kill me mercifully if they saw Bill with me. They knew him. So I invited him to come along.

We met three old men aged 105, 95, and 75, sitting in front of their shrine. "We want to become Christian!" They declared in unison. What? For real? I thought to myself. Then I asked them why? Now get this.

"When you challenged us, we took you on and got to work right away. We shot at you all the hexes, curses, and spells; charms, demons, and spirits, and all we have. But they all crashed in a wall of fire that burned around you. This is the first time in our lives and practice that we met a force we could not overcome. We are convinced it is your God who did that. We want to serve him as you do!" They confessed.

I heaved a sigh of relief. Nobody died in the contest, neither they nor I. On the contrary, three powerful spiritists surrendered to Jesus Christ, not through persuasion but on collusion with him. How gracious! How astounding! But that was the beginning. Amazing ripple effects took over.

Presently, the converted spiritists asked us to burn down their shrine, regalia, centuries of artifacts, medicines, and all. The bonfire reached the sky and blazed the waking town. It attracted the townspeople. They came rushing and asking. "What's going on? What's going on?"

The facts spoke for themselves. They spoke louder and clearer than anybody could. The dreaded shrine burned in leaping flames. Former terrorists of Christianity converted to it. They told their own story more eloquently by their looks. They exuded freedom, peace, and joy visibly. And word about their conversion resounded until every corner of the town heard it. Holy chaos and amazement gripped the town momentarily.

That ended our preaching and began never ending counseling sessions instead. Whole families and individuals who had relied on those men for protection hitherto, divulged secret allegiance. They saw no sense in keeping protective talismans, medicines, charms, etc., whose makers had switched allegiance. They fed them to the raging flames, and surrendered their lives to Jesus Christ.

For the next seven days, people poured in from neighboring towns to verify the conversion of those men. They too surrendered to Christ. On and on it went. From within 20-mile radius, people came. They saw the converted spiritists; they divulged protective charms and medicines they got from them and in turn surrendered their lives to Christ.

The bonfire blazed for seven days straight. The Holy Spirit re-enacted right before us Philip's experience in Samaria (Acts 8:2-13) and Paul's in Ephesus (Acts 19:11-20). He freed many people from the power and influence of the occult in ways that only he could. He gave life to the spiritually dead; hope to the lost; power to the powerless; and freedom to the imprisoned; joy and peace to the troubled and oppressed (cf. Luke 4:18-19).

The Holy Spirit and bold preaching of Jesus freed and retrieved whole communities from the domination of the occult.

Overnight, as it were, churches in 20-mile radius multiplied membership through genuine conversions. Spontaneously converts told their own story and invited others to experience Jesus for themselves. They broke free from deception and defeat in their lives. Churches swarmed, not into marginalized enclaves, but into noticeable living and caring communities of believers in Christ.

Lives transformed totally and self-evidently. Believers sought out people they had wronged and asked forgiveness. For the following weeks and months, pastors and priests across the board— Presbyterian, Methodist, Baptist, Apostolic, Pentecost, Assemblies, Roman Catholics, Seventhday Adventist—reported unprecedented ministerial freedom, and record giving in their churches.

For example, the pastor of the Presbyterian church reported that the collection taken on the day the 105-year old former spiritist was baptized exceeded his church's annual budget. Society never felt closer, freer, and safer, many people admitted.

After the event, I remarked that I planned a ten-day evangelistic crusade. It was too long for the Holy Spirit. He cut it short to three days. I planned it for a town. It was too small for the Holy Spirit. He extended it to 20-mile radius. How absolutely marvelous! Indeed, that was the Lord's doing (Psalm 118:23).

All over the place, group prayer meetings sprang up spontaneously. So did Bible study groups. Witnessing teams formed and took the gospel to towns that hadn't got it.

On one of our follow-up visits, we announced the venue and dates of our next outreach. Those churches came bringing us supplies unsolicited.

Missiological reflections

In hindsight, and with missiological eyes, I can see lots of things I couldn't see at the time. Beginning with the conversion of three spiritists, numerous people genuinely repented. They surrendered self-rule and committed to the rule of God in their personal lives.

Conversion occurred at the core of being. It was spiritual conversion. Therefore it affected people totally. They transformed inside out. Converts instantly personalized the good news. They reproduced themselves spontaneously. Churches became authentic, self-taught, self-supported and self-reproductive.

Unprecedented, denominational barriers disappeared. Roman Catholic, Baptist, Presbyterian, Methodist, Apostolic, Pentecost, etc., churches reached out together as the one Church of Jesus Christ should. Unity in diversity and love characterized the churches. For twenty years, goodwill toward one another, the fear of God, corporate prayer, and love for the word of God lingered visibly and effectively.

According to Romans 1:16, all that is to be expected when the good news is unsheathed appropriately. For it is indeed the power of God for the salvation of everyone who believes. Matthew, Zacchaeus, Nicodemus, Mary Magdalene, Paul, Cornelius, Lydia and numerous others evidenced it in the New Testament (Luke 5:27, Luke 19:1-10, John 3, Mark 16:9, Acts 10, Acts 16).

It didn't matter whether it was

- YHWHists like the three thousand who converted to Christ on the day of Pentecost (Acts 3)
- elitists theologians like Nicodemus and Joseph of Arimathea (John 3 and Luke 23:50-53)
- philosophers and the sophisticated like Dionysius, Damaris and Lydia (Acts 17:16-34, 16:14-15)
- military personnel like Cornelius (Acts 10)
- politicians like the governor of Cyprus (Acts 13:1-12), or

- social outcasts like Mary Magdalene and Zacchaeus (Mark 16:9, John 20:1-18, Luke 19:1-10).

Two facts remained unchanging. One, the good news was good and powerful to convert anybody. Two, the conversions were genuine. They led to self-evident total life transformation. God must expect that of the power of the gospel. The gospel is his total message addressed to the total human situation (John 14:6, Acts 4:12).

And you wonder! Why don't we see that reality often these days? Why is church so boring to many people? Why do Christians find it so hard to love people spontaneously and recklessly as the Bible says they should? Why don't Christians look significantly differently from non-Christians? Why are Christians so susceptible to false gospels— gospels that focus on self-improvement and self-aggrandizement, health and wealth, etc.? Why do so many Christians remain immature and non-productive for so long?

Why does Christianity look so dull, repelling and so self-defensive? We fiercely attack any and every appearance of cults, rather than affirm the truth through transformed lives, and let transformed lives speak for the truth.

Often, we attack cult-looking groups at what they are doing wrong. We compare their wrong beliefs, bad behaviors, seeming unfulfilled lives, not with visible counterparts in our lives. Rather, we pit the wrongness of cults against the surpassing greatness of Christ. In my mind, that is like comparing oranges with apples.

Do our attacks and the focus of their comparisons betray a lack of self-evident total life transformations to show for what we believe? If that is the case, why is that?

My personal observation is this. For many Christians, Christianity is not a personal relationship with Jesus Christ himself. Rather, it is a cultural expediency. This is what we grew up doing. For others, it is piecemeal lifestyle changes we make from time to time. Still for others, it is certain Christian sets of beliefs and values we accept intellectually and follow ritualistically. It is our church's way of worshipping God. And our church's way is all there is to God, no more.

All these bring about changes, no doubt. But these changes are all cosmetic and superficial. But because they look Christian, they blind us to true biblical Christianity. They in fact immunize us to biblical conversion—total life transformational conversion.

Our inability to accept and care for believers who differ from us culturally, racially, tribally, theologically or doctrinally; our fear of going all out for Jesus; our fear of taking God at his word; our fear of the unknown; our desire and insistence on being in control; our lack of spontaneous childlike trust; all these stem from those false starts. The cultural, lifestyle, religious/theological, false starts assume a life of their own debarring us from a vital personal relationship with Jesus himself.

It is not because we don't know enough Scripture; we don't pray enough; we don't go to church regularly; we don't do this or that churchly thing often. The fact is, perhaps, we have not met Jesus himself at the core of our being.

We may have impeccable intellectual view of Jesus. But that is different from a heart's view of Jesus. Intellectual view lacks the power to free people. At best, intellectual view of Christ tries to change us impossibly outward inward. On the contrary, a heart's view of Christ transforms us inside out precisely for this reason. Only a heart level encounter with Jesus opens the eyes of our hearts and causes us to see the glory of God as it is manifested in Jesus Christ (2 Corinthians 4:5-6).

When our hearts see Jesus as God, we convert to him at the core of our being. We fall in love with him. We transform inside out. We will never be the same again. We have seen Jesus with our hearts and converted there. The experience unites us eternally with him. Nothing can undo our union with Christ.

11

This has to be. For if Adam's rebellion and disobedience to God affected all of humanity so totally, Jesus Christ's submissive obedience to God must affect the repentant totally (Romans 5). Or it is not worth it.

What differentiates an encounter with Jesus Christ himself from assumed encounters with him is self-evident transformational conversion. When the townspeople of Sychar in Samaria experienced it, they at once exclaimed to the woman who brought them to Jesus. "We no longer believe just because of what you said; now we have heard for ourselves, and we know that this man really is the Savior of the world" (John 4:42).

So did the blind man Jesus healed. "Whether Jesus is a sinner or not, I do not know," he insisted in response to his interrogators. "One thing I know. I was blind but now I see" (John 9:25). The three spiritists and their victims and followers in Kedame exclaimed similarly. "It is good to know Jesus personally and be freed by him." A split second experience of Jesus himself powerfully transforms people so thoroughly, years of head knowledge— "crash-helmet religion" —without it, is a cruel substitute.

We may not know everything about Jesus. We can't ever. But we know what we have experienced of him and what we have become consequently. Once we were blind, unable to see God. But now we see. We see God, and are transformed by the glory of his face. Fact is, others see it in us as well. They can't deny the transformation they see and feel when they come around us.

Bands of the transformed and the transforming

Now, see masses of transformed and transforming people like that taking the gospel outside the church into communities and neighborhoods. Their marriages and families, their homes strongly speak love to the neighbors. See them at the workplace, facing the same pressures of work, just like anyone else, but responding with understanding, sincerity, truthfulness and care. They go out of their way to help colleagues with their work when they see the need. Or they ask for help unashamed when they need it, and admit failure when they have to.

See droves of missionaries land in missions exuding the fact that the love of Jesus does indeed transform lives. Their target people see and feel the love of Christ before they hear about it. They are not super-saints. They are very ordinary. But they are known for heart-felt sincerity, openness, understanding, patience, tolerance, and reckless love.

See churches springing up in missions known for one thing, love. Leadership as well as membership exudes love. Everywhere it is evident that the gospel of Jesus indeed transforms people inside out. Forgiveness, reconciliation, joy, peace and justice for all mark the churches.

See those churches quickly wean off their founders. They become rooted in their cultures and sub-cultures. They reproduce themselves spontaneously. They support themselves and lead themselves. See these other churches, in turn, propelled by love into missions! The cycle goes on unbroken and unstifled by prolonged mission control.

I don't see us debate any of that reality as contradictory to God's revealed expectation of the effects of our Lord Jesus Christ's death, resurrection, ascension and enthronement. But it seems to me, we are in danger of settling for the seldom occurrence as normative.

I vehemently disagree. I remain convinced that total life conversion and transformation are possible and contagious. The gospel of Jesus Christ still has the power to convert people at core level and transform them inside out self-reproductively.

I also remain convinced that God always uses people who model total life transformation to call others to experience the fact for themselves. The Holy Spirit continues to purify them for sure. But, for them, childlike trust and dependence on God, God's word and Spirit constitute a way of life. I recall a lesson I learned on that reality.

Learning in context

As part of university Christian students' evangelistic outreach, we went out in twos and threes to visit homes. My teammates and I visited an aged elder of my grandmother's church. He listened to us attentively as I led us in presenting salvation through Jesus to him. He seemed to have a good grasp of the Scriptures. For, he finished for us all the Scripture verses we quoted on sin, repentance and confession of sin, and receiving Jesus and trusting him, while we were still in the middle of each of them.

Before we knew it, his expressive knowledge of the Scriptures exhausted our stock. It silenced us and transfixed us nervously clueless before him. After fifteen minutes of discomforting silence, he graciously broke it with a question. Turning to me he said, "Tell me, son! Did you say Eugenia Sube is your mother?" [That was my mother's maiden name.]

"Yes, grandpa!" I affirmed.

"I witnessed her baptism. Your grandmother is my cousin. But tell me," he requested and then scanned me for a minute or so. "How did you come to have this unusual peaceful composure? It speaks so loudly. Tell me," he earnestly requested.

I heaved a sigh of relief. I explained that I wasn't aware of it. But if he felt some peace about me, it must be Jesus Christ.

And quickly, he demanded, "I want to have the same peace. Tell me how!"

So I told him that in addition to my meticulous Presbyterian upbringing I discovered at a very tender age a personal relationship with Jesus and have tried since then to keep it vital.

"How do you keep it vital?" he demanded straining forward as if to suck the answer out of me with his eyes.

"Oh, I read the Scriptures meditatively and convert what I understand into prayer and disciplined submissive obedience."

"Disciplined submissive obedience!" he repeated thoughtfully. "It makes a lot of sense. No wonder the Scriptures have transformed you so visibly. But I guess you love Jesus very much, don't you?" he pressed.

"You bet I do to the best of my knowledge. And, I am learning to love people the way he did," I said timidly.

"Will you please pray for me to dedicate my life to Jesus Christ? I want to be like you in serving him!"

Like me? How humbling! I thought to myself almost tearily. "Yes, of course, grandpa!" I said.

He prayed a most wonderful prayer of dedication thanking God for sending saints after him at the dusk of his life to bring him to faith in Jesus. Unbelievable! But that was just the beginning.

After his prayer, he ordered his household to suspend preparing their evening meal and come together. When they had gathered, he asked me to tell them everything I had told him so that they too would experience Jesus for themselves. I did. And they each said such heartfelt prayers, welcoming Jesus into their lives. Everything left my teammates and me speechless but joyful and humbled.

It was humbling indeed to realize that the Holy Spirit found my literal silence more useful than my parrotic, and perhaps heartless presentation of Jesus. How amazing! Since then, I have been learning this. The Holy Spirit has his way faster and more effectively with me, and through me to others when I hush literally and symbolically. Then he speaks through me instead. I commit to being more deliberate and conscious in running all I know, and all I can and want to do by the Holy Spirit and the Scriptures.

So it was that ripple conversions stunned me. Yes! But ripple healings and combinations of both also did. I had just learned to fast and pray for people whenever their suffering tugged heavily on my heart. Yvonne was one of the earliest ones at Accra, Ghana. She was one of several recent believers I discipled at the time. She collapsed in class and was rushed to emergency and had since returned home still unwell. I visited and learned that she had had the experience a few times previously. It appeared medical science had not helped her much. That saddened and burdened me.

Therefore I fasted three days and went to pray for her. Her mother welcomed me and took me to her bedside, saying, "Yvonne, Wilson is here" and she walked back out. Yvonne was awake but didn't acknowledge my presence. As I sat in the chair near her bed, I seemed to hear in my heart, "Drive away the demon from her!" What? A demon? How? I thought muddily.

For all I knew, Yvonne was several generations Presbyterian. And what was more she had received Jesus Christ as her personal Savior and Lord. How could a demon, if there was one, survive in that climate? I ignored what I thought I heard. So, I plunged into silent petitioning prayer for her healing.

"Lord, please heal Yvonne. You are the only one who can do what medical science cannot. With you all things are possible. Please, please heal her." I prayed over and over again. But Yvonne got no better.

Then I seemed to hear the same command on the inside of me a second time. "Drive the demon away from Yvonne."

But again, I disregarded it. I was totally convinced that it was impossible for a demon to be associated with a believer's sickness. Therefore I took what I seemed to be hearing as misdirection. Certainly it didn't come from God. I concluded and went right on petitioning God.

Right at the moment I clocked six hours of fruitless petitioning for Yvonne's healing, I felt a sharp pain on the right hand side of my neck. Simultaneously, these words pierced my heart, "You're being stiff-necked. Drive the demon away from Yvonne."

All of a sudden, Yvonne, who had lain on the bed facing the wall with her back toward me all that while, rolled over and flung out her left arm and queried, "Can't you see?"

Ouch! I was all goose bumped. But certainly, Yvonne could not have heard what I thought I heard in my heart. How could she? What was going on here? Sheer coincidence?

I stepped away from the inexplicable and faced the undeniable. My neck throbbed with unbearable pain. The goose bumps persisted. I began to shiver. Yvonne's gesture, the piercing look in her eyes and her query haunted me. Was I really disobeying God while busily representing him? But I had fasted and prayed for three days to God. And for the past six hours, I had petitioned God to heal Yvonne.

Compelled, and I think embarrassed as well, by the weight of the undeniables, I said this, "If there is a demon here, Jesus says go!" At once, Yvonne and the bed started rocking, first, rhythmically then violently and gently. Meanwhile I stood there not knowing what to do next. Thirty longest minutes crawled by and the rocking continued. Then I seemed to hear on my inside again, "Give the final command. Tell the demon to go away, now!"

So I said, "Jesus says, go! Now!" The bed rocking stopped instantly. And there was such calm, peace and a soothing feeling of the presence of God in the room. I basked in the light of God's working.

Yvonne's face shone brilliantly. As she sang hymns of praise, it was like several other voices sang with her. Then she prayed a most wonderful prayer of thanksgiving to God for her deliverance. She even thanked God for me. Me? What did I do? I thought to myself.

Then, directed by Yvonne, I went outside and invited her two younger sisters in to the room. She asked me to tell them what happened. "Let me see! Where do I begin?" I said that, playing for time, because honestly, I didn't know what to say.

"Go on!" Yvonne gently charged. "Tell them what happened!"

"Okay, okay!" I said.

I told them what I learned as I watched Jesus deliver Yvonne from a demonic oppression. And I invited them to look at, what they might have already seen anyway, the light that shone in Yvonne's face. That light evidenced what God had done for her. I stressed.

In response, both sisters received Jesus as their personal Savior and Lord right there and then. On a follow up visit three days later, I found Yvonne fully recovered, still radiantly cheerful and joyful. And she told me her mom and dad had also received Jesus as their personal Savior and Lord in response to her miraculous healing.

All that etched this message on my heart and mind. There was a lot I needed to learn about total freedom for the repentant. My schooling in transformational conversion barely began.

Several years later, after graduate school, I prayed for a Christian student in college in Wroclow, Poland. She was healed instantly from a knee problem she had had all her life. She got home to find that her mother and grandmother who also had the same problem got healed as well. When they compared notes, they realized that their healings occurred simultaneously.

In Colorado Springs, Colorado four years later, Del confided he had a nagging besetting bondage. He was ashamed of it and yet helpless against it. I fasted for a day. We met and prayed in a restaurant. A week later he reported two simultaneous deliverances, his and his son's. At the time we prayed in Colorado Springs, his son was away in Mexico. But he felt delivered from a similar bondage the same time his dad did.

One gospel for varied unsaved situations

Fruitless attempts to understand these happenings—God's mysterious responses to selfless fasting and heartfelt prayer for others—led me to quit trying. On the contrary, these happenings led me to take our Lord Jesus Christ's incarnation, crucifixion, resurrection, ascension and enthronement more seriously.

His own summary of the incarnation, crucifixion, resurrection, ascension and enthronement (Luke 4:18-19, cf. Ephesians 1:18-21) took on new meaning for me. He had declared that the Holy Spirit rested on him to

- proclaim good news to the spiritually bankrupt (verse 18a, re: Matthew 5:3)
- free the spiritually imprisoned (verse 18b)
- give sight to the spiritually blind (verse 18c, re: Acts 26:18-19, 2 Corinthians 4:5-6)
- free the spiritually oppressed (verse 18d) and
- proclaim that total life deliverance and transformation is now here (verse 19).

In Christ, then, God had provided everything needed to save, deliver, heal, reconcile and restore people to wholeness. That obligates us all, but particularly carriers of the good news, to ensure that everything in the package reaches everyone untampered with and undiluted (2 Corinthians 4:1-2). So that when the saved claim that Jesus—the Son of God—has freed them, they are indeed free. They know they are free, and they feel free (John 8:36).

But "everyone" includes many of us who were born and raised in church, like Yvonne. We might have been immunized against genuine conversion and a personal relationship with God through cultural, behavioral, theological changes—cosmetic superficial changes—without realizing it.

19

"Everyone" also includes varied unsaved and unchurched people. Some of these people are like Cornelius (Acts 10). They know God and consciously worship him. But they do not as yet know Jesus Christ. Therefore they remain unsaved. Others like the Athenians (Acts 17) vaguely know God and they largely worship him unconsciously. They do not know Jesus Christ and therefore they too remain unsaved.

Then, there are those others who know God and have worshipped him consciously according to the Scriptures. But for some mysterious reason, they willfully reject him and pick up the occult (Elymas, Acts 13), or refuse to accept Jesus as God (Paul, Acts 9). In addition, there are some people who unconsciously worship spirits and are consequently blinded by them to the gospel without knowing it (Acts 8, cf. 2 Corinthians 4:4). That makes their resistance to the gospel more demonic than sin.

But, irrespective of the unsaved situation, the gospel of Jesus Christ remains the power of God for the salvation of everyone and anyone who believes (Romans 1:16, Acts 4:12). It must be! And it is! However, it must be appropriately unsheathed, as indeed the apostles and disciples did.

Avoidable obstacles

What the Spirit of God began in Jesus Christ (Luke 4:18-19) he continued to do through the apostles (the book of Acts) and all over the centuries. He is here (2 Thessalonians 2:6-7) to do the same everywhere everyday when he is unresisted, ungrieved and unquenched (Acts 7:51, Ephesians 4:30, 1 Thessalonians 5:19).

One way we can resist and frustrate him looks like this. We slice up and fragment the gospel and make a preferred piece the whole gospel. Then the provision of food and shelter, sanitation and healing, or saving the soul while ignoring the rest of the body, etc., becomes the good news instead.

We can obstruct and misrepresent—grieve—the Holy Spirit when we franchise culturalized and parochialized views of God and transplant churches cross-culturally, or make "our" church the Church of Jesus Christ. Then "our" church takes center stage. We theologically, culturally and spiritually chisel members to fit "our" church at the expense of a personal relationship with God. Or we make the one synonymous with the other deceptively and counterproductively.

Then too, we can quench the Holy Spirit through restricting him to our comfort zone, prescribing his every move, act and expression according to our limits, theological view points, and sometimes biases. That was how my petitioning God to heal Yvonne resisted the Holy Spirit for six long hours, and would have quenched him, even after I had fasted for three days.

Meaning, one-size-fits-all formulas and methods we engineer may well be popular. But they miss the point. They part company with truly biblical methods and effectiveness. Unlike the truly biblical, they quick-fix the unsaved and the unchurched, and the churched but unsaved.

I am painfully aware of these tendencies and the way they obstruct transformational conversion. But I am also painfully aware of numerous inexplicable experiences I have had to the contrary. I am amazed at how well those experiences match New Testament models, particularly, the book of Acts, in transformational conversions. Therefore I resolve to keep on imitating Jesus on self-imposed limitation, and trusting and depending on God like an infant (Luke 18:17 and Matthew 10:16).

> *I tell you the truth, [Jesus said], the Son can do nothing by himself; because whatever the Father does the Son also does... By myself I can do nothing; I judge as I hear, and my judgment is just, for I seek not to please myself but him who sent me (John 5:19, 30).*

That even Jesus needed self-limitations and commitment to submissive obedience to God, and childlike trust and dependence on God, to please God, obligates us to do no less. In view of that reality, I strive to discern when to hush literally or symbolically, and when and what to speak, and how much.

That, I have realized, gets me out of the way so that the Holy Spirit can do what he must do. Refer to the conversion story of the Presbyterian church elder and his household cited above.

For only the Holy Spirit knows what it takes to unsheathe the message and power of the good news appropriately to convert people transformationally and reconcile them appropriately for continued total life transformation and spontaneous self-reproduction (Acts 26:18-19, 2 Corinthians 4:5-6). The next several chapters amplify. But first, what do God the Father and Jesus Christ have to say about all this?

Demand

2

God and Jesus on transformational conversion

Total life transformation, that is, inside out transformation in the way we think, feel and act, is absolutely impossible without transformational conversion. In other words, any part of a person that is not radically converted, can never transform radically. And transformational conversion, conversion that occurs at the core of being, is absolutely impossible without genuine repentance.

In genuine repentance, we admit that by our very nature, we are totally unlike God. By nature, we like to be independent of God and rule our lives away from him (Isaiah 53:6). That constitutes a bondage we cannot break free from by ourselves. We also cannot escape God's punishment for it. So we live in bondage to self-rule and in condemnation for it. But now we are willing to surrender self-rule and commit to the rule of God in our lives.

This results when God opens the eyes of our hearts to make us see the perfection of God in Jesus Christ side by side his substitutionary death in our place to set us free. That vision convicts us of our wretchedness and unworthiness. At once, we deplore living our lives without God. It is then that we desire to have God take over and be in charge of our lives. That is genuine repentance.

Only this kind of repentance receives God's forgiveness and results in core level conversion and reconciliation to God. And only in that context does God impart eternal life to start a personal relationship between God and the repentant.

The apostles couldn't miss Jesus' emphasis on genuine repentance. How could they? They knew that Jesus opened his public ministry with it. "Repent, for the kingdom of heaven is near" (Matthew 4:17). They felt his passion as he repeatedly warned that unless people repent, they were headed for inevitable eternal destruction (Luke 13:3, 5). They heard him when he charged them, after his resurrection and before his ascension, to preach repentance and forgiveness in his name to all the nations (Luke 24:47).

Therefore in their own public ministry, they emphasized the importance of repentance (Acts 2:28, 17:30, 26:20, cf. Matthew 3:2). It wasn't over yet.

In the transformation of the seven churches, Jesus invited individuals and whole churches to remember their former commitment to God, repent for abandoning it and return wholeheartedly to him (Revelation 2:5, 16, 12, 22; 3:3, 19). In tomorrow's God-sent, Holy Spirit directed worldwide revival, God would still remind us of the inevitability of heart-felt repentance (Isaiah 66:1-2)

So then, genuine repentance is as integral to core level conversion as core level conversion is to total life transformation. Said another way, there can be no conversion without repentance. And there can be no transformation—total life transformation—without core level conversion.

It revolutionized my evangelistic fervor when I discovered the way in which God the Father and Jesus Christ linked genuine repentance, core level conversion, and total life transformation to the person, presence and work of the Holy Spirit. They each stated the fact, then moved on to illustrate it so that we would not miss it.

God the Father's statement

25. I will sprinkle clean water on you, and you will be clean; I will cleanse you from all your impurities and from all your idols. 26. I will give you a new heart and put a new spirit in you; I will remove from you your heart of stone and give you a heart of flesh. 27. And I will put my Spirit in you and move you to follow my decrees and be careful to keep my laws (Ezekiel 36:25-27).

There it is! God gives to the repentant

- a cleansing for all impurities (verse 25)
- a new heart for the old (verse 26 a, c)
- a new spirit for the old (verse 26b) and
- God's Spirit to cause them to obey God totally (verse 27).

In using "I will," regarding cleansing, new heart, new spirit plus God's Spirit, God places the imperative on himself to make it happen. Even so, it is only after God adds his Spirit to the equation that acceptable obedience occurs, to indicate the presence of God's life. The cleansing, a new heart and a new spirit, though God given, could not produce the life of God in the repentant. Only God's Spirit could. To stress the point, God went right on to illustrate it.

God the Father's illustration

God used that which is humanly impossible, but altogether possible with God, to etch the message of transformational conversion on Ezekiel's mind, heart and spirit. He used disjointed heap of dry human bones becoming, not skeletons, not cadavers, but living persons to illustrate transformational conversion. Ezekiel 37:1-14 has the record.

1. The hand of the LORD was upon me, and he brought me out by the Spirit of the LORD and set me in the middle of a valley; it was full of bones. 2. He led me back and forth among them, and I saw a great many bones on the floor of the valley, bones that were very dry. 3. He asked me, "Son of man, can these bones live?"

I said, "O Sovereign LORD, you alone know."

4. Then he said to me, "Prophesy to these bones and say to them, 'Dry bones, hear the word of the LORD! 5. This is what the Sovereign LORD says to these bones: I will make breath enter you, and you will come to life. 6. I will attach tendons to you and make flesh come upon you and cover you with skin; I will put breath in you, and you will come to life. Then you will know that I am the LORD.'"

7. So I prophesied as I was commanded. And as I was prophesying, there was a noise, a rattling sound, and the bones came together, bone to bone. 8. I looked, and tendons and flesh appeared on them and skin covered them, but there was no breath in them.

9. Then he said to me, "Prophesy to the breath; prophesy, son of man, and say to it, 'This is what the Sovereign LORD says: Come from the four winds, O breath, and breathe into these slain, that they may live.'" 10. So I prophesied as he commanded me, and breath entered them; they came to life and stood up on their feet—a vast army.

11. Then he said to me: "Son of man, these bones are the whole house of Israel. They say, 'Our bones are dried up and our hope is gone; we are cut off.' 12. Therefore prophesy and say to them: 'This is what the Sovereign LORD says: O my people, I am going to open your graves and bring you up from them; I will bring you back to the land of Israel. 13. Then you, my people, will know that I am the LORD, when I open your graves and bring you up from them. 14. I will put my Spirit in you and you will live, and I will settle you in your own land. Then you will know that I the LORD have spoken, and I have done it, declares the LORD.'"

Verses 1-3, God ensured that Ezekiel saw and admitted that it was/is humanly impossible to give life to dry and disjointed human bones—symbolic of deadness.

Verses 4-6, God ensured that Ezekiel understood that only God could cause human deadness to hear and respond to his message of life.

Verses 7-8, God ensured that Ezekiel learned firsthand that even God's message communicated to human deadness without the Holy Spirit can only move lifelessness from one degree of lifelessness to another degree of lifelessness—from dry disjointed bones to skeletons to cadavers. This is case enough against fragmented gospels—other gospels. They generate temporal relief that is absolutely incapable of converting and transforming persons.

Verses 9-10, God ensured that Ezekiel realized that only God's Spirit could produce life in human deadness, to go from totally dead to totally alive.

The immediate application, of course, focused on the recovery of the Israeli nation exiled, dispersed and disintegrated in multiple foreign conquests and domination, and exiles and countries (Verse 11-14).

For as yet, the promised Messiah, the incarnated and anointed Son of God was not born. There has to be a nation of people among whom he would be born. Israel must be retrieved and resettled in the promised land to anticipate his birth, life and ministry. And through his incarnation, ministry, death, resurrection, ascension and enthronement, he draws all peoples to himself.

From those perspectives, the disjointed bones becoming, not skeletons or lifeless bodies (cadavers), but living persons has a universal application as well. The disjointed dry bones symbolized spiritually dead humanity condemned for its alienation from God. As with the dry bones in Ezekiel's vision, and Israeli nation, only the Holy Spirit can give life to spiritually dead and condemned humanity.

And just as the deadness and condemnation were real and thorough, the life giving would be. It too would be really real and thoroughly thorough. The Holy Spirit sees to it that it is.

He is the only one who convicts of raw implications and depth of sinfulness. He is the only one who knows whether repentance—response to the conviction—is genuine or not. He is the only one who ministers the comfort of forgiveness where repentance is genuine. He is the only one who converts the truly repentant accordingly at the heart—the core of being. And only the Holy Spirit imparts the life of God consequently to the genuinely converted to reconcile them to God and initiate a personal relationship between God and them.

A personal relationship with God consists of existence in which the repentant and converted are re-aligned spiritually and morally, mentally and emotionally, to God. Through that alignment, the aligned naturally transform in the way they think, feel and act. This is total life transformation.

God must expect total life transformation. For after all, Jesus Christ modeled it and he died to make it possible and available to all. His teaching, and all Scripture make that plain. And the Holy Spirit exists to make it happen.

But like God the Father, Jesus Christ also stated and illustrated transformational conversion. To miss it in our personal experience and teaching is inexcusable therefore.

Jesus Christ's statement

1. That same day Jesus went out of the house and sat by the lake. 2. Such large crowds gathered around him that he got into a boat and sat in it, while all the people stood on the shore. 3. Then he told them many things in parables, saying: "A farmer went out to sow his seed. 4. As he was scattering the seed, some fell along the path, and birds came and ate them up. 5. Some fell on rocky places, where it did not have much soil. It sprang up quickly, because the soil was shallow. 6. But when the sun came up, the plants were scotched, and they withered because they had no root. 7. Other seed fell among thorns, which grew up and choked the plants. 8. Still other seed fell on good soil, where it produced a crop—a hundred, sixty or thirty times what was sown. 9. He who has ears, let him hear."

10. The disciples came to him and asked, "Why do you speak to them in parables?" 11. He replied, "The knowledge of the secrets of the kingdom of heaven has been given to you, but not to them. 12. Whoever has will be given more, and he will have abundance. Whoever does not have, even what he has will be taken from him. 13. This is why I speak to them in parables: Though seeing, they do not see; though hearing, they do not hear or understand.

14. "In them is fulfilled the prophecy of Isaiah: 'You will be ever hearing but never understanding; you will be ever seeing but never perceiving. 15. For the people's heart has become calloused; they hardly hear with their ears, and they have closed their eyes. Otherwise they might see with their eyes, hear with their ears, understand with their hearts and turn for me to heal them.' 16. But blessed are your eyes because they see, and your ears because they hear. 17. For I tell you the truth, many prophets and righteous men longed to see what you see but did not see it, and to hear what you hear but did not hear.

18. "Listen then to what the parable of the sower means: 19. When anyone hears the message about the kingdom and does not understand it, the evil one comes and snatches away what was sown in his heart. This is the seed sown along the path. 20. The one who received the seed that fell on rocky places is the man who hears the word and at once receives it with joy. 21. But since he has no root, he lasts only a short time. When trouble or persecution comes because of the word, he quickly falls away. 22. The one who receives the seed that fell among the thorns is the man who hears the word, but the worries of this life and the deceitfulness of wealth choke it, making it unfruitful. 23. But the one who received the seed that fell on good soil is the man who hears the word and understands it. He produces a crop, yielding a hundred, sixty, or thirty times what was sown" (Matthew 13:1-23).

Jesus used four soil types to symbolize responses to the life-giving message of the good news. They are

- the wayside soil (verses 1-4)
- the rocky soil (verse 5-6)
- the thorny soil (verse 7) and
- the fruitful soil (verses 8-9).

He interpreted the soil symbolism like this. The wayside soil symbolizes people who hear the good news but misunderstand it. They abandon it just as soon as they hear it. Satan's pick vans get to work immediately. And it is gone (verse 19).

Another way of saying people abandon the good news for easy satanic snatching is that they resist or reject it. Most people who resist, reject or abandon the good news are often blind to it. Sources of their blindness include Satan, ideology, the occult, religion, sin, self, etc. They constitute prime candidates for Satan, the god of this age, to block and hinder from God's grace and truth, love and mercy, life and power, and forgiveness and reconciliation in and through Jesus Christ (2 Corinthians 4:4).

The rocky soil symbolizes people who hear the good news and quickly believe it. But as soon as they realize they must integrate it into their socio-cultural, socio-economic, socio-political, etc., and personal ways of thinking, feeling and acting, they abandon it (verses 20-21).

They highly esteem their socio-cultural and personal ways, to the point they believe the good news endorses them. In fact the good news comes to make them feel good about themselves. The God of the good news must be a family, tribal, cultural deity to do as they tell him, not the other way around. It surprises, repulses them when he demands change of character. The thinnest suggestion that he insists on change cues dropping him.

Therefore, the acceptance of the good news in that context amounts to a false start. Though cosmetic superficial, it parades as conversion. This masquerade immunizes people against genuine conversion. It betrays itself through massive resistance to spiritual matters. Romans 5:5-8 barely begins to describe.

> *Those who are dominated by the sinful nature think about sinful things, but those who are controlled by the Holy Spirit think about things that please the Spirit. If your sinful nature controls your mind, there is death. But if the Holy Spirit controls your mind, there is life and peace. For the sinful nature is always hostile to God. It never did obey God's laws, and it never will. That's why those who are still under the control of their sinful nature can never please God.*

The thorny soil symbolizes people who hear the good news and receive it half-heartedly. But they wholeheartedly humanize it through insistence on having the best of two worlds (verse 22).

For them, the good news doesn't call people to leave "all" and follow Christ. Rather, it promises forgiveness without repentance, conversion without transformation, eternal life without death to sin, the self and the world. It promises eternal bliss without forfeiting worldly bliss.

The wayside soil represents satanic domination. And the rocky soil represents fleshly domination. Similarly, the thorny soil represents worldly domination. That makes accepting the good news in that context another false start—cosmetic superficial change. Like the others, it too parades as conversion.

It betrays itself through modeling and insisting on allegiance to God and money. It christianizes moderation of morals therefore it sees biblical absolutes as legalism. It sees all belief systems as valid. Therefore it works toward ecumenism of all religious practices, etc. In short, it insists on being of the world while in it. That is defiance. Jesus insists on the opposite. It violates the very essence of the good news and affronts God.

For God and Jesus insist on "You shall worship the Lord your God and him only shall you serve" (Matthew 4:10, cf. Deuteronomy 6:4-5). All Scripture forbids the syncretistic blend that thorny-soil-Christians model and advocate. It is an insult to God. No, more than that, it is enmity with God.

> *You adulterous people, don't you know that friendship with the world is hatred toward God? Anyone who chooses to be a friend of the world becomes an enemy of God (James 4:4).*

In contrast, the fruitful soil symbolizes people who hear the good news and receive it wholeheartedly. They surrender self-rule and commit to the rule of God in their lives. That is genuine, core level, spiritual—transformational—conversion. The one and only conversion there is. And it is the one and only conversion that befits the good news of Jesus Christ (verse 23).

The fruitful soil also symbolizes freedom from the power of Satan and sin, and the power of the flesh and the world system without God. Accordingly, it results in total life transformation consisting of Christ-like thinking, feeling and acting, and Christ-like trust and dependence on God as a way of life.

Nothing could be clearer or emphatic. To expect people who received the good news half-heartedly to live it out wholeheartedly, is as futile as expecting those who resist or reject it to do so. For in time, those who received the good news half-heartedly would abandon it—reject it—or syncretize it—resist its transforming power and purpose.

Only people who receive the good news wholeheartedly can yield wholeheartedly to its transforming power, and commit wholeheartedly to its transformation purpose. To emphasize the obvious, Jesus like God, moves on to illustrate this fact after stating it.

Jesus Christ's illustration.

1. The Pharisees heard that Jesus was gaining and baptizing more disciples than John, 2. although in fact it was not Jesus who baptized, but his disciples. 3. When the Lord learned of this, he left Judea and went back once more to Galilee.

4. Now he had to go through Samaria. 5. So he came to a town in Samaria called Sychar, near the plot of ground Jacob had given to his son Joseph. 6. Jacob's well was there, and Jesus, tired as he was from the journey, sat down by the well. It was about the sixth hour.

7. When a Samaritan woman came to draw water, Jesus said to her, "Will you give me a drink?" 8. (His disciples had gone into the town to buy food).

9. The Samaritan woman said to him, "You are a Jew and I am a Samaritan woman. How can you ask me for a drink?" (For Jews do not associate with Samaritans.)

10. Jesus answered her, "If you knew the gift of God and who it is that asks you for a drink, you would have asked him and he would have given you living water."

11. "Sir," the woman said, "you have nothing to draw with and the well is deep. Where can you get this living water? 12. Are you greater than our Father Jacob, who gave us the well and drank from it himself, as did also his sons and his flocks and herds?"

13. Jesus answered, "Everyone who drinks this water will be thirsty again, 14. but whoever drinks the water I give him will never thirst. Indeed, the water I give him will become in him a spring of water welling up to eternal life."

15. The woman said to him, "Sir, give me this water so that I won't get thirsty and have to keep coming here to draw water."

16. He told her, "Go, call your husband and come back."

17. "I have no husband," she replied. Jesus said to her, "You are right when you say you have no husband. 18. The fact is, you have had five husbands, and the man you now have is not your husband. What you have just said is quite true."

19. "Sir," the woman said, "I can see that you are a prophet. 20. Our fathers worshipped on this mountain, but you Jews claim that the place where we must worship is in Jerusalem."

21. Jesus declared, "Believe me, woman, a time is coming when you will worship the Father neither on this mountain nor in Jerusalem. 22. You Samaritans worship what you do not know; we worship what we do know, for salvation is from the Jews. 23. Yet a time is coming and has now come when the true worshipers will worship the Father in spirit and truth, for they are the kind of worshippers the Father seeks. 24. God is Spirit, and his worshipers must worship in spirit and in truth."

25. The woman said, "I know that Messiah" (called Christ) is coming. When he comes, he will explain everything to us."

26. Then Jesus declared, "I who speak to you am he."

27. Just then his disciples returned and were surprised to find him talking with a woman. But no one asked, "What do you want?" or "Why are you talking with her?"   28. Then, leaving her water jar, the woman went back to the town and said to the people,   29. "Come, see a man who told me everything I ever did. Could this be the Christ?"   30. They came out of the town and made their way toward him.

31. Meanwhile his disciples urged him, "Rabbi, eat something."   32. But he said to them, "I have food to eat that you know nothing about."

33. Then his disciples said to each other, "Could someone have brought him food?"

34. "My food," said Jesus, "is to do the will of him who sent me and to finish his work.   35. Do you not say, 'Four months more and then the harvest'? I tell you, open your eyes and look at the field! They are ripe for the harvest.   36. Even now the reaper draws his wages, even now he harvests the crop for eternal life, so that the sower and the reaper may be glad together.   37. Thus the saying 'One sows and another reaps' is true.   38. I sent you to reap what you have not worked for. Others have done the hard work, and you have reaped the benefits of their labor."

39. Many of the Samaritans from that town believed in him because of the woman's testimony, "He told me everything I ever did."   40. So when the Samaritans came to him, they urged him to stay with them, and he stayed two days.   41. And because of his words many more became believers.

42. They said to the woman, "we no longer believe just because of what you said; now we have heard for ourselves, and we know that this man really is the Savior of the world" (John 4:1-42).

The posture (verses 7-8)

I envy the tact with which Jesus hitchhiked with the Samaritan woman and journeyed with her through her cultural, personal, and religious socialization layers until they arrived in the spiritual layer where he revealed himself to her. It all started when Jesus unthreateningly asked her for a drink of water.

The cultural (verses 9-14)

Quite confidently in control behind the "steering wheel," the woman responded by raising a typical cultural issue and objection. Jews and Samaritans were taught by both of their cultures to hate one another, though they lived in neighboring countries.

Jesus didn't deny or debate those cultural issues and objections in defense of his Jewish culture. No! He focused on God's gift of a person and eternal life in him, both of which were/are bigger and better than the best in any culture.

The personal (verses 15-18)

Still confident and feeling safe, the woman teased about a personal life issue through denial. She was a serial polygamist. But she wanted her hitchhiker to treat her as single.

Jesus didn't condemn her. Rather, he sensitively and tenderly disclosed to her that a serial polygamous lifestyle perpetuates singlehood. It makes marrying and divorcing intermittent. Jesus said this to reinforce his earlier assertion. God's gift of a person and eternal life in him not only transcend the best in all cultures. They are also bigger and better than the best in all prided preferred lifestyles.

The religious/theological (verses 19-24)

That assertion triggered off in the woman's mind a notorious and popular Jewish/Samaritan theological debate. "Our [Samaritan] fathers worshipped on this mountain, but you Jews claim that the place where we must worship is in Jerusalem" (verse 19).

Again, Jesus didn't ignore the woman's theological concerns. Neither did Jesus take sides in debates that reinforced misplaced priorities—insistence on the right place of worship at the expense of biblical insistence on the right object and manner of worship.

Instead, Jesus stressed that God is the right object of worship. The right way to worship him consists of worshipping in the Spirit and in sincerity—truth. Worshipping God in Spirit and in truth is bigger and better than the soundest and stoutest theological statements about the right place to worship God.

Spiritual hunger for God (verses 25-26)

Almost immediately, the woman affirmed a two-fold belief in God. First, she disclosed that she believed in the coming of the promised Messiah. Second, she affirmed that she anticipated that Messiah would finally settle all theological ambiguities. "When Messiah comes," she confessed, "he will teach us all things" (verse 25). That succinctly summed up a spiritual need that her cultural identity, personal lifestyle and theological conditioning had not met.

Human spiritual need or hunger is larger and deeper than cultural, personal and theological needs. Therefore only that which is bigger and better than the best theological, personal and cultural answers is capable of meeting the spiritual need of people decisively and incisively. And Jesus Christ is God's final and total answer to the ultimate human need—the spiritual.

When Jesus saw that the woman had admitted and confessed her spiritual need in terms of God's gift of a person—the Messiah—he revealed himself to her. "I who speak to you am he" (verse 26). With that self-revelation, Jesus met the woman's unmet spiritual need appropriately and adequately at the proper time in the dialog between them.

Did not her jaw drop in awe and amazement? Did not her eyes nearly ran out of the sockets in utter shock and surprise? Did she not think to herself?

"I know it! This is indeed the Messiah. No wonder he's so different. He hitchhiked with me into my life. Me! A Samaritan and a woman! He let me talk. And he listened! Amazing! How gracefully he talked and listened to me! He convicted me deeply but kindly. And now, all my anxieties about life have disappeared! My shame is all gone. The peace and joy bubbling in my heart is overwhelming. My chest is about to burst. I must tell someone. But first," turning to Jesus she worshipped him, and said, "Thank you, Lord! Thank you!"

He reassured her of the personal relationship she now has with God. She thanked him again and said, "This is all too much! There's something I've got to do right away! Can you wait here for a minute, please? I'll be right back!"

"Yes, of course! I will be right here!" Jesus assured her. And zoom, she flew on winged legs (verses 27-30).

Jesus must have known all along that the Samaritan woman, like all people, had the ultimate need, spiritual hunger for God. But wisely, he waited until she admitted and confessed that need at the proper time in the dialog between them. Why?

Why didn't Jesus go ahead to disclose himself to her right at the start, to force open all the doors into her life? He could have said, "Woman, I am Messiah. Do you get that? Now, give me a drink of water, will you?"

Or failing that, he could have taken the next opportunity. It came up pretty fast too. It was the cultural door to her life. Right here Jesus could have said something like this. "Shut up! Jewish or Samaritan culture makes no difference. What counts is following me. I am the Messiah. Believe in me and you are better off than many Jews who hadn't. Do you get that?"

But again, Jesus seems to have lost that opportunity as well, didn't he?

Quickly, another chance came up. The door opened to her personal lifestyle—a serial polygamist pretending to be single. Now, here, Jesus could have nailed her. "Poor thing! All these many men in your life, when will you cut it off? Haven't you realized it's not working? I am the Messiah. Give me a chance and I will fix you up, really well! Will you?"

But no! Jesus lost that too. Did he?

Then she let him into her theological life. How naive! She held out jaded doctrines of a mountain religion against time-honored doctrines of the worship of YHWH in the Jerusalem temple—The Temple. With one word, Jesus would have silenced and shamed her good. His refrain would have been, "Woman, you still don't get it, do you? I told you and I will tell you again. I am the Messiah. Get rid of all these jaded stuff and believe in me. When I save you, you'd be saved indeed."

Would she believe him? Would she accept him, as the Messiah that she had anticipated would settle all theological ambiguities?

Fact is, she would have shortchanged herself as well as the self-disclosed Messiah if she accepted him in the theological or lifestyle or cultural dimensions of her life. This is why.

One, accepting Messiah in one's socio-cultural dimension, makes him a socio-cultural activist. Changes made through his supposed presence would be ethnocentric and piecemeal, restricted to the social domain.

Similarly, two, accepting Messiah in one's lifestyle, makes him a behaviorist. Changes he brings about would be nothing more than peripheral short-lived personal lifestyle changes, much like a family doctor or clinical psychologist would prescribe.

Then, three, accepting Messiah in one's theological dimension, makes him a crusading theologian. Changes he might introduce would be culture bound and piecemeal, fit only for crash-helmet religion—the religion of the mind.

All these are forms of cosmetic superficial changes. They don't and can't touch the heart, let alone change it and convert people totally. Therefore none of them, or the combination of them, amounts to conversion. Yet, each of them poses as conversion. In that masquerade, they constitute religious vaccines. They immunize against genuine, spiritual, transformational conversion.

Christianity based on any of them resists God, God's word, and God's Spirit than all the demons and Satan put together. That was how the Pharisees became the bitterest enemies of Jesus Christ. For a fact, only supposed people of God could resist, grieve or quench the Holy Spirit (Acts 7:51, Ephesians 4:30 and 1 Thessalonians 5:19).

Jesus would have contradicted Scripture if he had disclosed himself as Messiah to the Samaritan woman in her socio-cultural, lifestyle or theological dimensions. For the Scriptures insist that it is the heart—the core of being—that must see, recognize and encounter Jesus Christ as God offered to redeem humanity.

That is why opening the eyes of the heart is so crucial for transformational conversion. God reserves to himself the right to open the eyes of the heart. And he opens the eyes of the heart only when the life and lips of Holy Spirit-filled carriers of the good news proclaim Jesus as the LORD (Acts 26:18, 2 Corinthians 4:1-6).

Therefore, the highest socio-cultural, behavioral or theological sophistry is not only a poor substitute. But it is rebellion and affront to God, for obvious reason. It does not and cannot convert people.

Were Jesus driven by less noble motives, he would have

- violated Scripture
- disclosed himself as Messiah to the Samaritan woman in her socio-cultural, behavioral or theological dimension, where he shouldn't
- caused her to make a cosmetic superficial change—false start—and
- proselytized her and positioned her to syncretize her knowledge of God.

But Jesus knew better. He always has noblest and purest motives. His desire and food, he said, were to do and finish the will of his Father (John 4:31-38). Therefore, sensitively and knowledgeably, scripturally and spiritually, Jesus responded to the Samaritan woman from within her multi-layer socialization context before disclosing himself to her. He converted her at the core of being—where the issues of life originate (Proverbs 4:23, cf. Mark 7:20-23).

No wonder the Samaritan woman instantly personalized the good news. No wonder she spontaneously reproduced herself in bringing her townspeople to Jesus Christ (John 4:27-30).

I could imagine her stand at street corners much like Jonah did in Nineveh. Over here, she climbed a tree. Over there, she climbed a rock. Wherever she found a strategic spot, she used it as a temporal mobile pulpit. In a trumpet-like voice, she called out to everybody. "Come, quickly, quickly! Come and see the Messiah. I have met him. He has changed my life. Come out and meet him. He's waiting at Jacob's well. Come! Come!" The shy, timid, self-conscious woman turned brazenly free, fearless, bold and articulate! Incredible!

The mayor, city officials and bureaucrats; factory owners and workers; flea market-stall owners, and customers; banks, tellers and customers; schoolteachers and students; spiritists and suppliants; amusement mongers, entertainers and audiences, everybody, dropped everything abruptly. They jammed the streets like locusts. They rushed to Jacob's well, unable to catch up with the woman preacher, who sprinted ahead of them in contagious ecstasy.

The crowd invaded and swamped Jesus and his disciples and Jacob's well in great expectation. The woman preacher approached Jesus. She said, "Lord Jesus, the audience is yours!" Jesus thanked her and took it. He talked about the kingdom of God. The townspeople absorbed everything he said.

They in turn believed in Jesus. They too converted transformationally. They turned to the woman who brought them to Jesus and said, "We no longer believe just because of what you said;

43

now we have heard him for ourselves, and we know that this man is the Savior of the world" (John 4:39-42). They asked Jesus to stay with them a little longer and teach them. He did (verses 40 and 43).

Which pastor, missionary, parent, Sunday school teacher, etc., wouldn't want to hear those words from their converts at church, home or missions? As for God, I think he doesn't hear enough of them. For Jesus had stressed that there is great joy in heaven anytime those words are sincerely spoken (Luke 15:7, 10 and 22-24).

Transformational conversion according to Jesus then is

- not socio-cultural borrowings or adaptations (verses 9-14)
- not personal lifestyle changes (verses 15-18)
- not religious/theological trade-ins (verses 19-24)
- but spiritual conversion (verses 25-26).

Spiritual conversion is transformational conversion. It is a direct, unhindered, personal encounter with Jesus Christ at the core of being. Only this encounter satisfies our spiritual hunger for God. And because it converts us transformationally, it also transforms us totally—inside out (as opposed to false starts impossibly changing us outward inward).

Naturally, transformational conversion leads to inside out—total life—transformation. It occurred at core of being. It is powerful enough to result in

- instant personalizing of the good news (verse 27-29)
- spontaneous self-reproduction (verses 27-30)
- multiple transformational conversions and personalizing of the good news (verses 39-42).

I chart below the statements and illustrations God and Jesus used to underscore spiritual conversion and distinguish it from cosmetic superficial changes—false starts—that are often mistaken for it. In their statements as well as their illustrations, both God and Jesus made it clear that only the Holy Spirit can produce life in conversion.

And it is only where he produces life that conversion occurs. Death remains wherever he hasn't.

Transformational conversion symbolism and illustration

God' Statement Ezekiel 36	*God's illustration Ezekiel 37*	*Jesus' statement Matthew 13*	*Jesus' illustration John 4*	*Missiological application*
Cleansing	Scattered dry bones	Wayside soil	Cultural adaptation	Rejection
New heart	Skeletons	Rocky soil	Lifestyle changes	Proselytization
New spirit	Lifeless bodies	Thorny soil	Rel/theo-logical trade-ins	Syncretism
My Spirit	**Living persons**	**Fruitful soil**	**Spiritual conversion**	**Transformational conversion**

In level one, on the chart, cleansing stands for incomprehensible experience of a spraying or sprinkling or splashing presentation of the good news. The effects soon vaporize leaving the sprayed, sprinkled and splashed as dead as disjointed scattered dry bones, and as fruitless as the wayside soil or mere cultural adaptation.

Like the pig that returns to mud after it is washed a million times (2 Peter 2:22), these end up where they had always been—resisting and/or rejecting the good news. Precisely, no amount of manipulative spraying, splashing or policed showering in the good news has any internal or eternal consequences.

Level two begins with a new heart. This could be a sudden drastic change of mind, maybe through a tragic accident or perhaps a change of diet in keeping with a diagnosis for say cancer. When the new heart becomes an end in itself, it remains as dead as a skeleton, and fruitless as the rocky soil, just another occasional lifestyle change. It amounts to proselytization—a cosmetic superficial change (Matthew 23:15, cf. 15:8-9).

The most deceptive false starts hibernate in level three. They start with a life-changing spiritual experience, insight, or one form of enlightenment or another. Their spiritual nature heavily endows them with the feeling of having arrived. But the feeling is as deceptive as animated cadavers groping in a mortuary or zombies walking about in church Sunday after Sunday. Like robots, they look real. But they are lifeless, deaf and speechless.

In the final analysis, absolutized spiritual insights or experiences, behave like the thorny soil and theological trade-ins. They lack divine life. Therefore, they cannot and do not produce the fruit of life—the Holy Spirit—which is love, joy, peace, and patience; kindness, goodness, faithfulness, gentleness, and self-control (Galatians 5:22-23). They can only produce syncretized likeness of it.

In sharp contrast, level four begins with "My Spirit." Spoken by God (Ezekiel 36:27), that means the Holy Spirit. As life-giver, he gives life to deadness, fruitfulness to barrenness, spiritual—transformational—conversion to imitations of it in the church, as well as varied unsaved situations outside the church.

After all the role of the Holy Spirit in all this is not incidental at all. This is his native territory. In the beginning, he was the one who hovered over everything before it was created. The prophets spoke under his hovering. He hovered over Mary to have Jesus Christ our Lord.

Our Lord Jesus Christ himself had to have the Holy Spirit hover over him for public ministry. And our Lord insisted that it is the Holy Spirit who hovers over people to convert them, and empower them for service. Accordingly, he ordered the apostles and his early disciples to wait for him to hover over them before they went out as his witnesses.

And at Pentecost, he did. The Holy Spirit filled and empowered them, and turned them loose.

From those perspectives, transformational conversions would elude us if we substitute

- higher degrees, specialized training, high-level orientations, psychological tests
- mission and vision statements, and preferred theologies
- neat formulas, projects, programs, strategies, etc., for the Holy Spirit.

William Henry Parker (1845-1929) in a beautiful hymn reminds us that only the Holy Spirit can make our praise, prayer and understanding of the Scriptures acceptable to God. Only the Holy Spirit can make us truly Christ-like—gentle, pure and kind—daily living to conquer the wrong while choosing the right.

Holy Spirit, hear us, help us while we sing; breathe into the music of the praise we bring.

Holy Spirit, prompt us when we kneel to pray; nearer come and teach us what we ought to say.

Holy Spirit, teach us when we read your word; shine upon its pages with the light we need.

Holy Spirit, give us each a lowly mind; make us more like Jesus, gentle, pure, and kind.

Holy Spirit, help us daily by your might, what is wrong to conquer, and to choose the right.

In my research into folk religion, occultism, witchery and Satanism, I met practitioners, who taught me that initiations transform initiates mentally, spiritually, emotionally, temperamentally and morally. They asserted that the transformation is so radical, were initiates' physical appearance to match it, even close relatives could not identify them.

Now, that is the power of initiation into anti-God, evil practices—union with evil spirits. Why must initiation into Christ be any less? At the best, occult or witchery initiation is identification with Satan. At the least, it fuses human and demonic lives into one. Why must identification with sublime life—the impartation of eternal life—in union with Christ scratch only the surface in supposed repentant people?

God the Father and Jesus Christ's statements and illustrations of transformational conversion (see above) leave us with a chilling ratio of 1:3. Meaning, out of every four supposed conversions, only one is transformational. But transformational conversions are self-evident. People, who convert transformationally, transform inside out—totally—self-evidently. They produce visible and invincible fruit.

Once I strayed into a church only to be greeted by a lady with these words. "I have been looking for you for the past three weeks."

"Looking for me? Where? Do you know me? Who are you?" I asked bewildered.

"My name is Betty. You and I don't know each other at all. But three weeks ago, you sat by me when you boarded Bus NT 500 on High Street. Your presence convicted me of my sinful life. I wanted to talk to you when we arrived at the bus terminal. But I lacked courage. I assumed that you live in the area where you boarded the bus. Therefore I went back there different times since then, hoping to catch you and talk to you. I am glad you showed up in my church today. Do you have time to talk? Please, don't say no!"

"Yes, yes! But this is all strange! I don't live on High Street. I only went to pray at a beach near there. And today, I strayed into your church when I missed my way to another church. This is all amazing!" I confessed.

"Yes, amazing indeed!" Betty echoed. But quickly she added, "God knows I must talk to you so he led you here. You didn't stray!" Betty comforted. We sat down to talk.

Betty was a banker and a single parent of three sons aged five, seven and nine. She sang in the church choir. Until that day on the bus, she had thought that she led a pretty good life. But the encounter turned on the button to screen her entire life to her in vivid colors. Each day each night those weeks, the screening ran. Every attempt she made to shut it off failed.

"For three weeks now, I have been under conviction that I had church but not Jesus Christ." She sobbed and asked me to lead her into a personal relationship with Jesus. "God must have prepared you for this. Please, teach me how to know Jesus personally!" She earnestly pleaded.

I did. And through her, four others came to know Jesus as their personal Lord and Savior. We started a neighborhood Bible Study that met weekly in her house. Today, Betty is a pastor in a Nazarene Church.

Thank God that he exposes false starts and leads people into genuine starts. Mary is another one he did in my experience.

Mary was the last to talk to me after a sermon I delivered at a school worship. She lived trapped in a harem of a supposed Christian benefactor who was sponsoring her through school. "I received Christ as my Savior when you challenged us to do so in your sermon. But I am trapped. Can you help me get out of my mess?" She requested with tears.

Her immediate desperate need of shelter, clothing, sponsorship and discipleship pierced my heart. So did the Scripture that insists that it is unbiblical to say, "Well, goodbye and God bless you; stay warm and eat well—but then you don't give that person food or clothing" in situations like that (James 2:14-17).

49

Presently, I assured Mary of my determination to solicit an all-rounded rescue and resettlement for her. Right after we parted, I looked for and found a number of friends who provided clothes, and sufficient financial commitment to relocate Mary to a boarding school. But everyone I contacted who could house her during school breaks couldn't do it at the time. The only option left was my place. But I was single and lived alone. I was concerned not to give the least appearance of evil.

To overcome that obstacle, I negotiated with a single admin assistant in my office to come and stay with us whenever Mary came on school breaks. She agreed. Soon, Mary graduated and taught school for a short while. Today, she is a missionary to the Gambia.

Jesus equates transformational conversion to spiritual birth. It leads to spiritual existence (John 3:5-6). Somewhere else, he calls it perpetual springs of water or living water or eternal life (John 4:14). He attributes all this to the indwelling Holy Spirit, visibly and invincibly gushing out the life of God in the repentant, forgiven and reconciled (John 7:37-39).

Paul calls it dying in Christ to live a brand new life in Christ (Romans 6:1-4). It is a new creation or re-creation in Christ (2 Corinthians 5:17, cf. Romans 5). Only recreation in Christ is powerful enough to lead to the surrender of self-rule and commitment to the rule of God as a way of life.

To repeat the obvious, only transformational conversion makes it possible for God to establish a personal relationship with repentant persons. For God is thrice holy (Isaiah 6). But people are totally sinful (Isaiah 53).

Only a vital personal relationship with God frees people from the bondage of divisive forces and influences of the world. Only a vital personal relationship with God bonds God's people from every culture, race, tribe and language into unity in diversity, and makes the unity an invincible witness against evil forces that engineer and promote

- rebellion against God
- division and hatred among people, and
- self-rule and self-destruction (Matthew 16:13-20, Revelation 7:9-12).

Unity in diversity among God's people is the clearest and loudest visible expression of God's wisdom, power and glory. It repeatedly reminds all God-hostile entities of their defeat in Christ (Matthew 12:29, Ephesians 3:10, Colossians 1:15-20). It must be the strongest and most credible objective for transformational evangelism and discipleship (Matthew 28:18-20, John 17:20-23).

Indeed, God wants a large crowd of the repentant, forgiven and reconciled from all cultures, races, tribes and languages

- to make up the Bride of Christ
- to participate in Christ's wedding to his Bride
- to participate in the revelation of the full glory of God (Revelation 19:7).

And the wedding of Christ, of course, ends the old order of things, characterized by sin, death, mourning, crying and pain (Revelation 21:14). Simultaneously, then, Christ's crowning and wedding usher in the new order. It is Christ's eternal rule of righteousness, peace, joy and justice for all.

God the Father and Jesus Christ both stated and illustrated the inevitability of transformational conversion to emphasize this fact. Only the Holy Spirit convicts sinful people to repent genuinely and receive forgiveness, reconciliation and eternal life as a free gift from God to cohabit with God eternally.

All this hinges on transformational conversion. Anything short of it wrecks the whole thing. But God whose plan and purpose it is, guards against wreckage. That means

- persistent hypocrisy—false starts, and

51

- persistent rejection—unregeneration would never slip through. No, never!

That obliges people who have been converted transformationally and are transforming—inside out—totally, to transmit and/or customize the experience and ensuing process of total life transformation for others.

Models

3

Immunizing false starts

The worst enemy of radical, transformational conversion consists of cosmetic superficial changes—false starts—parading as conversion. They begin as normal socio-cultural, lifestyle and theological changes in normal socialization (or evangelization) process. People grow up with them, believing and behaving as their family and community do.

They know all the right and acceptable things to do and they do them. And just as they become certain of, say, their sexuality, they do their relationship with God. They see their relationship with God as biological as their sexuality. But the God-human right relationship is not transmitted biologically (see chapter 2). That way of thinking, feeling and living is unbiblical. It constitutes false starts in relating to God. And yet, false starts give stout false assurance.

But the deadliest thing about false starts goes beyond false assurance. False starts immunize people against genuine knowledge of God and a vital personal relationship with him. They hide behind the comfort of the doctrine of sanctification and exploit it to legitimize the absence or little evidence of transformation.

This is the rationale. Sanctification equals perfection. But perfection isn't until Jesus returns. Until then, we can't help being who we are—frail and fragile, and weak but saved by grace. In that way sanctification becomes license to indulge the flesh. In leadership, false starts give unspiritual spiritual leadership.

What victims of false starts know of God largely consists of socio-cultural, subjective/personal and theological views of God. That those views could be biased, myopic, ethnocentric and limited is hardly debatable. Yet, people who grow up on them remain adamant that those views constitute solid basis for knowing God and relating to him.

So convinced are they that even when God himself jolts them to the contrary, they do not get it. In their immunity to the truth, they walk right passed God without realizing it.

Citing Jewish zeal for the law to illustrate the point, Paul laments that these kinds of people reject God while claiming to be following and serving him (Romans 10:1-4). But the goodness of the good news of Jesus Christ reaches out to such people as well. In Nicodemus we have a glimpse of that reality.

1. Now there was a man of the Pharisees, named Nicodemus, a member of the Jewish ruling council. 2. He came to Jesus at night and said, "Rabbi, we know you are a teacher who has come from God. For no one could perform the miraculous signs you are doing if God were not with him."

3. In reply Jesus declared, "I tell you the truth, no one can see the kingdom of God unless he is born again."

4. "How can a man be born when he is old?" Nicodemus asked. "Surely he cannot enter a second time into his mother's womb to be born!"

5. Jesus answered, "I tell you the truth, no one can enter the kingdom of God unless he is born of water and the Spirit. 6. Flesh gives birth to flesh, but the Spirit gives birth to spirit. 7. You should not be surprised at my saying, 'You must be born again.' 8. The wind blows wherever it pleases. You hear its sound, but you cannot tell where it comes from or where it is going. So it is with everyone born of the Spirit."

9. "How can this be?" Nicodemus asked.

10. "You are Israel's teacher," said Jesus, "and do you not understand these things? 11. I tell you the truth, we speak of what we know, and testify to what we have seen, but still you people do not accept our testimony. 12. I have spoken to you about earthly things and you do not believe; how then will you believe if I speak of heavenly things? 13. No one has ever gone into heaven except the one who came from heaven—the Son of Man. 14. Just as Moses lifted up the snake in the desert, so the Son of Man must be lifted up, 15. that everyone who believes in him may have eternal life.

16. For God so loved the world that he gave his one and only Son, that whoever believes in him shall not perish but have eternal life. 17. For God did not send his Son into the world to condemn the world, but to save the world through him. 18. Whoever believes in him is not condemned, but whoever does not believe stands condemned already because he has not believed in the name of God's one and only Son. 19. This is the verdict: Light has come into the world, but men loved darkness instead of the light because their deeds were evil. 20. Everyone who does evil hates the light for fear that his deeds will be exposed. 21. But whoever lives by the truth comes to the light, so that it may be seen plainly that what he has done has been done through God" (John 3:1-21).

Who they are

Nicodemus epitomized redeemable false starts in relating to God. The passage above says he went to Jesus, and must have returned converted at the core of his being. But how did it happen? Who was Nicodemus?

Verse 1 says Nicodemus was a Pharisee and a member of the supreme council of the Jews popularly called the Sanhedrin. Verse 10 adds that he was a Jewish teacher. Meaning, Nicodemus was a reputable evangelical theologian. He served on the highest Jewish council of religion. He was a popular conference speaker, teacher and preacher, and author. His name filled the stadiums and auditoriums to capacity. And his tapes, books, and essays roamed the country. They sold like hot cakes.

Therefore, he held his reputation in hand when he visited Jesus that night (verse 2). For at the time, the Sanhedrin had outlawed Jesus and his followers and all his associates (cf. John 5:18, 7:12-52, 9:22, 12:42). Shortly, though, Jesus too was going to warn people against Pharisaic blindness and hypocrisy.

The Pharisees, he would warn, succeeded Moses. "So practice and obey whatever they say to you, but don't follow their example. For they don't practice what they teach" (Matthew 23:1-2). Then Jesus amplified.

Pharisaic blindness

Pharisaic blindness cloaked false starts—cosmetic superficial changes—with the appearance of right standing with God. Understandably, Nicodemus partook of that blindness.

Pharisaic blindness derived from flawed theology. Though that theology started with God's word, it soon elevated itself above God's word. More than that, it subjugated God and God's word and purpose to itself (Matthew 15:1-9, 23:13-14).

Specifically, that theology granted that God gave the kingdom of God to Abraham and his descendants. But it insisted that Abraham's descendants must keep the law blamelessly to stay in the kingdom.

In their zeal to police impeccable obedience to the law, they substituted

- legalism for a personal relationship with God (Matthew 23:17, 19-21)
- circumcision for conversion to God (verse 15)
- ceremonial washing of hands, face and feet for inner purity (verses 25-28)
- tithing to include herbs for justice, mercy, faithfulness, fidelity and integrity (verse 23-24).

Pharisaic hypocrisy

Naturally, that reversal of things bred hypocrisy. Outward appearance mattered more than inner reality (verses 25-28). People's approval replaced God's approval. Obsession for social status, prestige and public opinion totally pushed God out of the picture. It placed the theologians right at the center of knowing and relating to God (cf. John 5:44). They became idolaters.

For, hypocrisy is hidden idolatry. Raw idolatry chooses and worships other gods overtly. Hypocrisy, on the other hand, chooses and worships other gods under cover. But blatant or concealed, idolatry pays hard wages. Idolaters become the gods they worship (cf. Deuteronomy 29:10-29). That is a natural course of things. For people who worship God their way, soon slip into worshipping the God they fancy. Before they realize it, they become that God.

No wonder the Pharisees saw Jesus as an imposter, and a deceiver of the people (John 7:12). He must be destroyed. Convinced that they served God while self-serving led to a dead end. It led to eternal separation from God (Matthew 23:33-39).

Somehow or other, the light of Jesus punctured Pharisaic blindness and hypocrisy for Nicodemus with a shock. The shockwaves led him to risk expulsion from the Jewish supreme council of religion. He went to check Jesus out for himself. He said to him, "Teacher, we all know that God has sent you to teach us. Your miraculous signs are proof enough that God is with you" (John 3:2).

Remarkably, Jesus didn't respond to the compliment. Instead, he focused Nicodemus' attention on entry into the kingdom of God. Why?

I think that Jesus saw in Nicodemus someone who got stuck. He got stuck in the trenches of outwardly imposed, sternly enforced regimen of starchy, dreary, wearying rules (cf. Buchanan 2001:11). That made up Pharisaic blindness and hypocrisy. Jesus saw a stuck and tired leader and teacher, preacher and speaker.

Beneath the surface, Jesus saw a hurting jaded leader who wasn't evasive about it. Rather, he risked reputation and all to do something about it. Very soon, Jesus would lead Nicodemus to convert transformationally, at the core of his being. But first, look at counterparts of Nicodemus in our time.

Contemporary examples

I personally commend Nicodemus because getting stuck on a false start in relating to God is easier than seeking out of it. Making it public when one abandons the masquerade and its shambles becomes even harder. Why?

John 12:42-43 says, "many people, including some Jewish leaders [Nicodemus' peers], believed in him [Jesus]. But they wouldn't admit it to anyone because of their fear that the Pharisees would expel them from the synagogue. For, they loved human praise more than the praise of God" (cf. John 9:22).

That is how tight false starts entangle victims. But the difficulty matches only pervasive and perennial occurrences of false starts. Recall Jesus' encounter with the Samaritan woman (John 4:1-42, see above). Remember how easy it would have been for Jesus to quick fix her and consequently entangle her in a credulous false start.

That encounter exposed the habitat of false starts. They normally originate in socialization or evangelization process. They include

- socio-cultural conditioning/adaptations
- lifestyle development/changes
- theological conditioning/swaps

taken as conversion. The following stories illustrate.

Socio-cultural conditioning/adaptation

One evening I strolled a neighborhood singing "In the old rugged cross…" softly to myself, I thought. A lady's voice called me from behind. "Young man, please come here a minute!"

I turned around and retraced my steps. I stood before the lady who called wondering what the issue was. She invited me to her house. Then she asked. "Would you please sing me the song you sang when I called you!"

"Yes, ma'am." I sang it. She asked for a repeat. I did. And another. I did. A fourth time, and I sang it again. She wept. She sobbed. She cried. Then she told me.

"My name is Kate. I am a pastor's wife. But I belong to Masonic Temple secret society. Pastors and priests, elders and deacons of churches, principals and schoolteachers, lawyers and medical doctors, the elite, belong to it. It is the thing to do around here if you want to belong to the in-group of society. It didn't pose a problem for my husband until recently. Three times he was due for promotion in the denomination but lost it because of my involvement in the secret society.

"I have risen fairly high in the ranks. I wasn't willing to give up everything just like that. The last time my husband and I talked about it, I threatened that I would more readily accept divorce than give up membership in the lodge. And that was where we left it.

"But the song you sang convicted me in two places. First, it is wrong for me to belong to a secret society. Second, I didn't really know God personally. I thought I did. As you sang the song over and over again, I surrendered my entire life to God. Who are you, anyway?"

61

I told her and added, "I am a second year university student."

"Thank you for what you have done for me. This very night I am going to cancel my membership. I am returning their robes, swords, books and all to them right away. Would you like to come with me? It's only 45 minutes away by boat" she gently requested.

"No, ma'am. I am sorry I can't. I am 60 minutes late for an appointment that would last all evening," I declined.

"I understand. Could you come back and see me tomorrow? Anytime of day is fine," she asked.

"Yes, ma'am," I committed.

Lifestyle development/changes

Several years later, I was a junior in the Master of Divinity degree program. I participated in an Art and Crafts show at a park in Spring, selling some paintings I had made.

Up until noon, I had made no sales. Then Stacie stopped by. "I like your paintings!" she complimented.

"Thanks!" I said.

"I'll like to buy those two," she said pointing at them. While I picked them, she asked, "You must be a Christian, aren't you?"

"Yes, I am. And you?" I asked.

"Oh yes! I am a 10th generation Presbyterian. My mom and dad serve as elders in my church. My brother, a year older, and I belong to the college and career group," she explained.

"But, tell me. Why did you ask if I were a Christian?" I queried.

"Oh, I just asked. This universal God we serve!"

Universal God? I thought to myself. Anyhow, we scheduled time to talk about this universal God.

At our rendezvous a week later, Stacie disclosed that she broke a wedding engagement a week to the wedding. And she became everybody's enemy, including her parents. She decided, 'they called the tune of hate, and hate it shall be. We'll all dance to it. It's that simple.' She thundered. I wasn't remotely part of it but I felt the heat of it in her tone of voice.

I prayed silently. Then I suggested, "Stacie, have you thought about what your parents must have felt? Wedding gifts had started coming in, hadn't they?"

"You, too? How strange! On whose side are you? I thought you were on my side. The guy is an unbeliever. I am a believer. Why doesn't anybody get that?" she protested.

"Stacie!" I began to say. "You know I am on your side. Give me a minute and I will show you that I am."

"You have it!" she said curtly.

"Stacie, put yourself in your parents' shoes for just a moment, okay? Here were Presbyterian elders, a medical doctor and a homey housewife. They raised two darling kids in strictest Presbyterian traditions for respectable right believing and living.

"One day, bright, blond and beautiful daughter, sweetheart Stacie came home with her boyfriend and proudly announced. 'Mom, dad! Chuck and I are engaged!' A year later, sweetheart Stacie calls off the wedding. Why? 'Chuck is an unbeliever. I can't marry him.'

"Now Stacie, think about this, will you? Why did it take you so long to admit Chuck was an unbeliever? You knew him all the way from high school and all the way through college. Had you thought you could change him and marry him? Had your attempts backfired?

How? And why? Was that what it was? Tell me the truth. Between you and me, you have nothing to lose." I stopped for a response.

After a long pause, Stacie said, "You're right. I should have known better. There was no way I could change him. Chuck was set in his ways. Moreover he hated Christians. To him Christians are all hypocrites."

"But you loved him and wanted to marry him, in spite of that, didn't you?" I jumped in rudely.

"Don't interrogate me!" Stacie protested.

"I am not! But you see, if you wrestle with that question and faithfully answer it at least to yourself, you'll discover why contrary to Scripture, you decided to marry an unbeliever in the first place." I pressed.

"You're a hard taskmaster, aren't you?" Stacie teased.

"Hard or soft, Stacie, you need to help yourself out of this death trap. It's killing you," I counseled.

"What trap?" Stacie inquired.

"Can't you see it? A smart, beautiful and young business executive had decided to kill herself to teach her parents, church and friends a lesson they would never forget. How does that square up?" I pushed.

"Kill myself? What do you mean by that?" Stacie queried.

"Look at it this way." I explained. "You were the one who knew and loved Chuck all the way from high school through college. You were the one who admitted belatedly that it was impossible to change him by marrying him. You were the one who cancelled the wedding a week before.

"Do you realize that you got your parents and their friends, your church and friends, everybody, into it all? Then you piously walked away leaving them to take care of the mess you created. And you're angry, bitter, and resentful, unwilling to forgive their embarrassment, pain and sorrow. You're trying so hard to justify your reaction while holding theirs against them.

"What kind of logic is that? What kind of a believer in Jesus Christ would do such things, conscience free?" I lamented.

There was another long pause. Then Stacie said, "I begin to see what you're saying. I need to take responsibility for my actions, don't I?"

"Exactly! And how would you describe your actions, in two words?" I tried to guide.

"I have been selfish and foolish!" Stacie said. At that she broke down and wept bitterly.

After she recomposed herself, I suggested, "Stacie, I think your repentance would be complete when you go back to your parents and apologize to them for the embarrassment and pain you caused them."

"Now, you've gone too far! Apologize to my parents? No way! I will never!" Stacie declared.

"Yes you will!" I calmly insisted.

"Will you make me?" Stacie said, looking defiant.

"No! How could I? You and I don't even know each other. But, if I were you, I would apologize to my parents for soiling their good name, and wounding their reputation in the church and community, among their friends and peers. Yes, I would." I proposed.

Stacie did. She and her parents reconciled. That ended her one-year self-exile. She and I met for a few times afterward. And from the

Scriptures I urged her to do personal heart-searching with judgment day honesty, using these pictures, to see whether she had a vital personal relationship with God.

One, from birth, and like all people, we all want to be self-taught regarding right and wrong, good and bad, and true and false (Isaiah 53:6). Most of us raised in Christian homes tend to think or assume that our Christian upbringing automatically takes care of that. We have believed the right things, done the right things all our lives, why not?

Two, a repackage of that insistence also exists. It is a stubborn unwillingness to yield our will, word, ways and works to God's will, word, ways and works. For some mysterious reason, we convince ourselves that we have sufficient justification by faith. We can take turns occasionally with God, God's word and Spirit on the last word in our lives (cf. Isaiah 55:8-9).

Tragically, in both situations, control is the heart of the matter. Neither of those situations shows surrender of self-rule and commitment to the rule of God in the way we think, feel and act. But, because we are many generations Christian, we are right with God. Maybe, we are God's favorites, why not?

Three, what Jesus Christ our Lord and Savior modeled and taught contrasts sharply with all that. He insisted on childlike trust and dependence on God as entry point to the kingdom of God (Luke 18:17). Then he modeled submissive obedience to God as the supreme sign of citizenship. Jesus imposed self-limitations on himself to submit to the Father, to love and obey him in everything all the way (John 5:19, 30). He left us the Holy Spirit to enable us be and do similarly (John 14:12-26).

Only from the third perspective can we relate directly vitally to God. Only from that perspective can the Holy Spirit have freedom to dwell in us, fill us, and produce his fruit of love in us. Then we would wholeheartedly love God (Mark 12:29-30), unconditionally accept and care for all believers (John 13:34-35), and selflessly love and pray for our enemies and persecutors (Matthew 5:43-48). Consequently, we would be effective witnesses of Jesus (Luke 24:48-49, Acts 1:8).

Stacie took the challenge!

On a business trip one of those days in a hotel room, Christ visited Stacie in a gentle quiet but unmistakable way. She wept tears of absolute surrender. She sang. She prayed. She thanked God profusely.

Moments later she called to tell me about it. She sounded so very different. She had become significantly different. She knew it. Today, several years later, her husband and kids, friends and colleagues at work know her as a godly wife, mother, manager, friend and discipler for Jesus.

Theological conditioning/swaps

At a conference for Christian student leaders, I presented a seminar on "The Holy Spirit and other spirits." Jeff waited until everybody else was gone. Then he confided.

"As you talked, I felt a choking lump rise in my belly. It gradually climbed up, up, up and finally went out through my mouth. I almost screamed when it got to my throat because it grew extremely painful then. But after the lump left me and was gone, I felt overwhelming peace and lightness I have never felt before."

I didn't know what to make of it so I asked Jeff. "Do you have a personal relationship with Jesus Christ?"

"Of course, I do. I am the president of my school chapter of IVCF. But do you know something? I have never felt this free, joyful and ready to explode. No! Never! Perhaps the lump had to do with dabbling in the occult," Jeff disclosed.

"Tell me about it," I inquired.

Jeff grew up a 4th generation Methodist. In junior high school, he dabbled in the occult. He contacted a spirit guide. The last year in

67

high school he rededicated himself to Christ. On and off through the first three years in college, he thought and silenced the thought about the occult dabble.

Most people he talked to convinced him that he had become a believer, and that took care of it. Demons and the Holy Spirit do not cohabit. He explained to them that he was a believer before he dabbled in the occult. Even so, his Christian "counselors" argued that theologically speaking, he had nothing to worry about. He should just believe it was all over with the occult. He had become a new creation (2 Corinthians 5:17).

According to Jeff, he dug the deepest theological pit and theologically buried his nagging thoughts about the occult in it, including his spirit guide. But the thoughts and spirit guide resurrected with a vengeance. They became nightmarish. He exhausted all the Christian help he could find. He continued to play his Christian roles as blameless as ever, while struggling secretly and silently against a stubborn spirit guide. Whenever he was overpowered, he secretly indulged his spirit guide.

"But, now," Jeff affirmed, "I am free. Free forever! Thank you!"

I led him through several related scriptural references like Deuteronomy 18:9-19, Matthew 12:43-45, Acts 19:11-20, Ephesians 5:11-19, Micah 6:6-8. Now, Jeff didn't have to muster up herculean faith to delude himself into possessing freedom he didn't have. He also didn't have to imagine the freedom he now had. Rather, he knew it as he experienced it at the very time Jesus gave it to him (cf. John 8:31-38).

Humanly speaking, it would be hard, near impossible, to debate Kate, Stacie and Jeff into accepting that they were victims of false starts. They would deny that they worshipped a socio-cultural, family, theological, denominational deity. He was a pampering doting god. He was sensitive and defensive to "their" cause. He was out to get all "their" enemies.

They would deny that they worshipped a deity who rescues but doesn't bother the rescued. He comforts but never disrupts the comforted. He sooths but doesn't disturb the soothed. He provides all "our" wants. But he doesn't intrude. He protects but never demands, judges, or meddles. He keeps his distance. And he doesn't crowd "us" (cf. Buchanan 2001:86).

But truly and sadly, Jeff, Stacie and Kate were victims of false starts. They had a god of their making, a god they could control. They could order him to do as they pleased. Typically, they ordered him to show them beyond reasonable doubt that

- he believed as they did that he belonged to them exclusively
- he sanctioned all their prescribed dos, don'ts, how-tos, and taboos, and
- he followed them to follow him in believing and living as prescribed.

Well, whether he indeed did and for how long, was another thing. Biblically speaking, though, all that contradicts everything about the LORD our God. For, Deuteronomy 10:14, and 17 says, "To God belongs the heavens and the heaven of heavens, and the earth and everything in it. The LORD our God is God of gods, Lord of lords. He is the great God, mighty and awesome. He shows no partiality and takes no bribes."

That God doesn't bow to any socio-cultural, lifestyle and/or theological sophistry. No! How could he?

However, in missions, Kate, Stacie and Jeff cannot conceal their cultural and/or theological bigotry and superiority complex for long. Therefore, they would run into two dangers that would plague their work for years.

One, they and the ethnocentric deity and gospel they present as God and the good news of Jesus Christ would be resisted and/or rejected by cultural and religious/theological bigots, self-sufficient, and self-satisfied elite. Understandably, their ethnocentrism does not intimidate, fascinate or dazzle people like that easily.

On the other hand, two, they would clone and append people they intimidate, fascinate and dazzle with supposed superior cultural, lifestyle and theological deity and gospel. The "appendices" do not constitute conversions in biblical terms. At the best, they are cosmetic superficial changes. But they would parade as conversions and boost conversion statistics accordingly.

Kate, Stacie and Jeff would have forgotten that it was right here that Jesus condemned Jewish missionaries. They had lost reality about right relationship with God long before they left home for missions. They could only produce after their kind with inevitable exception. Disciples made in error transcend their masters in error.

"Woe to you, teachers of the law and Pharisees, you hypocrites! You travel over land and sea to win a single convert, and when he becomes one, you make him twice as much a son of hell as you are" (Matthew 23:15).

Tragically, even when that becomes common knowledge with time—the church in missions remains woefully syncretistic and dependent on its founders—Kate, Stacie and Jeff would deny responsibility. Rather, they might scapegoat Satan, Islamic and demonic principalities and powers, and animistic, folk, religion treachery. The latter is too religious to convert.

Really?

That makes contemporary false starts as blind and hypocritical as the Pharisaic (Matthew 23). But, solemnly, Pharisaic blindness and hypocrisy, past and present, do not fall beyond the reach of the good news of Jesus Christ. If victims repent, they too would be converted transformationally (Romans 1:16). Kate, Stacie, Jeff and Nicodemus testify experientially.

Customized good news

This is another place where I envy our Lord Jesus Christ. So I am unlearning and learning to be more and more like him. Unpolluted by raw theological biases and raw humanity, he swiftly saw and speedily responded to the heart of the matter. Nicodemus' spoken and unspoken words told Jesus that it was the mystery about Jesus that attracted him. Therefore Jesus fiercely kept the focus right there and used it to lead Nicodemus to transformational conversion.

Jesus took Nicodemus from the mystery of Jesus—the mystery of the good news—that he had just confessed (John 3:2) and led him to four other mysteries closely connected with it. They include

- the mystery of the spiritual birth (John 3:3, 5-6)
- the mystery of the wind/the Spirit of God (verses 7-8)
- the mystery of belief (verses 9-16), and
- the mystery of disbelief (verses 17-21).

For brevity, I think John shortened the dialog between Jesus and Nicodemus. I retrieve it imaginatively, within context of course, to capture its earthiness regarding the issues.

The mystery of Jesus—the mystery of the good news (verse 2)

Nicodemus knew and taught enough of the Hebrew Scriptures. He knew that unique mighty acts, wonders and signs—unparalleled mystery—would distinguish the Messiah (Isaiah 29:18-19, 35:5-6, cf. Matthew 11:4-5, Acts 2:22). Many of Nicodemus' colleagues also knew that much. They had also seen and heard reports about Jesus doing them. And like Nicodemus, they had believed that Jesus was the Messiah. But unlike Nicodemus, they kept their belief secret to save face (John 12:42-43).

Therefore when Nicodemus risked expulsion from the Sanhedrin and went to see Jesus, what was he up to, really? Was it just to tell Jesus what Jesus already knew? "We all know that God has sent you to teach us. Your miraculous signs are proof enough that God is with you" (verse 2).

71

Typical of Jesus, he heard Nicodemus' spoken and unspoken request. Therefore he responded to the unspoken in terms of the spoken. Indeed he was/is Messiah—God incarnate. He had come as the only access to the kingdom of God. As mysterious as it is for God to become human temporarily, so it is for humans to become like God eternally. The process for the latter is the spiritual birth (verses 2-4).

The mystery of the spiritual birth (verses 3, 5-6)

Jesus described the spiritual birth to Nicodemus. The kingdom of God consists of spiritual existence. Spiritual existence demands spiritual birth. Just like physical birth gives people physical life and existence, so too spiritual birth gives people spiritual life and existence (Psalm 139:13-18). "You need to be born spiritually, Nicodemus," Jesus urged (verses 3, 5-6).

"This is puzzling!" Nicodemus muttered and continued. "It is a mystery. I don't get it!"

"No, you can't, Nicodemus. Mysteries are usually inexplicable. But, let me help you further." Jesus said and moved right into the mystery of the Spirit of God who makes the spiritual birth happen.

The mystery of the wind/the Spirit of God (verses 7-8)

"You didn't expect a neat formula when I talked about being born spiritually, did you?" Jesus queried.

"No! Not exactly, but...." Nicodemus stammered.

"Listen, Nicodemus. The spiritual birth is an act of God. Like all acts of God, it's unpredictable, anti-formula. It is mysterious. God suddenly breaks in to repentant people. In a split second, he recreates them from the heart. He imparts his life to them. And in that moment, they are born spiritually. Just like that! [cf. 2 Corinthians 4:5-6]. Humanly speaking, you can't predict or catch the exact moment it happens. It is like the wind.

"Once a rabbi took his graduating class of disciples on a simulation exercise trip to the flea market. He was teaching them about how to look for and receive obeisance in public. Suddenly the late afternoon hot winds came. Merchandize flew off lines, tables and stalls, littering the air. Before the rabbi knew it, the wind took the turban off his baldhead. The wind opened it and spread it out. It went dancing in the air.

"His disciples ran after it screaming, 'the rabbi's turban, the rabbi's turban, catch it, catch it!' But too late, the wind placed it beyond reach. It flew like a kite. You, see, the rabbi heard the sound of the wind. He saw merchandize and his turban snatched, swayed and swept along and away. But he didn't know where it came from or where it went.

"The Spirit of God works like that. Transformational changes he effects evidence his presence and work. They're self-evident. You can't miss them. Do you get it now, Nicodemus?" Jesus asked (verses 7-8).

"Y-yes! I think so" Nicodemus replied not quite sure he did.

Perhaps another mystery, a historical analogy, would help the historian theologian. Jesus moved into the mystery of belief in God.

The mystery of belief—saving faith in God (verses 9-16)

"Remember the last seminar you ran in the city hall on "Bronze snake therapy"? Jesus started.

"Ha-ha-ha!" Nicodemus laughed and asked. "You mean the bronze snake Moses made on the exodus journey?" (Numbers 21:4-9).

"Yes!" Jesus agreed.

"What has it got to do with it?" Nicodemus asked, bewildered.

"Everything." Jesus began to explain. But Nicodemus jumped in.

"How?" (John 3:9-13)

"The Bronze snake foreshadowed the mystery of saving faith in God and my imminent substitutionary death for the sins of the world. You see, Nicodemus, in the exodus incident, your ancestors rejected God and his servant Moses. They called God's deliverance death. They distrusted God's ability to keep them. They hated his daily provision of food. They wanted to go back to Egypt" (Numbers 21:4-5).

Again Nicodemus jumped in and asked. "Is that what it was? Was it that bad?"

"Oh, Nicodemus, yes! Had God not acted quickly, your ancestors would have killed Moses and appointed a disciple of Dathan as their leader. Under his leadership they would have headed back to Egypt."

"You think they would?" Nicodemus asked skeptically.

"Yes! They said so. Remember? But mercifully, God ordered poisonous snakes to break in on them and stop the madness. The snakes bit grumblers while they grumbled and complained and threw tantrums. Those bitten fell down, screamed, cursed, twitched and died. Funerals ran the clock.

"The vicious cycle of grumbling, snakebites, deaths, funerals, and tiredness wore everybody out. Then the survivors repented. They asked Moses to ask God to remove the snakes. They promised to behave themselves from now on" (Numbers 21:6-7).

"Do you know something?" Nicodemus began to say.

"What?" Jesus asked.

"I never saw the snakebites as an act of mercy. I saw it as punishment. But now I see it differently. But for the snakebites, our ancestors would have headed back to Egypt. Egypt? Wow!" Nicodemus conceded.

"Well, Nicodemus, the mercy associated with the bronze snake transcended the mercy associated with the snakebites. It offered the gift of life. Those bitten would live if they looked—simply looked— at the bronze snake. But that required a deliberate act of faith. Those bitten must believe that indeed they would live when they looked at the bronze snake after live snakes had bitten them.

"And as you know, those who looked at it lived. That is the mystery of belief" (Numbers 21:8-9).

"But I bet, the idea of looking at a bronze snake to live after being bitten by poisonous live snakes didn't make sense to everybody. Therefore some refused to look and died foolishly" Nicodemus expressed, wondering.

"Of course!" Jesus added. "And that is the tragedy of disbelief. It too is a mystery. I will tell you about that in a minute. But you see, the bronze snake and the pole foreshadowed my imminent crucifixion. You remember Caiaphas' popular series on 'One death for many lives'? [Isaiah 53, cf. John 11:49-53, 18:14].

"Caiaphas emphasizes the death of one for many lives. But you know, because he is so vague about who dies for 'many lives,' he misinterprets 'many lives' as Abraham's biological descendants only. Were he biblically thorough, he would have realized that the one who dies for 'many lives' is 'the Son of Man' as well as 'the Son of God.' And 'many lives' includes people from every culture, race, tribe and language.' He would interpret Isaiah's prophecy (chapter 53) in terms of Daniel's prophecy (chapter 7:13-14) in his seminars.

"Since you're so familiar with Isaiah 53, let me remind you of Daniel 7:13-14. Daniel said,

In my vision that night I looked, and there before me was one like a Son of Man, coming with the clouds of heaven. He

75

approached the Ancient of Days and was led into his presence. He was given authority, glory and sovereign power; all peoples, nations and people of every language worshipped him. His rule is eternal—it will never end. His kingdom will never be destroyed.

"I am God who incarnated as the Son of Man to die as the Son of God for the sins of the world—the world. Those who believe in me will receive forgiveness of sins and eternal life as a free gift from God. They will be reconciled to God. This is what the bronze snake on the pole pointed to. Do you believe that, Nicodemus?" Jesus asked (John 3:13-16).

"Yes, I do, Lord! I am confounded. We claim to know so much. Yet, we know so very little. My books and tapes are all over the place. How can God ever forgive us, teachers, for how we tend to misrepresent him? Please forgive me. I hate what I am and have done." Nicodemus pleaded.

"Of course! You're forgiven. That's why I came. Since you are a teacher, let me tell you about the mystery of disbelief briefly before you go." Jesus said.

"It's getting late but who cares? I can listen to you all night. But I am wondering, how can disbelief be a mystery?" Nicodemus confessed.

The mystery of disbelief (verses 17-21)

"My Father sent me into the world so that he would save the world through me. Those who believe in me, as I told you, will be saved. But those who don't are already condemned. Do you know why?" Jesus asked (verses 17-18).

"No!" Nicodemus replied.

"To believe or disbelieve is a deliberate choice between light and darkness—life and death. Death is living without God. And the world had lived in darkness until I came as the light and life of the world.

But people who do evil hate the light. They know that welcoming the light means they must surrender the life of evil and its practices. They resent that. Therefore they reject the light.

"But in rejecting the light, they reject me the only way out of darkness and death. They reject me not out of ignorance, but in defiance. That is the mystery, right there. Given a choice between light and darkness, life and death, who would choose darkness and death instead of light and life? But people do that all the time. That is the ultimate expression of the mystery of evil" (verses 19-21).

"That makes love of evil as stubborn as death, doesn't it?" Nicodemus remarked insightfully.

"There you have it, Nicodemus." Jesus said. They got up to go. As they shook hands, Jesus added, "It was nice talking to you, Nicodemus!"

"The pleasure was mine!" Nicodemus replied.

"Give my love to your friend Joseph of Arimathea!" Jesus expressed.

"I sure will!" Nicodemus said.

Three scriptural references indicate that Nicodemus converted transformationally on that visit. One, he boldly withstood, and two, openly dissociated himself from, the Sanhedrin's condemnation of Jesus Christ. Then, three, he boldly and openly accompanied Joseph of Arimathea to claim the dead body of Jesus, provide for and participate in giving it an aristocratic funeral (John 7:50-52, 19:38-42, cf. Luke 23:50-56).

Appropriate good news carriers

What Jesus was and how he went about things emerged as key to leading Nicodemus to convert transformationally. Jesus was God incarnate. He represented the kingdom of God. He was/is the only way into the kingdom of God. He more than anybody knew most perfectly, saw clearest, how perverted and distorted views of the kingdom of God had programmed supposed people of God and others against God. He, more than anybody, could counter those views most effectively.

But, his initial face-to-face encounter with Satan (Matthew 4:1-11, cf. Luke 4:1-13) showed that he more than anybody could also sabotage the kingdom of God most severely and eternally.

As the fulfillment of all the Scriptures, the final piece in God's self-revelation to humanity (Hebrews 1:1-4), God incarnate and redeemer of lost humanity, Jesus could snatch the kingdom of God for himself. And that would have been it. God had lost. Jesus had become self-declared king of the kingdom of God. Jesus faced that temptation all the way to the very day he ascended to heaven (Matthew 16:13-23, John 6:14-15, Acts 1:6-9).

But he declined each time because he didn't see equality with God in terms of snatching it. Rather, he put self-limitations on himself. He served God as one who had no rights. He obeyed God submissively right into dying like a notorious criminal (Philippians 2:5-11).

Were Jesus less preoccupied, and therefore self-seeking, he would have heard only Nicodemus' spoken words—his compliment of the Messiah. Taken on face value, Jesus would have heard articulated flawed theology about Messiah—teacher and miracle worker only.

And knowing that Nicodemus was an evangelical theologian, Jesus would have indulged himself in a deserved opportunity to straighten out, or floor, a flawed evangelical theologian and author, leader and teacher, and preacher and speaker. This was his chance to get even. The theologian asked for it by coming.

Self-justification parading as justified theological preoccupation would have prevented Jesus from

- hearing Nicodemus' personal admittance to the wonder that emanates Messiah as consistently biblical
- hearing Nicodemus' personal yearning to participate in the wonder and purpose of Messiah as also consistently biblical.

To quick fix the flawed evangelical theologian, Jesus might use theological big guns like

- the doctrine of Messiah and the trinity
- the doctrine of Messiah and the incarnation
- the doctrine of Messiah and justification
- the doctrine of Messiah and sanctification
- the doctrine of Messiah and...

While busy quick fixing—flooring—the flawed theologian, Jesus would have missed the opportunity to convert a desperate seeker of the kingdom of God. He would have pushed Nicodemus back into the theological quagmire he was trying to get away from. How tragic for the life-giver to snuff out life in that way!

But Jesus knew better. Therefore he modeled what we could imitate to carry the good news appropriately to false starts that parade as conversions. Jesus listened to Nicodemus. He read his lips and body language. He took seriously the time of day Nicodemus chose to come and see him—night. He saw and took Nicodemus for whom he was, a seeking jaded leader and teacher. He loved him for himself.

Jesus heard Nicodemus' heart. He focused the issues for him through taking him beyond what he knew intellectually. He helped him scripturally and spiritually to experience God firsthand, convert transformationally, have and know that he had a personal relationship with God, and transform inside out—totally.

Jesus' fierce commitment to discerning to follow after God in doing God's will in all things played the major part in all this. Therefore Jesus' attitude constitutes a clarion call for us to imitate him and do similarly. Then we too would see transformational conversions among false starts that parade as conversions.

But the word discernment sends the shivers. Discernment? Not for me! Most of us like to think that way. It is a monopoly reserved for a few. I am learning differently. To a very large extent, we could all discern most situations pretty accurately. Our biggest problem, I have discovered, is our tendency to stereotype people, situations and what we see, hear or feel. But stereotyping is another form of discernment. I call it "sugar-bowl" discernment.

I was guest in a home in Buffalo New York one weekend. Life began very early Monday morning for my host and hostess. Therefore, Sunday night, my hostess schooled me about Monday breakfast procedures. "We will be gone before you get up. But we'll get your coffee going!" she ended.

Everything in the kitchen showed that my host and hostess had their breakfast on the run. Now was my turn. I poured out my first cup of coffee. And convinced that I could tell a sugar bowl with my eyes closed, I shoveled in sugar and stirred it. Sip, it was salt, not sugar. And down the drain the first cup went.

I reached out for another familiar sugar bowl and went through the ritual. But that too was salt. A third time I did, absolutely convinced that I knew what I was doing. How can you go wrong when you read "sugar" on the bowl? But alas, the contents here too were salt. So the drain drank all my coffee and wanted more.

What was the problem? I knew a sugar bowl. And in someone else's home, what I knew—stereotyped—failed. More than that, it abused my intelligence. That is the way of stereotypes, and stereotyping. Sugar bowl discernment is a mocker.

It is easy to "sugar-bowl-discern" socio-cultural, lifestyle and theological false starts parading as conversions. We can smell them a mile away. We know how they look like, speak like, stand and sit like; and how they think and smell like. We know just what they need. They need straightening up.

Consistent with sugar bowl discernment, we might recommend

- a charismatic church to shatter the spell of liturgical lethargy
- a little wine to heal parched peptic ulcers of total abstinence
- a secular psychologist to ditch years of hyper-calvinistic honing, and so on and so forth.

Or, we might see ourselves as divinely appointed, gifted, trained and commissioned on oath to straighten up victims of false starts. And by God, we will. Straightening up means, "chiseling" to fit our one-size-fits-all program, project, and plan—formula. And so with hammer and chisel, we chisel life to fit a formula.

According to Jesus, sugar-bowl discernment, strategy and ministry put us on top and our target persons down. They give us unlimited power and box God up. They kill not only our "victims." They kill us. They blind us to our victims' real needs and the purpose of God as well as our better judgment.

Therefore Jesus instructed and warned. Be careful what and how you hear. If you stereotype people—sugar-bowl-discern them and their problems—they too would stereotype you and your solutions for them (Mark 4:24). Reciprocal responses include resistance and/or rejection, or proselytization and/or syncretism. Ouch!

But we can help false starts seeking help if we are

- childlike in trusting and depending on God (Luke 18:17, see also sheep, snakes and doves in Matthew 10:16) and
- Christ-like in submissively obeying God (John 5:19, 30).

Transformational conversion requirements

Nicodemus, and Jeff, Stacie and Kate (see above) are typical victims of false starts that parade as rightness with God. Therefore, under normal circumstances, they are not the kind you walk up to with a neat formula or keys to being right with God. They had either authored or taught some of those keys and formulas. Or, they had been there done that with the rare and popular versions. They are often masters and distillers of the "right" information about knowing, worshipping and serving God.

Similar to willful haters of God (see chapter 6), they need to come to the end of themselves. The basis of their self-efforts and self-righteousness must corrode, evaporate or bomb-out, leaving them unsure, shaky and feeling abandoned. In addition, they must feel desperate about it. When they do, they know at once where they must not turn for help—self and its allies of socio-cultural or family, denominational doctrinal deity and gospel.

Simultaneously, they know where to go—the Lord, of course. But often, they cannot pinpoint their problem. Other times, they do but they're afraid they would be ridiculed if they admit the true truth. Therefore they approach a would-be counselor purposely vague. They would test the waters first to find out if it's safe to confide, to be vulnerable. They want to know if they would be accepted, loved and helped without being condemned first.

Therefore, judgmental legalists, and ungraced, ruthless purists would fail to see, name and zero in on the real issues—bombed out false starts seeking the biblical out.

On the other hand, selfless Christ-centered, Scripture loving, prayerful, spiritually sensitive, empathetically humble Holy Spirit-filled believers would help tremendously for four reasons.

One, they know how to get out and stay out of the way of the Holy Spirit. And they do it. Two, they know how to help people focus their heart and mind on God expectantly. And they do it. Three, they know how to keep appropriate biblical pressure on gently but firmly until the light dawns. And they do it. Four, they can and do recognize it when the Holy Spirit intervenes. Sometimes he does in unprecedented ways. But they recognize it timely. They lead off or join in the celebration.

Meaning, repentant victims of false starts need to be positioned properly to experience the mysterious transforming power of the good news directly. This is all the work of the Holy Spirit (see Jeff, Stacie and Kate above). Co-workers he uses must be sensitive to his leading as a way of life. Crash helmet—mind—religion experts frustrate the Holy Spirit and the seekers.

And as we have seen, our Lord Jesus Christ modeled this so perfectly for us in leading Nicodemus to transformational conversion. Therefore John 3:1-21 constitutes a model for leading victims of false starts to convert transformationally—at core of being.

Model

Victims of false starts parading as conversions, convert transformationally when selfless, Holy Spirit-filled persons, consciously or unconsciously, position them to experience the mystery of the transforming power of the good news directly for themselves.

Principles for implementing the model

One: Be sure you have been transformationally converted. You had met Jesus Christ at the core of your being; you have fallen in love with him. Consequently, you have a heart's view, not an intellectual view, of Jesus. You are transforming totally (2 Corinthians 4:5-6).

Two: Be sure it is the love and the Spirit of God motivating you to guide seeking victims of false starts to transformational conversion. And make sure it is not a critical, self-righteous, vindictive spirit driving you to straighten up fallen pastors, missionaries, seminary professors, conference speakers, evangelists, etc. who should know better.

Three: Be sure your every move is self-evidently childlike trust and dependence on God, and Christ-like submissive obedience to God, his word and Spirit.

Four: Avoid debating false starts. Do not try straightening out their theology or behavior either. It would feel like being chiseled.

They would recoil, and even self-exile from following Jesus altogether.

Five: Avoid witch-hunting. Neither "sugar-bowl-discern" false starts or their particular problem. You'd end up stereotyping them and their problem. Then you would resort to stereotypical one-size-fits-all formulas, keys, recipes, etc., to quick fix them fruitlessly.

Six: But prayerfully discern their heart's cry behind their brash behavior or self-flagellation, blame slipping and shifting, exaggerated success and unfulfillment, superiority complex and veneered ethnocentrism. Take time off to pray and expect God to show you what the issues are beyond the issues.

Seven: Be loving and understanding but firm. Be cautious and tender but persistent to keep the focus on the heart of the matter. Help false starts to hear God for themselves.

Eight: help them to hear, see, feel, face and deal with the chasm they had fixed between

- *Their head—crash-helmet religion—and their aching and famished heart, hurting to experience God*
- *The god they had theologically figured out and the transcendent God they can never fathom*
- *The parochial, ethnocentric god they had known, controlled and bullied into subjection and the universal God they have not bothered to know, love, worship, and serve through unconditional acceptance and care for believers from all cultures, races, tribes and languages*
- *The god of academic pursuit they had dissected and pieced together scientifically and the God who inhabits the high and lofty place but desires to establish a God-human relationship with the repentant and humble*
- *The god transfixed in exotic doctrines fit for winning theological debates and the LORD God to experience as closer than human breath, loving, forgiving and merciful, but*

demands and deserves absolute obedience, and rejects expedient and convenient obedience.

Nine: Guide, don't push, false starts to see, face and deal with the subtle neglect, fear, scorn, suspicion they had nurtured into fierce resistance and rejection of the mystery of God, evidenced in avid indulgence in numbers, formulas, recipes, keys, —the measurable, predictable and controllable.

Ten: Guide, don't push, false starts to see, face and deal with the gulf they had fixed between the comfort of kingdom doctrines and the responsibilities of kingdom citizenship, e.g., joy and peace, forgiveness and reconciliation, unity in diversity, which only believers in Christ can know, experience and model in a hateful, suffering and divided world.

Eleven: As appropriate, share how a heart's view of Christ, as opposed to a purely intellectual view of him has freed, empowered and transformed you so much so that you are loving God more, trusting and depending on him more, obeying him more, etc.

Twelve: Use a personal experience or two to show how a growing understanding of the simplicity of the good news of Christ has freed and helped you to hold lightly all you know, e.g., theology, missiology, etc.

Thirteen: By the same token and when appropriate, show how like Paul, you are more deliberate and proactive in leading people away from putting their trust in human wisdom, but in the wisdom of God. Gently, but firmly challenge comfort zone dependence on formulas, keys—the tried and tested—, and unwillingness to let God be God consequently.

Fourteen: Prayerfully and scripturally place seeking false starts before God so that they wrestle with the issue of control in their lives. Who has it, God, God's word and God's Spirit or self or popular opinion?

Wilson Awasu

Fifteen: Using one or two personal experiences, illustrate surrender of self-rule and commitment to the rule of God as inevitable expressions of genuine repentance and saving faith.

Sixteen: As appropriate, use one or two personal experiences to illustrate the presence and work of the Holy Spirit in your life. Show how he has continued to transform the way you think, feel and act since he has taken residence in you. Show how with his help, you have matured in loving God, all believers as well as your enemies.

Seventeen: Through a personal experience, show seeking false starts how easy it is to lip service saving faith and live a life of disbelief for the most part.

- *Saving faith consists of childlike trust and dependence on God to save and keep; therefore surrenders ambitions and expectations to God, discerns and follows God's will, word, ways and works.*
- *Disbelief consists of childlike trust and dependence on human reasons that admit God can save but can't really keep; so "we" must do "something" to keep us going, hanging in there pursuing our will, word, ways and works.*

Eighteen: Similarly, paint the thin line that lies between a being identity and a doing identity.

- *Being identity consists of God-grace-faith orientation. It takes pressure off "us" and unleashes peace, calm confidence in God, joy and hopeful perseverance.*
- *Doing identity consists of human-works-merits orientation. It puts pressure on "us" and unleashes anxiety, frustration, burnout, a feeling of readiness to quit but unable to, a compelling feeling of guilt and need to prove self.*

Nineteen: Be sure you are filled and are being filled—empowered and controlled—by the Holy Spirit as a way of life (Galatians 5:16, 25).

Twenty: Remind yourself constantly that you are privileged to be co-laboring with the Holy Spirit. Therefore always discern and follow his leading. Be careful not to resist or quench him through unbelief/disbelief. Disbelief is actually rationalistic belief that God can do all things, but he won't do certain things at certain times and places.

Twenty-one: On the scale 1-5, functionally rate 4 or 5 in being prayerful, teachable, Spirit-filled, spiritually sensitive, scripturally knowledgeable, ministerially flexible and Christ-centered in all things.

4

Unsaved conscious worshippers of God

Among other things, Cornelius' conversion reveals that good news carriers could stand in God's way and hinder the good news and frustrate prospective converts to Christ without knowing it.

For, God knew that Cornelius worshipped him consciously. God had actually sent an angel to tell Cornelius that he had approved his prayers, and gifts to the poor. Accordingly, Cornelius knew he worshipped God consciously.

The good news, for all times, remains God's power for saving everyone who believes (Romans 1:16). "Everyone" includes people like Cornelius, who worship God consciously but are unsaved.

But unfortunately, carriers of the good news carry with them a deep-seated pre-conditioning that tends to negate all of the above or make no sense out it all. Therefore that pre-conditioning has to be exposed and dealt with biblically. Or it would resist God, blunt the power of the good news, and obstruct prospective recipients of the good news. Or failing that, it would proselytize or carve them in its own image unconsciously.

And that was exactly where Christ laid emphasis in freeing and equipping Peter adequately before sending him to Cornelius.

For indeed Peter needed freedom from himself before he could see, accept and treat Cornelius as God did. Very seriously, Peter needed to be equipped with truly biblical views of all people, not the least, Cornelius. It was in the process that Peter picked up and followed a thread of acts God had initiated and orchestrated to convert Cornelius transformationally.

All that makes Cornelius' conversion experience an illustrative case story. It is the case story for leading unsaved conscious worshippers of God to salvation in Jesus Christ.

This case story is one of many New Testament-approved approaches to cross-cultural evangelism. It and they emphasize that God is more thorough and particular and intentional about transformational conversion than we are conventionally.

1. At Caesarea there was a man named Cornelius, a centurion in what was known as the Italian Regiment. 2. He and all his family were devout and God-fearing; he gave generously to those in need and prayed to God regularly. 3. One day at about three in the afternoon he had a vision. He distinctly saw an angel of God, who came to him and said, "Cornelius!"

4. Cornelius stared at him in fear. "What is it, Lord?" he asked. The angel answered, "Your prayers and gifts to the poor have come up as a memorial offering before God. 5. Now send men to Joppa to bring back a man named Simon who is called Peter. 6. He is staying with Simon the tanner, whose house is by the sea."

7. When the angel who spoke to him had gone, Cornelius called two of his household servants and a devout soldier, one of his personal attendants. 8. He told them everything that had happened and sent them to Joppa.

9. About noon the following day as they were on their journey and approaching the city, Peter went up on the roof to pray. 10. He became hungry and wanted something to eat, and while the meal was being prepared, he fell into a trance. 11. He saw heaven open and something like a sheet being let down to earth by its four corners. 12. It contained all kinds of four-footed animals, as well as reptiles of the earth and birds of the air. 13. Then a voice told him, "Get up Peter. Kill and eat."

14. "Surely not, Lord!" Peter replied. "I have never eaten anything impure or unclean." 15. The voice spoke to him a second time, "Do not call anything impure that God has made clean."

16. This happened three times, and immediately, the sheet was taken back to heaven.

17. While Peter was wondering about the meaning of the vision, the men sent by Cornelius found out where Simon's house was and stopped at the gate. 18. They called out, asking if Simon who was known as Peter was staying there.

19. While Peter was still thinking about the vision, the Spirit said to him, "Simon, three men are looking for you. 20. So get up and go downstairs. Do not hesitate to go with them, for I have sent them."

21. Peter went down and said to the men, I'm the one you're looking for. Why have you come?"

22. The men replied, "We have come from Cornelius the centurion. He is a righteous and God-fearing man, who is respected by all the Jewish people. A holy angel told him to have you come to his house so that he could hear what you have to say." 23. Then Peter invited the men into the house to be his guests.

The next day Peter started out with them, and some of the brothers from Joppa went along. 24. The following day he arrived in Caesarea. Cornelius was expecting them and had called together his relatives and close friends. 25. As Peter entered the house, Cornelius met him and fell at his feet in reverence. 26. But Peter made him get up. "Stand up," he said, "I am only a man myself."

27. Talking with him, Peter went inside and found a large gathering of people. 28. He said to them: "You are well aware that it is against our law for a Jew to associate with a Gentile or visit him. But God has showed me that I should not call any man impure or unclean. 29. So when I was sent for, I came without raising any objection. May I ask why you sent for me?"

30. Cornelius answered: "Four days ago I was in my house praying at this hour, at three in the afternoon. Suddenly a man in shining clothes stood before me. 31. And said, 'Cornelius, God has heard your prayer and remembered your gifts to the poor. 32. Send to Joppa for Simon who is called Peter. He is a guest in the home of Simon the tanner, who lives by the sea.' 33. So I sent for you immediately and it was good of you to come. Now we are all here in the presence of God to listen to everything the Lord has commanded you to tell us."

34. Then Peter began to speak: "I now realize how true it is that God does not show favoritism 35. but accepts men from every nation who fear him and do what is right. 36. You know the message God sent to the people of Israel, telling the good news of peace through Jesus Christ, who is Lord of all. 37. You know what has happened throughout Judea, beginning in Galilee after the baptism that John preached— 38. how God anointed Jesus of Nazareth with the Holy Spirit and power, and how he went around doing good and healing all who were under the power of the devil, because God was with him.

39. We are witnesses of everything he did in the country of the Jews and in Jerusalem. They killed him by hanging him on a tree. 40. But God raised him from the dead on the third day and caused him to be seen. 41. He was not seen by all the people, but by witnesses whom God had already chosen—by us who ate and drank with him after he rose from the dead. 42. He commanded us to preach to the people and testify that he is the one whom God appointed as judge of the living and the dead. 43. All the prophets testify about him that everyone who believes in him receives forgiveness of sins through his name."

44. While Peter was still speaking these words, the Holy Spirit came on all who heard the message. 45. The circumcised believers who had come with Peter were astonished that the gift of the Holy Spirit had been poured out even on the gentiles. 46. For they heard them speaking in tongues and praising God.

Then Peter said, 47. "Can any one keep these people from being baptized with water? They have received the Holy Spirit just as we have." 48. So he ordered that they be baptized in the name of Jesus Christ. Then they asked Peter to stay with them for a few days (Acts 10:1-48).

Who they are

Cornelius is typical of people who consciously worship God but are unsaved. He feared God and worshipped him consciously with his family (verse 2a). He gave generously to people in need (verse 2b). He prayed regularly to God (verse 2c).

Through an angel God disclosed to Cornelius that he had endorsed his gifts and prayers. He linked him with Peter to lead him into transformational conversion experience (verses 5-8, 17-33). Soon, he, his family and friends would hear a straightforward telling of the story of Jesus and convert transformationally (verses 34-43). They would receive the Holy Spirit in evidence of converting transformationally.

They would receive initial follow up instruction in their newfound relationship with God (verses 44-48).

Essentially then, people who consciously worship God but are unsaved know God but do not as yet know Jesus Christ. Credible witnesses of Jesus Christ discern that knowledge accurately. Then they link the knowledge of Christ biblically to it. The marriage between the prior knowledge of God and the current knowledge of Jesus Christ results in transformational conversion as it should.

The Ethiopian eunuch makes another New Testament example (Acts 8:26-40). But Old Testament examples include Melchizedeck (Genesis 14:17-19, compare Hebrews 6:13-7:28), Jethro (Exodus 2:15-22, 4:18-20, 18:1-27), Balaam (Numbers 22-25), and Job (the book of Job).

Contemporary examples

Like their Old and New Testaments counterparts, contemporary examples do not just have a vague idea about God. They know God. Some register as "priests" and/or "prophets" of God similar to Mechizedeck and Balaam (see above). Their priestly acts parallel the Levitical priesthood without any prior influence from the latter.

Similarly, their prophecies point to the transcendent God, the uncreated Creator, his unparalleled power, providence and mercy. They point to eternal salvation in him alone. They demand unqualified unrivalled worship of God.

Since numerous works, like Don Richardson's "Eternity in their hearts" (see recommended reading), exist on this global phenomenon, I cite only the following. Pachacuti ruled Inca (Peru) civilization from 1438-1471. He did not only teach his people to pray to Viracocha—the uncreated Creator God. He also taught them to pray to him with deepest awe and humility (Richardson 1984:38).

Then, there was Kolean, a Santal of Calcutta, India. He was one of many who kept alive Santal traditional belief in Thakur Jiu—the genuine God. His testimony led western missionaries, Lars Skrefsrud and Hans Borreson to see Thakur Jiu as the right Santal name for God.

When Skrefsrud and Borreson connected the story of Jesus Christ to the knowledge of Thakur Jiu in their preaching, they averaged 80 joyful Santal baptisms per day. Santal believers spontaneously passed on the message of the good news among their people. Phenomenal conversions followed (see Richardson 1984:41-54).

Prophets of Karen, a Burmese people, on the other hand, had hymns they taught their people about Y'wa—the true God. Themes of those hymns
- extolled the eternity of Y'wa's being
- appreciated Y'wa's redemptive visit to people
- emphasized people's duty to love Y'wa and one another
- invited sinners to repent and return to Y'wa for mercy
- predicted Y'wa's return as king, etc. (see Richardson 1984:73-85).

Phenomenal self-reproductive conversions among Karen taught Adoniram Judson, a pioneer American missionary to Burma and his colleagues, about the validity of that prior deposit and preparation for the good news of Jesus Christ. The reality exploded as Judson led Ko Thah-byu, a Karen Burmese, to Christ while he worked for him.

Sooner than later, Ko Thah-byu led the way and worked with George and Sarah Boardman, Jonathan Wade, and other western missionaries to ready harvest among the Karen. Karen converts became missionaries to spread the good news still further among their own people almost as quickly as they converted to Christ and were baptized.

Ko Thah-byu distinguished himself. Francis Mason, another colleague of Judson, called him "The Karen Apostle" (see Richardson 1984:91-96).

Other forms of contemporary examples exist. They take into account individuals whose experiences parallel the blind man Jesus healed through saliva, mud and washing in the Siloam pool (John 9:6-7). Medical science and all conventional methods of healing had written them off. A long torturous life and public ridicule or painful slow death stirred them in the face.

In bleakest hopelessness, God came to their rescue, through a dream, a voice, an angel or an impression on the mind, specifically instructing them to do something and get well. They did and got well.

Others had dramatic angelic visitations giving them messages from God to deliver to specific people, sometimes to total strangers, at certain times and places. Still others had detailed visions of future events, and were directed to pray about them, tell or warn particular persons, or people of a given society. And there were others who died clinically but came back to life with stories about encounters with a blinding light, angels, or Jesus, who gave them a "mission" to return and carry out for God.

While growing up, I sat two or three times in audiences that listened spellbound to Sedem as she delivered messages she had received from God through trances. But I didn't make much of her or her messages until I graduated from college. Actually, it was a series of recent deaths, fulfilling predictions Sedem had made in my childhood, that drove me to go talk to her personally.

Sedem disclosed that she started receiving and delivering messages from God in her youth. Like Jeremiah, she protested vehemently. But God told her she would go to whomever he sent her and deliver whatever message he gave her. Accordingly, she had delivered messages from God to individuals, families and clans, and towns and whole tribes. Some of the messages predicted famines and deaths.

The famines and deaths were eventual punishment from God for individual and corporate refusal to repent for sacrificing animals to

95

rivers, mountains, and rain and sun gods; for chronic land disputes, and protracted clan feuds.

In time, devastating famines and sudden deaths wiped out extended families, whole clans, and communities as Sedem predicted. But for all practical purposes, Sedem remained marginalized in her church. She hanged in there scornfully, but joyfully, until she died at 95 in the strength of a 30-year old. She predicted her death.

On the day she died, I was told; she cooked her last meal early evening and had it with her husband. She took a shower, and went to say goodbye to her son and daughter and their families living two, three blocks away respectively. Back home she said goodbye to her husband. She entered her prayer room. Unlike at other times, she left the door wide open. And that was it. Husband entered moments later. And there she was, dead on her knees.

I recently met Maria. Her church threw her out of church when it had run out of ways, including public humiliation and torture, to stop her from dreaming and foretelling future events that happened with mathematical precision.

For example, through nightly visions she saw, and later exposed, the church leadership's entrenchment in extra marital affairs, the practice of necromancy, misuse of church funds, etc. She warned that insanity, bleeding boils, and poverty would come as God's punishment on the unrepentant and remain in family lines for years.

"The fatigued and disillusioned church leadership got rid of the 'dreamer'," Maria lamented, "but internal corruption continued to plague the church." According to Maria, God gave her the gift of visions/prophecy at age eight when he resuscitated her after she had been declared clinically dead.

Job, Jethro, Balaam, and Mechizedeck, the John-9-blind-man, the Ethiopian eunuch, and Cornelius; Parchacuti, Karen prophets, Sedem and Maria, plus countless others would always meet formidable skepticism, resistance and rejection among supposed people of God. The following explains.

For some mysterious reason, we tend to deny God's Spirit and word the chance to give us needed light and guidance in these and similar matters. Rather, we rely heavily on conventional wisdom. Its light and comfort convince us that we know, "Such people don't belong here!" Therefore we push them out or reject them.

Perhaps because of the reality, God initiates and orchestrates fresh acts, with or without cooperation from his supposed people, to save or nurture such people. Though illiterate, both Sedem and Maria amazed me with their knowledge of Scripture. And consistent to fact, Jesus took initiative to look up and convert the former blind man following his rejection from the Synagogue (John 9:35-38).

And similarly, it was Jesus who exposed Peter's inhibiting "excess baggage"—Jewish ethnocentrism—to him, to face it and deal with it biblically before he sent him to Cornelius.

Numerous Corneliuses exist out there. Christ may well be calling you and me to get ready before he sends us out to tell them the story of Jesus. Our willingness or unwillingness to face our cultural, theological, and spiritual views and attitudes, and deal with them biblically is the measure of our love for Christ. That is a disturbing thought!

Customized good news

The bridge between conscious knowledge and worship of God and conscious knowledge of Jesus Christ is the shortest ever. Understandably, intimate knowledge of God predisposes these kinds of God-worshippers to identify Jesus Christ rather quickly.

To underscore this reality, God disclosed in Isaiah 66:1-2 that he is transcendent but he esteems people who are humble and holy and, who submissively obey his every word.

Not surprisingly, Peter opened his sermon by affirming that fact to Cornelius and his family and friends. "I now realize how true it is that God does not show favoritism, but accepts people from every nation who fear him and do what is right" (Acts 10:34-35). Then he moved on to tell them a customized story of Jesus Christ as follows.

You must have heard that not long ago, the God you know incarnated himself in Jesus Christ in Israel. God made Jesus Christ Lord of all things and the embodiment of peace with God.

You also must have heard that John the Baptizer signaled Jesus Christ's public ministry. It all began in Galilee and spread through Judea.

God anointed Jesus Christ with the Holy Spirit and with power. So Jesus went around doing good and healing all who were oppressed by the devil, for God was with him. I am one of his closest friends. My colleagues and I went in and out with Jesus Christ when he did all these things throughout Israel and in Jerusalem. Then our religious leaders (and Rome) crucified him.

But God raised him to life three days later. God restricted his resurrection appearances to those of us whom Jesus had chosen beforehand to be his witnesses. We ate with him and drank with him after he rose from the dead. He charged us to proclaim everywhere that God had appointed him the judge of all the living and the dead.

All the prophets—the Scriptures—spoke about him. They emphasized that everyone who believes in him will be forgiven their sins through his name (see verse 36-43).

Suddenly, the Holy Spirit fell on all who heard Peter's message. They audibly spoke in foreign tongues, praising God (verses 44-46). Amazed, Peter ordered them all to be baptized with water in the name of Jesus Christ. Unanimously, they asked Peter to stay with them for a few days. And he did (verses 47-48).

The customized good news that transforms unsaved conscious worshippers of God focuses on the link between God and Jesus, highlighting

- Jesus as God
- Jesus as God incarnate
- Jesus as God's anointed one
  o doing good, healing the sick and exorcising demons
- Jesus as the redeemer through
  o death and bodily resurrection
- Jesus as central theme of all the Scriptures
  o pardoning the genuinely repentant
  o giving the Holy Spirit to the transformationally converted
- Jesus as the judge of the living and the dead
- Jesus to be proclaimed by credible witnesses (verses 36-48).

Appropriate good news carriers

Typical of God, he orchestrated several players and factors to convert Cornelius transformationally. They include

- God himself (verses 1-6)
- an angel of God (verse 3b-6)
- Cornelius (verses 1-6, 24-33, 44-48)
- Cornelius' family, attendants and friends (verses 2, 7-8, 17-23, 27
- the Holy Spirit (verses 19-44), and
- Peter (verses 9-48).

There could not have been a better carrier of the good news to Cornelius, an early gentile convert, than Peter. Peter knew Jesus firsthand. He was one of the twelve apostles. He participated in the ministry of Jesus and witnessed his crucifixion from within. He fellowshipped with the resurrected Jesus and saw him ascend to heaven.

Then, Peter experienced Pentecost and the formal birth of the Church firsthand. Therefore if anyone ever converted transformationally, Peter did. The cleverest disguised miniature form of it could not fool him.

In addition, Peter had somewhat integrated his transformational conversion theologically. Freed by that integration and subsequent modification in his theological thought, word and deed, he had fearlessly withstood Sanhedrin intimidation. He boldly insisted that Jesus, whom the Sanhedrin killed but whom God raised from the dead, was/is the only means of salvation (Acts 2:14-42, 3:12-26, 4:1-37). As a result, Peter had had an effective ministry among the Jews, with bitter persecution, of course.

But from those very same perspectives, Peter most qualified to misrepresent Jesus and the good news to short-change transformational conversion among non-Jews. He could most effectively transmit cultural overtones as part of the good news.

He might make exuberant reference to his close association to Jesus Christ to impress people. But unlike Christ, he would refuse to associate with non-Jews. If he had to, like in the case of Cornelius, he would on the basis of their willingness to become Jewish. Without realizing it, he would build conditions necessary for becoming Jewish into the good news. Then transformational conversion becomes synonymous with becoming Jewish.

What a negation of the incarnation and atonement, resurrection and ascension, and enthronement of Jesus Christ! For in Jesus Christ, God reconciles all things, and people of all cultures, races, tribes and languages to himself and to one another (Colossians 1:15-20, Revelation 7:9-12).

Unfortunately, theological, cultural and spiritual changes that Peter failed to make in himself, would seriously discredit the good news. Does it indeed convert people of all cultures, races, tribes and languages tranformationally and reconcile them to God and to one another? Peter's ethnocentrism would render the good news' claim to counter the world's hate and divisions in diversity with love and unity in diversity meaningless. And it would make it impractical.

Accordingly, Peter would either clone non-Jews in his own likeness or shoo them away. Those he cloned would take becoming Jewish externally as being converted to Christ internally. And those he shooed would consist of people who resented and rejected his ethnocentric gospel parading as the good news of Jesus for obvious reason. It asked them to cease to be who they were culturally, deny any previous knowledge about God, become Jewish, then God would save them.

How tragic that Peter, who knew Jesus so intimately, would have damaged his cause that severely! How tragic that Peter, whom Jesus had trained and equipped with his word and the Holy Spirit would have walked into Cornelius' house, totally unable to see and build on what God had done in preparing Cornelius for transformational conversion!

Precisely to avoid those tragedies, God alerted Peter to them. He jolted him to his need to integrate his transformational conversion culturally. God especially jolted Peter to see his cultural, theological and spiritual blind spots and deal with them to become an effective cross-cultural carrier of the good news. The process started "pre-field" and continued "on-field."

First, in a vision, God used an obvious violation of levitical dietary law to catch Peter's attention and draw him into dealing with any vestiges of Jewish ethnocentrism he harbored. Contrary to that law (Leviticus 11), God ordered Peter to kill and eat unclean animals. As a matter of course, Peter rejected, "Surely not, Lord! I have never eaten anything impure or unclean" (Acts 10:1-14).

It must have shocked Peter when God said, "Do not call anything impure that God has made clean" (verse 15). For emphasis, this happened three times. Then the vision ended. Momentarily, Peter wondered what it meant (verses 16-17).

Right then, God showed Peter the meaning of the vision and the application of its message. The implications of transformation in Jesus transgress cultural bigotry. Said another way, ethnocentrism has no place in transformation in Jesus Christ. For God shows no favoritism. Presently, God instructed Peter to welcome three messengers who have just arrived from a gentile and a military officer serving contemporary Jewish conquerors—Rome. He did and learned their mission (verse 17-23).

Peter confessed cultural changes he had made accordingly. To Cornelius and the audience in his house he said, "You are well aware that it is against our law for a Jew to associate with a gentile or visit him. But God has showed me that I should not call any man impure or unclean. So when you sent for me, I came without raising any objection" (verse 28-29).

Second, God used the fact of his endorsement of a gentile's pre-conversion godly acts—generous gifts to the needy and regular prayers to God—to catch Peter's attention and draw him into dealing with his theological biases (verses 22, 30-33, cf. verses 1-8).

For the wildest misinterpretation of the rabbinical theology that raised Peter would fail to hint that God would do such a thing. What was more, God had actually sent an angel to a gentile to deliver the message of God's acceptance of those godly acts. And not the least, it was the same angel that disclosed Peter's exact name and exact lodging. He was Simon Peter lodging Simon the tanner, whose house was by the sea (verses 30-33, cf. 3-7, 17-23).

Sheer weight of evidence that God was in all this, led Peter to make needed theological, cultural and spiritual changes. He confessed, "I now realize how true it is that God does not show favoritism. But he accepts people from every nation who fear him and do what is right" (verses 34-35). But it wasn't over yet.

Third, God let the Holy Spirit fall on Cornelius, his family members and friends while Peter was still telling them the story of Jesus. In a sense, the visible and audible falling of the Holy Spirit on them announced God's acceptance of their repentance and conversion and the moment both happened (verses 44). That also caught Peter's attention and drove him into dealing with any spiritual pride or superiority complex he might have harbored.

It certainly astonished the Jewish believers who accompanied Peter "that the gift of the Holy Spirit had been poured out even on Gentiles. For they heard them speaking in tongues and praising God" (verses 45-46).

When Peter recounted this incident later in Jerusalem, he disclosed that the Holy Spirit actually cut his sermon short. He said, "As I began to speak, the Holy Spirit came on them as he had come on us at the beginning" (Acts 11:15). Meaning Peter was astonished just as his Jewish colleagues were.

In view of the new light the phenomenon shed, Peter made further theological and spiritual changes. He confessed, "Can anyone keep these people from being baptized with water? They have received the Holy Spirit just as we have." Accordingly, he ordered them to be baptized with water in the name of Jesus Christ (verse 47-48).

So then, Peter needed to make certain changes in the way he thought, felt and acted culturally, theologically and spiritually to become an appropriate carrier of the good news to unsaved conscious worshippers of God. It goes without saying that if Peter needed to make those changes in himself, we too need to make them to be appropriate carriers of the good news to similar people.

The changes that Peter had to make in the way he thought, felt, and acted cross-culturally, as said earlier, followed

- his three-year apprenticeship to Jesus Christ (Mark 3:13-19)

- his firsthand experience of Jesus' life, ministry, crucifixion, resurrection appearances, and ascension (Matthew 16:13-17:21, 26:36-75, John 20:1-10, Luke 24:36-53)
- his firsthand experience of Pentecost and aftermath (Acts 2:1-47)
- his firsthand experience of being repeatedly refilled with the Holy Spirit (Acts 4:23-37)
- his effective ministry in terms of numerous transformational conversions, healings, exorcisms and discipleship (Acts 2-5).

That forbids us to put confidence in our higher education, personal spiritual and ministry experiences, superior technology, much money, and the like. Rather, our confidence must be in God and God alone. Then, we would be truly biblical, being filled with the Holy Spirit, spiritually sensitive, teachable, and flexible methodologically.

Transformational conversion requirements

God took pains to ensure that Cornelius, his family and friends converted transformationally. The narrative leaves us in no doubt that they met Jesus at heart and converted at the core of being. Therefore they could transform inside out. Instantly personalizing the good news, they could spontaneously lead others to convert transformationally.

The narrative makes it abundantly clear that the importance of the spiritual and scriptural fitness of carriers of the good news comes next only to the presence and work of the Holy Spirit. Without that fitness, carriers of the good news could indeed resist, grieve and quench the Holy Spirit through misguided allegiance to cultural and theological bigotry.

Therefore it behooves them to make changes in the way they think, feel and act culturally, theologically and spiritually to be biblically effective (see above).

Put together, then, Acts 10:1-48 constitutes a biblical model for leading unsaved conscious worshippers of God to transformational conversion.

Model

Unsaved conscious worshippers of God convert transformationally when an appropriate carrier of the good news links up for them the knowledge of God and the knowledge of Jesus Christ (Acts 10:1-48, see above).

Principles for implementing the model

One: Be sure you have been transformationally converted. You had met Jesus Christ at the core of your being, you have fallen in love with him. Consequently, you have a heart's view, not an intellectual view, of Jesus. You are transforming totally (2 Corinthians 4:5-6). God made certain that Peter cleared that with himself.

Two: Be sure it is the love of God motivating you to lead unsaved conscious worshippers of God to transformational conversion. And make sure it is not a misguided mission obsession to swell the statistics of heathen converts enlightened "our way" that is driving you. God made certain that Peter cleared that too with himself.

Three: Be sure your every move is self-evidently childlike trust and dependence on God, and Christ-like submissive obedience to God, his word and Spirit. This too God ensured that Peter cleared in himself.

Four: Beware of negative cultural and theological stereotypes you have regarding religious experiences. Desist projecting them on people (verses 9-20, 34-35, cf. Galatians 2:11-16).

Five: Cultivate and keep cultivating truly biblical views of people and of the Church of Jesus Christ (verses 28, 34-35, cf. John 17:20-23 and Revelation 7:9-12).

Six: Constantly and scripturally scrutinize—review and reinterpret—your cultural and theological views in ministry context (verses 30-35).

Seven: Don't project a pre-determined—easy to handle—category of the unsaved on prospective converts. Open-mindedly listen to their religious experiences—religious life-story—(verses 1-8, 30-35). Don't pre-judge people's religious experiences or religious life story. Prayerfully assess them in terms of Scripture.

Eight: Be careful you are not bedazzled by people's religious experiences either. Soberly discern

- *how much knowledge about God is revealed in them (verses 1-8, 30-35) and*
- *how much knowledge of Jesus Christ—the good news—is needed to supplement the knowledge about God (verses 36-43).*

Nine: Accurately discern and interpret possible sovereign interventions of the Holy Spirit—his promptings, leadings, directing, etc.—as you tell the customized story of Jesus Christ. Watch and listen carefully and test all things scripturally. Promptly obey the Spirit lest you resist or quench him through disobedience based on ignorance and/or unbelief/disbelief (verses 44-48).

Ten: Be sure you are filled and are being filled—empowered and controlled—by the Holy Spirit as a way of life (Galatians 5:16, 25).

Eleven: Remind yourself constantly that you are privileged to be co-laboring with the Holy Spirit. Therefore always discern and follow his leading. Be careful not to resist or quench him through unbelief/disbelief. Disbelief is actually rationalistic belief that God can do all things, but he won't do certain things at certain times and places.

Twelve: On the scale 1-5, functionally rate 4 or 5 in being prayerful, teachable, Spirit-filled, spiritually sensitive, scripturally knowledgeable, ministerially flexible and Christ-centered in all things.

Adaptive implementation of these principles prevents presumptuous denial of knowledge about God to God-fearers. For we would either confirm and build on God's prior work in prospective converts to Christ or we would audaciously attempt to corrode it.

Adaptive implementation of this model helps us to avoid working against God while working for him. Herein lies the wisdom of biblically classifying the unsaved and biblically connecting them directly to God for him to convert them transformationally.

5

Unsaved unconscious worshippers of God

Several years ago if you asked me what Christ did while on earth, this is what I would have said. He announced the kingdom's arrival; he restored and redefined Israel's hope; and he enacted salvation for the whole world. Along with that, he cast out demons, healed the sick, and raised the dead. He gathered and trained those who, after he was gone, would carry on his work of announcing, building, and teaching (cf. Mark Buchanan 2001:101).

Should you ask me if I was finished, I would have said, "Y-yes! That covers it all, I think!" Give me additional time to add anything else I recall, I might add that Jesus met and conquered Satan as God had said he would. And he walked experientially in our shoes.

What wouldn't come to mind readily is Jesus Christ's one-on-one conversions. I stumbled over them later in my personal study of the life of Jesus Christ in the Gospels. And how refreshing, challenging and motivating to see Jesus use diversified methods to convert different people one-on-one.

For example, he used theological discussion, not debates, to lead Nicodemus a conservative theologian to conversion experience. Through socialization he led Matthew and Zacchaeus, tax collector and chief tax collector respectively, to it.

He converted Mary Magdalene through exorcism. But it was through laidback chit-chat that he led the Samaritan woman to conversion at Jacob's well. As for Paul, he suddenly blinded him and handed him over to Ananias of Damascus to finish the job. Ananias restored Paul's sight and helped him to be filled with the Holy Spirit. On and on and on Jesus' one-on-one conversion stories go!

Jesus treated each person differently. Rather, uniquely, I should say. No wonder each one converted transformationally. The apostles closely followed Jesus' example. And they too saw transformational conversions. So shall we if we allow unsaved situations to dictate the method we use to connect people directly and appropriately to Jesus who converts them at the core of being.

How Paul discerned, responded to and treated the Athenians to lead them to transformational conversion (Acts 17:16-34) illustrates further.

> 16. *"While Paul was waiting for them in Athens, he was greatly distressed to see that the city was full of idols. 17. So he reasoned in the synagogue with the Jews and God-fearing Greeks, as well as in the marketplace day by day with those who happened to be there. 18. A group of Epicurean and stoic philosophers began to dispute with him. Some of them asked, "What is this babbler trying to say?" Others remarked. "He seems to be advocating foreign gods." They said this because Paul was preaching the good news about Jesus and the resurrection. 19. Then they took him and brought him to a meeting of the Areopagus, where they said to him, "May we know what this new teaching is that you are presenting? 20. You are bringing some strange ideas to our ears, and we want to know what they mean." 21. (All the Athenians and the foreigners who lived there spent their time doing nothing but talking about and listening to the latest ideas.)*
>
> 22. *Paul then stood up in the meeting of the Areopagus and said: "Men of Athens! I see that in every way you are*

religious, 23. For as I walked around and looked at your objects of worship, I even found an altar with this inscription: TO THE UNKNOWN GOD. Now what you worship as something unknown I am going to proclaim to you.

24. "The God who made the world and everything in it is the Lord of heaven and earth and does not live in temples built by hands. 25. And human hands do not serve him, as if he needed anything, because he himself gives all men life and breath and everything else. 26. From one man he made every nation of men, that they should inhabit the whole earth; and he determined the times set for them and the exact places where they should live. 27. God did this so that men would seek him and perhaps reach out for him and find him, though he is not far from each one of us. 28. In him we live and move and have our being. As some of your own poets have said, 'We are his offspring.'

29. Therefore since we are God's offspring, we should not think that the divine being is like gold or silver or stone—an image made by man's design and skill. 30. In the past God overlooked such ignorance, but now he commands all people everywhere to repent. 31. For he has set a day when he will judge the world with justice by the man he has appointed. He has given proof to this to all men by raising him from the dead."

32. When they heard about the resurrection of the dead, some of them sneered, but others said, "We want to hear you again on this subject." 33. At that, Paul left the Council. 34. A few men became followers of Paul and believed. Among them was Dionysius, a member of the Areopagus, also a woman named Damaris, and a number of others.

Who they are

Athenians, then, are typical of people who worship God unconsciously. Typically, they worship many gods including God (verse 16). But God does not just happen to be one of the gods they worship.

Historical facts, not speculations or imaginations, led the Athenians to the name, "The Unknown God." For on Mars Hill, six centuries earlier, Epimenides, a Cretan poet/prophet, prayed to God and he stopped a plague that would have wiped out Athens. Consenting to Athenian pressure to enshrine the event for future generations, Epimenides directed that "agnosto theo"—to an unknown god—be written on the altars that consumed the sacrifices to that God.

Therefore, it was historicity and reverence that preserved at least one of those altars until the first century A.D. The historicity of the event, and the altar and its name anticipated our Lord Jesus Christ. Providentially, God had intervened—reached out—in the history of Athens to preserve life when all Athenian known gods had failed.

Little wonder that Athenians adopted Epimenides' teaching that people are creatures of God—"We are his [God's] offspring" (Acts 17:28). [Again, for a fuller treatment of the topic, read Richardson (1984:9-132).]

Athenians communicated a loud message when they claimed to descend from "The Unknown God," and not from any of their numerous other gods. It was this. Beyond their philosophical sophistry lay belief in a Creator God. History well taught them that they could only know him through self-revelation, not philosophical manipulation.

It was only left for a diligent and appropriate carrier of the good news to discern that belief accurately, interpret it correctly, and use it effectively to establish the biblical link that exists between the God they knew subconsciously and worshipped unconsciously and the God they should know consciously and worship consciously (verses 22-23). Paul proved to be a diligent and appropriate carrier of the good news to the Athenians. And he did exactly that (verse 24-34).

Most New Testament conversions occurred when Jesus, Peter, Philip, Paul, etc., discerned and targeted conscious or unconscious knowledge people had about God. In either form that knowledge constitutes God's prior work in people.

The Athenians (Acts 17) constitute people who had unconscious knowledge about God. But examples of people who had conscious knowledge about God include the Samaritan woman Jesus met and converted at Jacob's well (John 4), the 3000 YHWHists who converted to Christ on the Day of Pentecost (Acts), Cornelius (Acts 10), etc.

Contemporary examples

Acts 14:15-17, 17:24-31, Romans 1:18-32, insist that God had revealed himself to all peoples. People largely store their perception of God in names they call him. For example, those names describe God as the uncreated Creator God, the Master of Heaven, the Sky God, the Supreme God, the true or genuine God, or simply, the Great One, and so on and so forth.

Accordingly, he is Theos to Greeks; Deus to Romans; Viracocha to the Incas of Peru; Shang Ti to Chinese; Hananim to Koreans; Gud to Norwegians; Thakur Jiu to Santal of India; Magano to Gedeo of Ethiopia; El elyon to Cannanites; and Karo to Mbaka of Central Africa Republic (compare Richardson 1984:1-132).

He is Mawu to Ewe of West Africa (Geoffrey Parrinder 1950); Nyame to Akan of West Africa (J.B. Dnaquah 1944); Olodumare to Yoruba of Nigeria (E.B. Idowu 1962); Y'wa to the Karen of Burma; and Karai Kasang to the Kachin, also of Burma (Richardson 1984:73-96).

In addition to names people call God, these other forms store and reveal knowledge about God among peoples around the world: Folklore enshrines historical events of unprecedented mass deliverance from death, chaos, catastrophe, etc., as divine interventions and/or encounters (Jacob Spieth 1906 and Awasu 1988).

Indeed as God had prepared the good news for people, he had also prepared people for it. They may or may not be aware of their prior preparation for it. Therefore, it goes without saying that when good news carriers take pains to discover the form, content and local meaning of that prior preparation and match it appropriately with the good news, they would be working God's works after him. Phenomenal conversions would result.

But the role of the Holy Spirit in all this cannot be overemphasized. Only his filling, empowerment and leadership unleash the wisdom of God to hush human wisdom. God's wisdom in the filled, empowered and led cannot help but marry God's prior work in people to the good news of Jesus Christ.

That is what motivates me to draw critical attention to these models of New Testament conversions. Moreover, I know they still work. I have used them (see the conversion stories I cite throughout the book).

Customized good news

Unlike conscious worshippers of God, the unconscious worshippers of God need a longer bridge to connect them experientially to Jesus Christ. The raw materials for building that bridge often lie beneath the veneer of philosophical sophistry. That was exactly where Paul found the Athenian concept of God.

He discerned and picked it up in two places. The first was the name Athenians called God, "The Unknown God" (verse 23). How their folklore enshrined belief in God— "We are his offspring" — constituted the second (verse 28).

Paul scrubbed the Athenian concept of God scripturally and spiritually. Then he expanded and extended it biblically (verses 23-24). He engineered it an apologetic bridge focusing on the sovereignty of God and the progressive self-revelation of God. He soft-paddled the centrality of Jesus to salvation, and inevitable judgment without him but he didn't sacrifice either of them (verses 29-34). Here's his message.

(Greetings, illustrious) Athenians! I noticed that you are very religious. As I walked your streets, I saw many altars. One of them had this inscription on it— "To the Unknown God." Listen to me as I tell you about this God you have been worshipping without knowing who he is.

He is the God who made the world and everything in it. Since he is the Lord of heaven and earth, he doesn't live in temples people build. Neither can people serve his needs. The fact is, he has no needs. He himself gives life and breath to everything. He satisfies every need there is.

From one person, he created all the peoples throughout the whole earth. He decided beforehand which should rise and fall, and he determined their boundaries.

His purpose in all of this was that the peoples—nations— should seek after God and perhaps feel their way toward him and find him—though he is not far from any one of us. For in him we live and move and exist. As one of your own poets says, "We are his offspring." Since this is true, we shouldn't think of God as an idol designed by craftsmen from gold or silver.

God overlooked people's former ignorance about these things. But now he commands everyone to turn away from idols and turn to him. For he has set a day for judging the world with justice by the man he has appointed. And he proved to everyone who this is by raising him from the dead (verses 22-31).

Connotations of the word "resurrection" suddenly split the audience and ended the meeting. Some people laughed. Others said, "We want to hear more about this later." But others, among them

Dionysius and Damaris, joined Paul and became believers in Jesus Christ (verses 32-34).

In a word, the customized good news that led unconscious worshippers of God to transformational conversion looks like this. The Unknown God is the Creator God of the universe. He has revealed himself in

- the world of nature, elements, spirits and people
- the human conscience
- people's folklore and poetry [and the arts]

He is Lord of the universe and everything in it—all existence derives from him and depends on him. He had revealed himself (more especially) in the Hebrew Scriptures. He incarnated himself in a person—Jesus Christ. Through Jesus Christ he invites all peoples to

- turn away from idol worship and
- turn to him in wholehearted worship or
- face judgment for idolatry hereafter.

He raised Jesus from the dead as proof of all this (verses 22-32)

Capsulated, the customized good news that led unconscious worshippers of God to transformational conversion was an apologetics consisting of God revealed in

- creation
- conscience
- folklore/poetry
- Scriptures and
- Jesus Christ.

Delayed and instant acceptance marked the effectiveness of Paul's message. Those who delayed acceptance simply needed more information about the God who incarnated himself, died and resurrected, and more time to think things through. The delayed acceptance didn't have to do with miscommunication.

Miscommunication would have consisted of mismatching Jesus Christ to "The Unknown God" through audacious disregard for God's self-revelation in creation, conscience and folklore. The Athenians needed the apologetics Paul used because their knowledge of God was largely subconscious. Precisely for that reason, conscious worshippers of God, like Cornelius, do not need an apologetics to convert transformationally.

Obviously, then, a blanket approach to the unsaved does two things at least. One, it mocks God through disregarding his prior work in the unsaved. Two, it generates external conformity devoid of internal—core level—conversion. That results in outward inward changes—cosmetic superficial changes fraught with syncretism.

Appropriate good news carriers

Several things made Paul an appropriate carrier of the good news to philosophically sophisticated people who worshipped God unconsciously. One, Paul thoroughly educated in both Greek philosophy and Hebrew theology. But he later learned not to put confidence in human wisdom of any kind. He learned to let human wisdom serve the wisdom of God, so that his converts put their faith in God and God's power instead of human wisdom.

Two, he converted tranformationally in a dramatic post resurrection-ascension encounter with Jesus Christ. Three, he was and remained filled with the Holy Spirit. Four, he now had a thorough understanding of the Scriptures and the purpose of God. Five, Jesus especially assigned Paul as a carrier of the good news to non-Jewish elite.

Six, Paul remained God-focused and Christ-centered; Holy Spirit empowered, controlled and directed; scripturally balanced and sound, and methodologically flexible. Seven, he was motivated and guided by the love of God for Jews and non-Jews. Eight, through deliberate and conscious effort, Paul disciplined himself to make the good news relevant and understandable to Jews and non-Jews as well.

Nine, Paul diligently and vigilantly retained Jesus Christ at the heart of the good news. His thought, word and deed demonstrated that, indeed, the good news was/is the power of God to save repentant Jews and non-Jews alike (Acts 26:9-23, Romans 1:16-17). And not the least, ten, Paul persistently sought to know the mind of Christ and the schemes of Satan (1 Corinthians 2:16, 2 Corinthians 2:11)

Consequently, eleven, Paul saw numerous transformational conversions leading to total life transformation—from absolute rebellion against God to submissive obedience to God (Romans 15:18-21).

Certainly, Jesus Christ remains our perfect model in all things, including leading others to transformational conversion, and total life transformation. But Paul stands as a pristine human example we do well to copy.

One area in particular is Paul's emphasis on self-preparation and readiness to be used and usable by God (1 Corinthians 9:24-27). In this, Paul, John the Baptizer and Jesus Christ agree that we could be the worst enemies, hindrances, to the good news while we busily communicate it.

Accordingly, Jesus Christ insists that when we ourselves do not transform totally in thought, word and deed

- we would minimize and pamper our besetting sins
- we would sniff out and hyperbolize negligible flaws in the lives of target people
- we would overestimate our ethnocentric solutions for stereotypical problems we project on target people, and underestimate their power to fight back for encroachment (Matthew 7:1-6).

Similarly, John the Baptizer urges, You want to connect people directly to God, then,

- fill out all valleys of doubts in your own life first—cultivate childlike trust and dependence on God
- level out all mountains of pride and conceit in your own life first—be truly humble
- straighten out all crooked, deceptive and insincere ways in your own life first—be self-evidently sincere and honest
- smoothen out all the rough edges in your own life first—be truly loving, forgiving and winsome.

Then, all people would see, desire, accept and experience the goodness of the good news for themselves (Luke 3:4-6).

Everything shows that Paul took John and Jesus seriously on this. He rid himself of any and everything that would hinder people from seeing, desiring, accepting and experiencing the Lord Jesus Christ for themselves. Accordingly,

- he refused to use shameful and underhanded methods— manipulation and intimidation born out selfish ambition and superiority complex
- he refused to trick people [with clever and persuasive but meaningless God-talk]
- he refused to distort God's word [with personal, liberal or evangelical pet agendas].

Rather, he painfully told the naked truth of knowing, loving and worshipping God wholeheartedly, with God and his audiences as witness (2 Corinthians 4:1-2)

Do any less than that, and transformational conversions would continue to elude us. In their place, short-lived cosmetic superficial changes would keep mocking our evangelistic and discipleship efforts.

Transformational conversion requirements

God is always working ahead of us. In view of that Jesus insisted that we didn't choose him. He chose us. He appointed us and placed us in places of lasting fruitfulness. And he guaranteed us answered prayers (John 15:16). Our appropriate response to that reality divides into two.

One, we need to be sure others or we didn't call us to divine office. That often happens. Two, being totally certain it is God who called us, and being sure we are where he wants us and when, leave us with one more thing to be certain about.

It is to make sure we study and accurately discern and correctly interpret all the forms in which our target people disclose or repress their hunger for God. With that, we study and accurately discern and correctly interpret all the ways in which God had revealed himself in the culture of target people. Both of these are culturally consistent. Therefore they defy and elude ethnocentric stereotyping parading as universal or conventional characterizations.

The narrative (Acts 17:16-34) shows that Paul made certain about all that. He repeatedly reminded himself and others that he was a servant of God and Jesus Christ. Then too the narrative shows that Paul discerned the Athenian concept of God through firsthand and fresh study and interpretation. And it was freshly derived internal evidence that determined corresponding method and message.

If anyone could boast of one-size-fits-all, high-powered sermons, or one-size-fits-all, tried and tested methods, Paul certainly could. But he didn't. In fact, he never did.

All those pieces make Acts 17:16-34 a biblical model for leading unconscious worshippers of God to a conscious knowledge of him; and the link between him and Jesus Christ; and finally to transformational conversion.

Model

Unconscious worshippers of God are converted transformationally when an appropriate carrier of the good news effectively links up their culturally expressed forms of hunger for God to the knowledge of God revealed in creation, conscience, folklore/poetry, Scriptures, and Jesus Christ.

Principles for implementing the model

One: Be sure you have been transformationally converted. You had met Jesus Christ at the core of your being, you have fallen in love with him. Consequently, you have a heart's view, not an intellectual view, of Jesus. You are transforming totally (2 Corinthians 4:5-6).

Two: Be sure it is the love of God motivating you to lead unconscious worshippers of God to transformational conversion. And make sure it is not a misguided mission obsession to swell the statistics of heathen converts enlightened "our way" that is driving you.

Three: Be sure your every move is self-evidently childlike trust and dependence on God, and Christ-like submissive obedience to God, his word and Spirit.

Four: make sure you do not impose premeditated—universal or conventional—categorizations on unsaved situations. Study each new situation afresh, noting

- *names for the Transcendent, Creator, True, Genuine God, Unknown God, Unknowable God, etc. in their languages; desist dubbing them with foreign categories*
- *honorific expressions about the Transcendent One in everyday language and folklore/poetry (verses 28b)*
- *attitudes toward those names and expressions*
- *symbols of worship; desist calling them gods; they might not be (verse 16, 22-23a); find out local meanings and stories connected to the symbols.*

Five: Accurately discern target people's concept of God and correctly interpret it, allowing meanings to be internally derived and validated. Desist imposing premeditated anthropological or theological or religious definitions and categories, e.g., "animism," "polytheism," etc. (verse 23). Imposed categories, names and meanings reject local ones perilously.

Six: Open-mindedly discern how target people

- *have misperceived and/or mislabeled knowledge about God and*
- *have ignored and/or misdirected hunger for God (verses 16, 18-21 and 28b).*

Seven: Tactfully isolate elements of truth in target people's concept of God, see how those elements naturally lean away from or lean toward

- *the sovereignty of God and*
- *progressive revelation of God*

before deciding how to beef up those elements in plain biblical terms (verses 23-26).

Eight: Though an apologetics is most natural to this type of situations, don't let it be a premeditated—universalized—apologetics. Rather, let it be

- *internally derived and*
- *consistently customized*

to take target people from where they are in their knowledge about God to where they should be in their knowledge of God.

Nine: While biblically and consistently expanding target people's knowledge about God (verses 23-26 and 28b), i.e.,

- *God revealed in creation*

- *God revealed in human conscience and*
- *God revealed in folklore/poetry*

establish that, knowledge about God obligates humanity

- *to seek God wholeheartedly*
- *to depend absolutely on God and*
- *to worship only God (verses 27-29).*

Ten: Then introduce

- *God revealed in the Scriptures and*
- *God revealed in a person—Jesus Christ—*

as the final pieces in God's progressive self-revelation (verses 30-31).

Eleven: Impress it on target people that with the final piece of God's self-revelation—Jesus Christ—God commands

- *a genuine break with the past—vaguely knowing/relating to God and*
- *a clean acceptance and commitment to the present— knowing/relating to God through Jesus Christ or*

face inevitable condemnation for idolatry (verses 29-31).

Twelve: If you prayerfully and scripturally communicate the good news of Jesus Christ in the power of the Spirit to unconscious worshippers of God in this manner, you can be sure that their rejection of it would not be blamed on miscommunicating it (verses 32-34).

Thirteen: Be sure you are filled and are being filled—empowered and controlled—by the Holy Spirit as a way of life (Galatians 5:16, 25).

Fourteen: Remind yourself constantly that you are privileged to be co-laboring with the Holy Spirit. Therefore always discern and follow his leading. Be careful not to resist or quench him through unbelief/disbelief. Disbelief is actually rationalistic belief that God can do all things, but he won't do certain things at certain times and places.

Fifteen: On the scale 1-5, functionally rate 4 or 5 in being prayerful, teachable, Spirit-filled, spiritually sensitive, scripturally knowledgeable, ministerially flexible and Christ-centered in all things.

Adaptive implementation of these principles prevents audacious corroding of God's prior work in people who worship God unconsciously. Rather, knowing that God works ahead of us obligates us to discern his "footsteps" and plant ours in them. In that way we would gladden heaven and ourselves more frequently with transformational conversions.

6

Willful haters of God

Contemporary examples of who they are

Ever had the hardest time eating your most favorite dish when it sat before you moisturizing your face, nostrils and mouth? I did once at college. I was in my second year. And for 13 months, the experience haunted me. More than that, it turned nightmarish.

Actually, it wasn't just because the experience snatched my appetite and compelled me to eat up a dish I once enjoyed but now detested. No! Rather, it was what triggered it off.

Friday lunchtime arrived in usual fashion with great expectations of temporal relaxation and recreation for tired students. I got my food and sat at an almost full rectangular table designed to sit 16 people. The hassle and bustle of noisy students hungrily waging silverware to devour their food grew wilder and more deafening every minute. Soon the wild symphony would crescendo and crash into normal weekend campus desertion and dispersion.

I bowed my head, in usual fashion, and silently prayed. While praying, I overheard a couple of voices across the table remark, "Look at this guy! He's praying here in the dining room!"

My eyes met several eyes that looked but didn't stare at me as I raised up my head. Then came this remark from one person who didn't look. "Don't mind him. They're all hypocrites. Believe me, I know them!"

The remark stung like a bee. The venom reached my bones in seconds. It almost paralyzed me when I realized that it was David, a fellow believer, who injected the poison.

David, yes David! He and I belonged to the campus chapter of Inter-Varsity Christian Fellowship. He and I had sat on several subcommittees of IVCF. Barely three months ago, he and I and Jane were teammates visiting homes during a summer IVCF evangelistic outreach to his hometown. When did he desert Jesus Christ? When did he become a betrayer of the faith? When did he become a persecutor of fellow believers? These and similar questions raced through my mind all at once.

Suffocating tension raged in and around me momentarily. The within and without tensions crashed into wild waves. The waves hit mercilessly. They tossed me to the edge of abandoning my lunch. To comply would communicate a loud message I would rather not communicate. But to tough it out and eat my lunch was a hardest thing I ever did. Every bite, beginning with the first, navigated drowning waves and landed on a rougher "shore," my stomach.

David dropped out of IVCF. He barricaded every possible road to him with barbwire and landmines. He avoided me like the plague. Meanwhile my heart ached. I wavered between bitterness and empathy, anathema and pardon, hate and love for David.

David didn't just backslide. His every move on campus showed that he was deliberate and conscious

- in forsaking the faith he once enjoyed and propagated, and
- in persecuting that faith and its adherents.

Think of a fellow missionary who risked the lives of his wife and three and two year old kids alongside of you in a creative accessed country for ten years. Back home on furlough, he did not only divorce his wife. He did not only leave the mission. He did not only abandon the faith he propagated in restricted countries. He picked up occultism.

You know that though his wife has custody of their kids, now 13 and 12, the court granted him visitation rights. What happens to the kids when they visit dad? How about his former wife, would the churches and individuals who supported them in missions be sensitive and helpful to her in her sudden nightmare? What becomes of the former Christian missionary who has turned occultist? Is his doom eternally sealed as Christian gossip and abandonment indicate?

Pastor Larry Lovelace makes another scenario. If names describe people, his definitely did. His church members loved him and hanged on his every word. He preached biblical truth pastorally. He was handsome and winsome in every way. A bleeding leakage of an extra marital affair with one of the ladies in the choir snatched the pulpit and the pastorate from him. His marriage split over it.

He pumped gas for a while. The next time you heard about him, he's been initiated into the practice of witchcraft. Not only that, he writes and pens his name to scripts for Hollywood productions that satire clergy.

Here is another. Two doors down the hallway from you is Dr Gil Denken, professor of Psychology. He knows that you are a devout Christian. In a chat one day he discloses to you that he was a missionary kid. But now, he is into Meditation. He organizes weekly meetings for meditation "trips" off campus. Several students you are currently discipling attend. They rank high on Dr Denken's list of adept small group leaders in Meditation.

He confesses to you, "For the first time in my life, I am free, really free to be me. I intend to help free as many as I can from the kill-joy menace you people call Christianity." How would you respond and not only react as this situation hits you?

These are not made up stories. No! They are all true stories.

Willful haters of God are not clichés or relics. People who know God, love him and worship him but deliberately and consciously drop him and choose another god are not a thing of the past. Neither are they a rare occurrence as we might wish. Nor are their effects on humanity taken care of by a neatly crafted cold theological explanation.

As said earlier, they are not your casual occasional backslider who might be deficient in Christian assurance and/or discipleship. No! Some of these pass for seasoned evangelical disciplers. They didn't slide into doubt, confusion and despair about God and relating to him. Rather, they purposefully willfully

- rejected God
- chose another god—idolatry and
- decided to spite God and God's purpose.

History bleeds and speaks in evidence. For example, one, today, popular Christian theological thought and behavior worldwide succumbs to subtle influences of Darwinism/secularism/evolutionism. But Charles Darwin (1809-1882) was a pastor's kid.

Two, Communism as a political ideology may well be dying out since the wall fell in 1989. But Marxism remains strong. And like Darwin, Karl Marx (1818-1883) too was a Rabbi-Christian kid.

Three, Adolf Hitler (1889-1945) was a church-boy. Four, so was Anton LaVey, high priest of Satan, currently resident in San Francisco, California. This is the man who sold Hollywood on glamorizing and popularizing satanic ideas and views and their pervasive acceptance as harmless and normal way of things in everyday life in video games and cartoons, for example.

Why LaVey, Hitler, Marx and Darwin, and numerous others like them abandoned the God they once knew and chose another god could only be speculated this late. But the effects of their lives defy speculation. So the question comes.

How do you get such people for a Christian dialog, an apologetics perhaps, or a dosage of an evangelical quick fix formula or capsule or an intellectual zap? How do you retrieve and restore such people to the faith they calculatedly rejected and (sought) are seeking to eat up cancerously? David, my colleague enlisted in that crusade.

Honestly, even if evangelical quick fixes abundantly existed and I fancied them, for two months, my own motives remained mixed. I might resort to them for the wrong reason. My love for David muddied at that time.

Campus Christian gossip didn't help either. Every corner of our tightly knit chapter of IVCF currently steamed with gossip about David and the like of him. I barely escaped enticements to vent and wallow in it. I doubt if any prayers I said for David in those two months escaped the pollution and hindrance of self-righteousness.

Momentarily, the experience enrolled me in an extended course in "Willful haters of God." I began to learn that willful haters of God indulge in power rampage. They reject the God who denies them indulgent power and they defect to the god that lavishes it on them. And usually, it is running power bankrupt that either turns the defecting prodigals homeward or drives them further away from home.

Was I not overjoyed when David tracked me down eleven months later and said, "I need to talk to you!"

"Me? What's up David?" I asked, expecting the worst.

"I need something for my personal devotion. What do you recommend?"

I didn't believe what I heard. But David's every look confirmed every stroke of his request. I think he noticed my bewilderment. So he spoke again. "I went away from the Lord Jesus Christ. I went after my heart's wildest desires. For a while, I had them. But for some time now, I have hit rock bottom. It hurts. I need out. Can you help me? Please do!"

I think I passed the course I took in "Willful haters of God." Perhaps I made a "B+" or even an "A." Not because David, my live class project, had a happy ending, and I got to hear about it from his own lips. But because of this, after the initial two months of self-pity and self-righteousness, I repented. For the next eleven months I prayed wholeheartedly everyday for David. When he came to talk to me, it was like God telling me, Your prayers for David are answered! See the answer for yourself!

Biblical examples of who they are

Luke 15 recorded Jesus' teaching on three types of lostnesses and their usual remedies. Usually, it is the shepherd who goes to look for and recover the consciously lost—the lost sheep (verses 1-7). And usually, it is the owner who searches and finds the unconsciously lost—the lost coin (verses 8-10).

And though the father's heart aches for the willfully lost—the lost son—, it is the prodigal who decides to return home and does, after he has come to a stinging end of himself (verses 11-24). Understandably, the willful, unlike the conscious and unconscious, know where and what home is and could retrace their way back to it.

Unusually, however, God orchestrates direct and indirect power confrontation in pursuit of willful haters of God. Whenever he does, he invites the defectors to a power match. He lets them pit their preferred power against the wooing, not brutish, power of God in an open contest.

Elijah's contest with the prophets of Baal constitutes such power confrontations. Indirectly through Elijah, God challenged the power of the prophets of Baal to expose its impotency, and woo Israel back from Israel's willful rejection of YHWH, their God.

Elijah proposed that the prophets of Baal and he kill a bull each, flay it and put it on a designated altar. Then they each should pray to their respective God to consume the sacrifice by fire. The God who did, would distinguish himself as the real God.

What a proposal! What a contest! All the people said, agreeing.

The prophets of Baal went at it first. They prayed and danced; they cut themselves and raved all morning, all afternoon until evening. But there was no reply, no voice, and no answer.

Then came Elijah's turn. He repaired the altar of YHWH in the sight of the massive crowd of Israelites. He dug a trench around the altar large enough to hold about three gallons of water. He piled the wood on the altar, cut the bull in pieces and laid them on the wood. At his direction, attendants poured water over the offering and the wood until it soaked them and ran off filling and overflowing the trench. Then Elijah walked to the altar and prayed.

O YHWH, God of Abraham, Isaac, and Jacob, prove today that you are God in Israel and that I am your servant. Prove that I have done all this at your command. O YHWH, answer me! Answer me so these people will know that you, O YHWH are God and that you have brought them back to yourself (1 Kings 18:36-37).

Immediately the fire of YHWH flashed down from heaven and burned up the sacrifice, the wood, the stones, and the mortar. It even licked up the water in the ditch! When the people saw it, they fell on their faces and cried out "YHWH is God! YHWH is God!" (verses 38-39, read also verses 1-46).

The spiting prodigals confessed self-evident exhaustion of their preferred power. They recommitted to the God they had abandoned. In Jeremiah's description,

- they admitted self-devaluation—worthlessness (2:4 and 21)
- they abandoned death—broken cisterns, and
- they returned to life—fountain of living water (verse 13).

But Paul's Damascus road experience constitutes a direct power confrontation. Paul met Jesus Christ directly. Typical of willful haters of God, Paul went on a power rampage, uttering threats with every breath, determined to annihilate the followers of Jesus. Then he collided with Jesus himself.

The encounter convicted Paul beyond all doubts that the authority he had and was wielding derived from anti-God sources. He and the Sanhedrin that empowered him had actually rejected God and chosen another god. Their real god was their traditions—a rigid lifeless code of ethics that they mercilessly policed to self-serve. It had assumed ultimacy to which God's word and God himself had to submit or be rejected for failing to (Matthew 15:1-9).

Paul's face-to-face encounter with Jesus on the Damascus road melted his piece of that power fast. It started to melt when a brilliant light suddenly beamed down on Paul from heaven. Saul was his name at the time. His horse went crazy at the light, and tossed him several feet high in the air and down to the ground like a bag of potatoes. He heard a voice saying to him, "Saul! Saul! Why are you persecuting me?"

"Who are you Lord?" Saul asked.

The voice replied, "I am Jesus, the one you are persecuting. Now get up and go into the city, and you will be told what you are to do."

Paul's companions heard the sound of someone's voice, but they saw no one. When Paul got up, he realized that he was blind. His companions led him by the hand to Damascus. And for three days, he remained blind.

Apparently, Jesus had appeared to Ananias in Damascus. He directed him to go

- open Paul's eyes
- deliver Jesus' marching orders to Paul, and
- help him to be filled with the Holy Spirit.

This happened on the third day. Accordingly, Paul regained his sight, was filled with the Holy Spirit, and was baptized with water.

Consequently, Paul did not only become a closest follower of Jesus Christ and a chief apostle of him. He also became a most avid imitator of Jesus Christ. To the extent, he asserted that he had the mind of Christ (1 Corinthians 2:16b). And conversely, he also knew the schemes of Satan (2 Corinthians 2:11b). He asked his converts to imitate him (I Corinthians 4:16, 11:1). How bold! Yet Paul's boldness derives from and is based on Christ.

Appropriate good news carriers

With adept agility, Paul flexed methods to connect people directly to Jesus for him to convert them at the core of being. In Acts 17:16-34, see above, he used an apologetics to connect Greek philosophers to Jesus Christ. In Acts 13:13-43, he used the law and the prophets to connect practicing Jews to Jesus Christ. But in Acts 13:6-12, we see Paul using power encounter to confront evil acts of a defected Jew who had become an occultist. This was Elymas. The account reads,

> *6. They traveled through the whole island until they came to Paphos. There they met a Jewish sorcerer and false prophet named Bar-Jesus, 7. who was an attendant of the proconsul, Sergius Paulus. The proconsul, an intelligent man, sent for Barnabas and Saul because he wanted to hear the word of God. 8. But Elymas the sorcerer (for that is what his name means) opposed them and tried to turn the proconsul from the faith. 9. Then Saul, who was also called Paul, filled with the Holy Spirit, looked straight at Elymas and said, 10.*

"You are a child of the devil and an enemy of everything that is right! You are full of all kinds of deceit and trickery. Will you never stop perverting the right ways of the Lord? 11. Now the hand of the Lord is against you. You are going to be blind, and for a time you will be unable to see the light of the sun."

Immediately mist and darkness came over him, and he groped about, seeking someone to lead him by the hand. 12. When the proconsul saw what happened, he believed, for he was amazed at the teaching about the Lord.

Like the prophets of Baal, and the Sanhedrin and Paul prior to his conversion, Elymas

- deliberately rejected the God whom he knew, and
- consciously defected to another god whom he didn't know (Acts 13:6-7).

For, like all Jews, Elymas must have been painfully taught

Hear, O Israel: YHWH our God YHWH is one. Love YHWH your God with all your heart and with all your soul and with all your strength (Deuteronomy 6:4-5). I am YHWH your God, who brought you out of Egypt, out of the land of slavery. You shall have no other gods before me (Exodus 20:2-3).

If a prophet, one who foretells by dreams, appears among you and announces to you a miraculous sign or wonder...and says, "Let us follow other gods" (gods you have not known) "and let us worship them," you must not listen to the words of that prophet or dreamer...

If your very own brother, or your son or daughter, or the wife you love, or closest friend secretly entices you saying, "Let us go and worship other gods" (...gods of people around you, whether near or far...) do not yield to him or listen to him. Show him no pity. Do not spare him or shield him. You must certainly put him to death. Your hand must be the first in putting him to death, and then the hands of all the people. Stone him to death, because he tried to turn you away from YHWH your God... Then all Israel will hear and be afraid, and no one among you will do such an evil thing again (Deuteronomy 13:1-11).

But contrarily, Elymas did not only forsake the God of Abraham, the God of Isaac and the God of Jacob. He picked up the occult (Acts 13:6). He didn't stop there. Through occultic means, he tried to block a prospective gentile convert from believing in Jesus (Acts 13:7-8). Paul discerned this and responded swiftly. Just like Elijah did the prophets of Baal, see above, Paul challenged Elymas' occult power to expose its impotency compared with God's power.

The stage opened with Elymas attending the Roman governor, Sergius Paulus at his court (verses 6-7). Sergius Paulus had present, Barnabas and Saul to tell him the good news. Through occultic means, Elymas tried to divert the governor from the faith (verse 8). But filled with the Holy Spirit, Paul discerned this (verse 9).

Paul characterized Elymas declaratively:

- You are a child of the devil (verse 10a).
- You are an enemy of all that is good and right.
- You are a masquerader full of deceit and trickery (verse 10a).
- You are a pervert of the ways of the Lord (verse 10b).
- You are headed for a head-on collision with the Lord (verse 11a).

For that, you are going to be physically blind for a brief time (verse 11b). And immediately Elymas became blind (verse 11c).

I think Paul used the term, "the Lord," deliberately. He was a Jew talking to a fellow Jew become an occultist. In using "the Lord," he appealed to Elymas' knowledge of YHWH (the LORD) whom he had deliberately rejected and defected from (verses 6, 10-11). Both Paul and Elymas knew that choosing another god was punishable by death for Jews (see passages cited above). Indirectly, Paul reminded Elymas about that.

But from experience, Paul knew that Jesus Christ reduced the death sentence to three days' physical blindness for him when he had substituted the traditions for the LORD (cf. Acts 9:1-20). Therefore sternly but mercifully as well, Paul made Elymas blind for a brief time (verse 11).

But this wasn't a quick fix formula Paul reproduced unthinkingly. In part, his knowledge of the Old Testament teaching on the issues guided him (see above). The Holy Spirit also guided him (verse 9).

It was the Holy Spirit who led him to discern and expose Elymas' currently acquired identity—son of the devil—and his entanglement in it (verse 10). It was with the Holy Spirit's help that Paul accurately discerned that Elymas engaged spiritual forces to obstruct Sergius Paulus from hearing to understand and receive the message of the good news (verses 8-10). And it was the Holy Spirit that led Paul to curse Elymas to be blind momentarily. And because he led Paul, he also effected the blindness on Elymas (verse 11).

We do not have the privilege of knowing whether Elymas, like Paul, saw the light of Christ after a brief time of darkness. But we know three things. They are most revealing. First, Elymas' occult power conceded defeat. It couldn't prevent Elymas from becoming blind instantly. Simultaneously, second, Elymas' occultic spell on Sergius Paulus snapped. Only the Holy Spirit could

- attack Elymas, the occultic oppressor and
- free Sergius Paulus, occultic victim

at one and the same time (verses 7b-12).

And third, Sergius Paulus didn't believe in Jesus Christ through intimidation or persuasion by Paul. Rather, he did through amazement, wonder, awe, "at the teaching of the Lord" (verse 12). Therefore an evangelistic method that ignored the occultic influence

135

put on by Elymas, and focused exclusively on Sergius Paulus would have failed to lead him to conversion (verses 6-12).

By the same token, it would have been wrong to blame Sergius Paulus solely if he rejected the good news he wanted to hear. The real culprit would have been the occultic hindrance Elymas secretly imposed on him. It operated beyond Sergius Paulus' awareness and control. On the other hand, Sergius Paulus' acceptance of the good news under those circumstances would have amounted to cosmetic superficial short-lived change, not conversion.

There could not be a better-suited carrier of the good news to that situation. For Paul had been there done that with the elements that made up that situation. And Paul's ability to depend utterly on the Holy Spirit further qualified him as a most appropriate carrier of the good news to willful haters of God.

Having said that, I must hurry on to add that Paul had two other forms of support in addition. The first was his missionary companion, Barnabas (verses 2-3). For Barnabas "was a good man, full of the Holy Spirit and faith" (Acts 11:24). That constitutes an invaluable form of support. But second, Paul and Barnabas (and Mark at the time) also had the spiritual support of the church in Antioch (Acts 13:1-3)

The church in Antioch inhabited unity in diversity, worship, fasting and prayer, and attentiveness to the Holy Spirit (Acts 13:1-2a). It witnessed the Holy Spirit's choice and appointment of Barnabas and Paul as messengers of the good news (Acts 13:2b). It bathed their calling and appointment in more fasting and prayer. Then it laid hands on them and sent them on their way (verse 3).

Meaning, the church in Antioch, Barnabas and Paul, and the Holy Spirit entered into spiritual partnership. It must have been with eager anticipation that the church in Antioch prayed for Barnabas and Paul, welcomed them back, and celebrated with them the transformational conversions they reported (Acts 14:24-28). This is another invaluable form of support Paul had.

But in addition, I think, locating and touching base with God's prior and current work in the city of Salamis in Cyprus educated and informed their praying, planning and procedures (verse 5). That contact eliminated counterproductive duplication, presumption and competition in ministry.

That Barnabas and Paul met Elymas and knew him as a Jew become an occultist before they met him with Sergius Paulus (verses 6-8) tells me something else. It is this. They ethnographically, scripturally and spiritually looked for signs or clues to schemes that Satan was using to battle the purpose of God in the city. That helped them further in focusing their prayers and plans for effective and relevant communication of the good news.

In this way, Paul lived out his claim to know what Christ is doing where and when, and what Satan is doing to resist Christ there and then (1 Corinthians 2:16 and 2 Corinthians 2:11).

Customized good news.

Willful haters of God know God. They had related to him. They know the Scriptures. In some cases, they had served him in ministry. It wasn't ignorance or deficient information that drove them away from God. It was a willful choice to be gone from him.

They went on a power rampage. To return to God requires that they experience power bankruptcy, and feel freed from its entanglements. This constitutes a first step toward retrieval and restoration of prodigals to the God they had abandoned and spited through defection.

The usual route to that life changing experience consists of a stinging "hit-rock-bottom," genuine repentance and a commitment to return home (e.g., the prodigal son, see above). The unusual route divides into direct and indirect power confrontation.

Elijah's contest with the prophets of Baal represents the indirect form of power confrontation. God challenges the defectors' newfound power through a messenger of God (see the prophets of Baal and Elymas above). But Paul's encounter with Jesus on Damascus road makes up the direct form of power confrontation (see above). God does it himself without going through a messenger.

Whether direct or indirect, the power confrontation is never brutish. But it engages the conscious involvement of defectors. Defecting prodigals need to experience the impotency of the power to which they defected, how totally incomparable it is to God's power. Then repentance would be genuine, and cleavage and return would be thorough, expediting restoration.

Restoration comprises of unlearning, relearning, and healing. These form integral parts of their discipleship. But there is no substitute for unconditional welcome, acceptance and care for the returnees among the community of believers.

Transformational conversion requirements

Over all, willful haters of God often defect to spite God and his purpose. Most times, defection is triggered off by bitter disappointment at God, Christians, the church, or even self. But the brunt of the blame is usually put on God. It is he who proved too slow, too distant, too silent, and too powerless. He was the one who didn't show up when and how he should.

Some of the specifics blame God for letting a long awaited only child die on her fourth birthday; a life dream shatter on the horizon, injustice prevail; the innocent suffer while the wicked prosper. It was he who rewarded righteousness with bitter persecution, and sacrifice with unrecognition.

It was he who let 84-year old righteous Jane char in an apartment fire. It was he who let unfaithful pastors and self-serving theologians control the hearts and minds of thousands. It was he who let Christian publishers become restricted country clubs, etc., etc. Yes God is to blame for all this, who else? He could have let justice and truth win and prevail, but he didn't. Why?

This was the logic Job vehemently rejected as his friends sought to drown him in it (see the book of Job). But it makes perfect sense for defectors. Therefore defectors justify defection straight face.

However, without realizing it, the swinging of the pendulum makes them returned prodigals to Satan, the power of sin, the power of the flesh, and the power of the world system without God. All these gleefully welcome reversed prodigals back with

- renewed empowerment and boldness for self-worship
- limitless opportunities and appetite for self-expression and
- reinforced hatred and defiant opposition to God and God's purpose.

Indeed, there is ecstasy in Satan's kingdom whenever one such prodigals returns. What invaluable tools at Satan's disposal! For one thing, defectors hardly see themselves as taking Satan's side. Though grossly involved in promoting Satan's cause while resisting God's in every way, they take full responsibility for all their actions. In fact, they take pride in escalating influence and acclaimed notoriety they enjoy in fueling bad press about God.

Therefore Satan empowers defectors especially and uses them extraordinarily. Consequently, one willful hater of God who defects to spite God sweeps thousands into idolatry. See biblical and contemporary examples cited above.

Soon, their newly acquired identity develops accompanying vocabulary for self-expression. Characteristically, it consists of power, pride, prestige, competition and being number one; must always win, subjugation, domination and triumph; defiance, lust and greed; self-justification and self-gratification; zero tolerance for fair play; aptitude for seeing wrong as right, bad as good, false as true, and vice versa; a drive to promote treachery, vulgarity, violence and, self-justified use of brutish power; isolation and insulation to human pain and suffering, etc., etc.

That situation makes the language of power the only one they now understand. Therefore, only power confrontation can catch their attention and perhaps hold it. The power confrontation must be such that it engages their conscious involvement and conscious experience of self-evident defeat (see prophets of Baal, Saul of Tarsus and Elymas above).

When self-evident defeat floors them, they might concede defeat and think home like prodigals. Or, unable to swallow their pride, they might deny the undeniable and sink further into deception and live in suicidal denial.

Similarly, self-evident defeat momentarily frees victims and followers of defectors and offers them an out option. They could take it as the followers of Baal prophets, and Sergius Paulus did, or reject it.

In all of this, carriers of the good news play a key role. They should

- accurately discern the situation
- correctly interpret it and label it, and
- appropriately match it with the power confrontation it deserves.

Take Elijah for example. Everything from before he pronounced the drought to the time he called fire from heaven, showed that he acted according to perfect discernment of the situation.

One, standing squarely on scriptural basis, Elijah discerned that as nationally organized idolatry hardened the hearts, minds and wills of citizenry,

- it galvanized the sky into bronze
- it petrified the ground into iron and

- it vaporized the rain into powder and dust (1 Kings 17:1, 18:17-18. cf. Deuteronomy 11:13-17, 28:15-24).

Two, from Israel's defection to Baal, Elijah discerned a willfulness that God wanted to confront redemptively with power confrontation. So he prayed that God answered him to prove that his proposal of power contest came from God (1 Kings 18:17-18, 21-22, cf. verses 36-37).

Similarly, it was from scriptural perspectives that Paul discerned, interpreted and labeled Elymas—a defected Jews—as a child of the devil (see above, Acts 13:6 and 10). At least, Exodus 20:2-3, Deuteronomy 6:4-5, 13:1-11 taught Jews to kill defected Jews. Paul and Elymas agreed on that.

From New Testament perspectives, Paul knew that defected people (Jews and non-Jews) perilously affront Jesus Christ. But experientially, Paul knew that Jesus Christ reduced the death sentence to temporal physical blindness for him (Acts 9:1-19, see above). Elymas could benefit from that mercy as well. Therefore he made him blind temporarily (Acts 13:6-12).

I think it was for emphasis that the Scriptures said that Paul was filled with the Holy Spirit before he burned his eyes into Elymas and his current occultic identity and activity (Acts 13:8-10). For without the Holy Spirit, years of gazing at Elymas would fail to reveal to Paul Elymas' entanglement in satanic identity and activity at the time (see above).

And without the Holy Spirit, any curses Paul pronounced would have had no effect on Elymas, making Paul a charlatan. But because Paul acted as the Holy Spirit directed him, Elymas became blind instantly. The Holy Spirit countered Elymas' occultic power. Simultaneously, he freed Sergius Paulus from Elymas' occultic spell.

At once, three things we could do become obvious. Of the three, only one is biblical. First, we could unbiblically ignore willful haters of God, declaring them God-forsaken or unreachable by God. Then we have the like of Darwin, Marx, Hitler and LaVey, etc., plaguing generations of humanity with horrific recycling woes and anti-God thinking and behavior.

Second, we could presumptuously engage willful haters of God in a power confrontation like the seven sons of Sceva, the high priest, did. Then like them, we collide with humiliating backfires (Acts 19:11-17).

But third, we could learn to submit our much learning (and self-righteousness) to the scrutiny of the Scriptures and the Holy Spirit. Then learn to follow the Holy Spirit's leading to engage willful haters of God timely and appropriately in redemptive power confrontation.

One form calls for selfless, sacrificial, sustained intercessory prayer and fasting for the prodigal to hit rock bottom self-evidently, repent and return to God, e.g., the prodigal son (Luke 15:11-24). That was what I did for David, my colleague at college. That was how he returned to the Lord Jesus Christ. Or, fast and pray fervently for them to encounter the Lord Jesus Christ directly in a dramatic way as Paul did (Acts 9:1-19).

The other form, of course, consists of Elijah and the prophets of Baal, and Paul and Elymas—an open power contest as the Lord might direct in the thick of it. Recall my power contest with spiritists at the beginning of the book.

So then, Luke 15:11-24, Acts 9:1-19, 13:6-12, cf. 1 Kings 18:20-39 constitute a model for drawing willful haters of God into a redemptive power confrontation with God. When they concede defeat and return, the church gains a check. Their awe at the grace of God and subsequent loyalty to it is contagious.

Model

Situations created by willfully hating God, and defecting to spite God, require appropriate good news carriers to confront them redemptively through power confrontation. The power confrontation should engage the conscious involvement of defectors, as well as their conscious experience of self-evident defeat (Luke 15:11-24, Acts 9:1-19, 13:6-12, cf. 1 Kings 18:17-39).

Defectors who concede defeat and return to God are awed indelibly at the transforming power of the good news (Romans 1:16). They appreciate the depth of the grace of God than most and remain avidly loyal to it.

Principles for implementing the model

One: Be sure you have been transformationally converted. You had met Jesus Christ at the core of your being, you have fallen in love with him. Consequently, you have a heart's view, not an intellectual view, of Jesus. You are transforming totally (2 Corinthians 4:5-6).

Two: Be sure it is the love of God motivating you to lead willful haters of God to transformational return to God. And make sure it is not misguided, presumptuous, self-righteous zeal.

Three: Be sure your every move is self-evidently childlike trust and dependence on God, and Christ-like submissive obedience to God, his word and Spirit.

Four: Ensure that you have strong, committed and updated prayer support going for you (Acts 13 1-3).

Five: Cultivate and maintain

- *a vital personal relationship with God, demonstrating love, forgiveness and reconciliation*
- *a vital habit of praise and thanksgiving, fasting and praying to God (verse Acts 13:2a and 3a).*

Spontaneously and habitually intercede for believers and non-believers.

Six: Learn all you can firsthand from existing work of God— groups and individuals—at ministry locations. Prayerfully and ethnographically, scripturally and spiritually discern expressions of

God's current presence in the place, striving to know the mind of Christ (Acts 13:5-7, cf. 1 Corinthians 2:16).

Seven: Scripturally and spiritually discern signs and clues to schemes Satan is using locally and currently to battle God, God's purpose and God's people, striving to know the schemes of Satan (Acts 13:6-8, cf. 2 Corinthians 2:11).

Eight: Cultivate and maintain the habit of discerning and promptly obeying the leading of the Holy Spirit in your personal life and ministry (Acts 13:2, 4 and 9).

Nine: Desist dubbing seeming resistance with preconceived notions. Rather, let internal evidence and the leading of the Holy Spirit direct you in interpreting the resistance, to label it correctly as "willful haters of God."

Ten: Let the Holy Spirit lead you to discern whether in addition to rejecting God, willful haters of God have defected to another god, and if so, how are they spiting the God they knew with allegiance to the god they are currently serving without knowing him

- *through persecuting current worshippers of God and/or*
- *through obstructing prospective worshippers of God (Acts 13:6-8).*

Eleven: If you would pray and listen and wait and watch for answers in the thick of it, God may well surprise you with responses that would shame your comfort zone but perfectly match situations with freshly redemptive release of the presence and power of the Holy Spirit (Acts 13:9-11). Incredible retrieval of willful haters of God and incredible transformational conversions would delight you and gladden heaven in the face of prevailing resistance (Acts 13:12).

Twelve: You would experientially discover the truth of, "For my thoughts are not your thoughts, neither are your ways my ways, declares the LORD. As the heavens are higher than the earth, so are

my ways higher than your ways and my thoughts than your thoughts"
(Isaiah 55:8-9).

Thirteen: Be sure you are filled and are being filled—empowered
and controlled—by the Holy Spirit as a way of life (Galatians 5:16,
25).

Fourteen: Remind yourself constantly that you are privileged to
be co-laboring with the Holy Spirit. Therefore always discern and
follow his leading. Be careful not to resist, grieve or quench him
through unbelief/disbelief. Disbelief is actually rationalistic belief
that God can do all things, but he won't do certain things at certain
times and places.

Fifteen: On the scale 1-5, ensure that you functionally rate 4 or 5
in being prayerful, teachable, Spirit-filled, spiritually sensitive,
scripturally knowledgeable, ministerially flexible and Christ-centered
in all things.

7

Victims of the occult

Jesus and the Samaritan woman; Peter and Cornelius; Paul and Dionysius and Damaris; Elijah and the prophets of Baal and the Israelites, Jesus and Saul of Tarsus, and Paul and Elymas and Sergius Paulus (see preceding chapters), constitute varied contexts in which people converted at the core of being. They converted transformationally.

Therefore they could transform totally. They could integrate the good news into the way they thought, felt and acted. They could worship God wholeheartedly. Unreservedly, they would love God with their spiritual, emotional, mental and physical energies. And unconditionally, they would accept and care for all believers; they would model forgiveness and reconciliation (Mark 12:29-31)

But Elijah, Jesus, Peter, and Paul, didn't follow ready-made neat formulas. No! Each of them accurately discerned the unsaved situation before them and appropriately matched it with the life-giving message of God in the power of the Holy Spirit.

This biblical evidence and teaching paint for us a picture and a message, an imperative and an expectation that we must take seriously if we would see transformational conversions. As the rest of the current chapter shows, Philip did. He too saw transformational conversions in humanly impossible situations.

Philip, we know, was one of the seven disciples the apostles assigned to daily distribution of food in the early church in Jerusalem. The martyrdom of Stephen followed by bitter persecution cut short their work and drove him and others out of Jerusalem and scattered them all over the place (Acts 6:1-8:3).

Imagination fails to predict that someone suddenly dispossessed of job, ministry and all belongings, running for dear life would

- temporarily forget about all that and
- temporarily bring a notorious occultist and his victims to transformational conversion to Christ.

But Acts 8:1-24 says Philip did. The account is fascinating!

> *1. On that day a great persecution broke out against the church at Jerusalem, and all except the apostles were scattered throughout Judea and Samaria. 2. Godly men buried Stephen and mourned deeply for him. 3. But Saul began to destroy the church. Going from house to house, he dragged off men and women and put them in prison.*
>
> *4. Those who had been scattered preached the word wherever they went. 5. Philip went down to a city in Samaria and proclaimed the Christ there. 6. When the crowds heard Philip and saw the miraculous signs he did, they all paid close attention to what he said. 7. With shrieks, evil spirits came out of many, and many paralytics and cripples were healed. 8. So there was great joy in that city.*
>
> *9. Now for some time a man named Simon had practiced sorcery in the city and amazed all the people of Samaria. He boasted that he was someone great, 10. And all the people, both high and low, gave him their attention and exclaimed, "This man is the divine power known as the Great Power."*

11. They followed him because he had amazed them for a long time with his magic. 12. But when they believed Philip as he preached the good news of the kingdom of God and the name of Jesus Christ, they were baptized, both men and women. 13. Simon himself believed and was baptized. And he followed Philip everywhere, astonished by the great signs and miracles he saw.

14. When the apostles in Jerusalem heard that Samaria had accepted the word of God, they sent Peter and John to them. 15. When they arrived, they prayed for them that they might receive the Holy Spirit, 16 because the Holy Spirit had not come upon any of them; they had simply been baptized into the name of the Lord Jesus. 17. Then Peter and John placed their hands on them, and they received the Holy Spirit.

18. When Simon saw that the Holy Spirit was given at the laying on of the apostles' hands, he offered them money 19. and said, 'Give me also this ability so that everyone on whom I lay my hands may receive the Holy Spirit.'

20. Peter answered: 'May your money perish with you, because you thought you could buy the gift of God with money! 21. You have no part or share in this ministry, because your heart is not right before God. 22. Repent of this wickedness and pray to the Lord. Perhaps he will forgive you for having such a thought in your heart. 23. For I see that you are full of bitterness and captive to sin.

24. Then Simon answered, "Pray to the Lord for me so that nothing you have said may happen to me" (Acts 8:1-24).

Who they are

How does a city saturated with occult presence, power and performance look like, smell like, feel like? How do people dominated by the occult look like, speak like, smell like? The passage gave us scant clues. They center on Simon.

One, Simon was a distinguished occultist. He lived in a commercial city in Samaria. He claimed to be powerful. And he confirmed his claims with a long practice full of mind-boggling miraculous acts (verses 9 and 11). So influential was he that, two, the townspeople, from the least to the greatest, often spoke of him as "the Great One—the Power of God" (verse 10). All the townspeople revered him (verse 11).

Now, that was something! Rarely do construction workers and lawyers, garbage truck drivers and medical doctors, models and politicians, etc., agree on who are famous. Uncommonly, Simon enjoyed consensus that he was the incarnated power of God. That means, apart from the laurels of a lucrative practice, Simon enjoyed allegiance that politicians would envy (verses 9-11).

How did Simon earn his popularity and fame? Certainly it did not come through philanthropies, or sports, or the arts. No! Rather, he earned it through occultic acts that amazed the freckle-minded and tough-minded alike. Verse 11 says, "They followed him because he had amazed them for a long time with his [superhuman acts]."

Those acts took the form of

- esoteric power (superhuman power) and
- esoteric knowledge (knowledge beyond the senses).

For a long time, the townspeople both heard and saw Simon perform those acts.

Meaning, Simon was not a charlatan. The burglars he cursed for breaking into his house, died soon afterward. The serial rapist he hexed became crippled almost instantly. The spell he placed on a ruthless bully converted him, his children and grandchildren into beggars. Wars, famines, economic crashes, etc. he predicted came true.

Simon was at home in the human and spiritual worlds. With ease, he invoked spirits of the dead and communicated with them in the sight of all. He channeled and connected dabblers to spirit guides. He fused witch-spirits with the spirits of aspiring witches. He dewitched witches. He exorcised the demonized. Simon physically lived in Samaria. Equally physically, Simon inhabited a climate of surrealism.

Seeing and experiencing esoteric power (superhuman power); and hearing and experiencing esoteric knowledge (knowledge beyond the senses) took their toll on Simon's townspeople. The esoteric shaped the way they viewed and related to the world around them. The human and spiritual realms were active and interactive. Simon adeptly probed both realms and gave needed guidance and counsel for meaningful and peaceful co-existence, much like meteorologists do the weather.

Strangely enough, however, neither Simon nor the townspeople hinted that the visible and invisible, human and spiritual worlds were arbitrary. This is how. Simon didn't claim he was God. He simply claimed that he was "someone great" (verse 9). Why?

In calling Simon, "the Great One—the power of God," the townspeople betrayed belief in a transcendent God (verse 10). Simon was great. But that God transcended him. He also transcended the human and spiritual worlds that Simon probed so excellently. Simon was an incarnated power of the transcendent God.

Contemporary examples

Contemporary examples of Simon and his townspeople similarly simmer belief in God. But, functionally, they believe in ancestral spirits, spirit guides, spirits of the dead, witch spirits, Satan, demons, angels, etc.

They include

- dabblers and practitioners of the occult, diviners, necromancers, witches, and Satanists

- descendants and victims of practitioners and dabblers
- users of necromancy, ouijaboards, tarot cards, palm reading, horoscopes
- (in short) those who dabble or delve into esoteric power and knowledge.

The attraction and fascination consist of chance to experience or benefit from esoteric power and knowledge, mediumism, divination, fortune telling, future predictions, spiritual healing, herbalism, protective medicine or charm, etc.

Accordingly, shamanism and animism form only a fraction of this crowd. For not all people who indulge in esoteric power and knowledge are religionists. In fact, many who do, aren't. But the quest for the esoteric always and everywhere nullifies or represses belief in God.

Customized good news

Bumping into superstitious bands of people while fleeing persecution constitute a time and place for two forms of shoddy evangelism. The one is to spray or sprinkle the good news and run off. Who knows, persecutors might be close at your heels.

The other is to quick fix a superstitious people who wouldn't know the difference anyway, with a one-size-fits-all message. Time is life and delay is death.

But if pressure of time and fear for one's life dominate, then, of course, bypassing a superstitious people—too slow to understand anything anyhow—would be most sensible. And God would grant that. Of course!

On the contrary, Philip behaved differently. Controlled, directed, and motivated by the Holy Spirit (cf. Acts 6:1-7, 8:1-8), he deliberately and consciously stopped in that city of Samaria. He told the story of God who incarnated himself as the Messiah (verse 5). He ordered demons out of the demonized. They screamed as they left victims. He made the paralyzed jump up and walk (verse 7).

The effects were immediate and phenomenal. One, the crowds listened intently to Philip because of

- what he said—the good news of the kingdom of God and Jesus the Messiah—the incarnated God (what they heard) and
- what he did—exorcisms and miraculous healing of the paralyzed (what they saw) (verses 6-7 and 12).

Two, the crowds believed the message and were baptized (verse 12). Three, Simon also believed and was baptized. He followed Philip around, totally amazed by Philip's miracles and signs (verse 13, cf. 9-11). So, four, there was great joy in that city (verse 8).

Who would have imagined that a "fugitive" in transit could topple a stubborn occult domination so incisively and decisively?

I recall. Tim Hessel was a godly principal of an engineering school in Ghana. On a field trip with some of his students, he bumped into an occult dominated town. From time to time during the trip, he took time off to research the occult ridden town and townspeople.

He sensed a depressing cloud of death suffocating life and vitality out of everybody and everything in sight. It left old and young, educated and uneducated, rich and poor; people, animals and vegetation, everything, gaunt, writhen, and depressed. Life looked blighted. His heart broke. He wept and prayed.

He talked with a few pastors in the town. Their response was, "No use! There is no life in this place. There has never been life here. And there will never be!"

"Why?" Tim asked?

"So long as those occultists dominate life here, nothing, nothing, would change. Only death survives here" pastor Lully, one of the pastors, said, despairingly.

"Who are the occultists? What do they do? Why are they allowed to kill life here?" Tim asked, outraged!

"Allowed," pastor Passy began to explain. "Nobody allowed them. They just snatched it. They intend to kill it. Everybody and everything lives at their mercy."

"Why do you let them go on like that?" Tim queried.

"What can anyone do? There's nothing anybody can do. Life is gone from this place. And nothing, nobody can bring it back. It's all over here" pastor Lully said in despair.

"I disagree! There can be life here again!" Tim thundered.

"How!" pastor Skip asked skeptically.

"I know a young preacher. He seems to connect vitally with God. God may well use him to snap this death thing you live with here. Life will return to this place and amaze everybody, including the occultists!" Tim proposed.

"Let's see, 'a young preacher,' you say?" pastor Passy inquired.

"Yes!" Tim agreed.

"The traditional rulers and council of elders of the town would be hard to sell on that proposition, 'a young preacher,' I mean" pastor Passy explained.

"You and I are talking about different things, sir! You're talking about impossible traditional protocol to beat. I am talking about bringing possible life to a lifeless town." Continuing, Tim urged, "Promise me one thing, all of you. Go pray; talk with other pastors in the town. Together, go talk to the traditional leaders about giving God a chance to turn their town around for the better. This is my card. Call me and give me feedback in a week." Tim slammed the card in pastor Passy's hand, somewhat indignant.

The pastors accepted the challenge. They got back in touch with Tim, saying, "The traditional leaders Okayed your proposal. But they want to meet and counsel the 'young preacher."

I was the "young preacher." Tim had briefed me. His conviction, burden and compassion for "a lifeless town" of about 3,000+ people were contagious. He and I took short unannounced trips there within the week for me to see and size up the situation for myself.

However, at the sight of me, the traditional leaders unanimously took back their consent to have me preach there. A spokesperson for them explained. Turning to the pastors, who had accompanied Tim and me to the meeting, he said.

"When you mentioned 'a young preacher,' we didn't think of a teenager. You know what you are doing? You are going to throw a teenager—a lamb—to those wolves. [He meant Simon's counterparts.] How do you account for his blood? What do you tell his parents? Cut off a young life, in an audacious attempt to free a town from fateful lifelessness? No! We would not be part of your conspiracy!" he vehemently protested on behalf of the others.

Needless to say the rulers and elders were adamant. They sent us away without allowing us to say as much as a word. Three such meetings fruitlessly followed. "You heard us. No more of this!" the spokesperson said the last time around.

After a month of prayer and self-examination, Tim and I went by ourselves to see the leading ruler by himself. I thanked him for their love and concern for me. I recounted a few experiences I'd had in dealing with situations similar to theirs. [A typical one is the story at the beginning of this book.] Then I pleaded.

"Please, look at this whole thing as God handling a humanly impossible situation, using a child so that it would be seen that God alone is the doer. Please, please, please, give him a chance. He will not fail you!" I earnestly pleaded.

"I hear you, son. I feel your passion!" the leading ruler began to say thoughtfully. And he continued. "I will talk with the council of elders. Come back in a week and meet with all of us again."

The rulers and council of elders finally gave us their blessing. But they counseled me to be very cautious in what I said and how I said it. "And by all means, don't attack those occultists. Leave them alone. Or they will fight back with spells and hexes and curses. They might even kill you just like that. Drumming signals the commencement of their counterattacks. As soon as you hear the first beat, stop! Duck, cower and return to your seat. Our scouts would be right there to whisk you on guard to the palace," the spokesperson firmly counseled.

"God bless you, son," the leading ruler consoled.

"Thank you sir!" I responded. By this time Tim and I had put several prayer groups in place. They prayed fervently for us all the way.

A massive crowd turned out for our first open air meeting. The mass singing was poor. So I sang a few songs accappella just before I preached. As I pulled out my sermon outline, I felt a strong urge to put it aside. Rather, I should invite people with inexplicable, medically incurable, chronic, and terminal sicknesses forward and pray for them to be healed.

I panicked! This early in the scheme of things! I thought a place like that needed an introductory sermon about the real God, dissociating him from misconceptions of him. But I was mistaken. I suddenly lost all the confidence I had. My heart began to pound wildly, rattling my ribcage, rather shamefully, if people noticed it.

I silently panned the audience, while examining and re-examining the source of the prompting. I checked my spirit, my mind, and my motives for being there at all! Where was this prompting coming from, what for? On and on and on I went re-examining the prompting again and again to be sure it came from God. In my faithlessness, I felt a soft, gentle, easily negligible urge directing me to go ahead. I knew that was God. Satan pushes. God, on the other hand, leads.

So I did. Crowds came forward. I repeated that I didn't want people with on and off headaches, stomachaches, fevers, flu and the like. But I wanted the demonized and the bewitched, the charmed and hexed, the terminally ill and suffering. Pastors walked through the crowd and sampled case histories.

Then I sat a straightback wooden chair on a wooden table in the center of the crowd. I climbed and stood on the chair so that everybody would see me all around and know that I wasn't playing any games or tricks.

I told the story of Jesus as God incarnate, as our redeemer and Lord. He suffered the pain for all our sins and all our sicknesses so that we wouldn't have to suffer them. "Believe him as I pray!" I urged.

Then I prayed that God should free people for them to know that

- he is God
- he had freed them in Jesus Christ, and
- he had turned their hearts back to himself in Jesus Christ.

Then I said, Amen! But I didn't hear it.

A deafening holy chaos made up of screams, dancing for joy, singing, praying, laughing, skipping and jumping around, etc, presently exploded. It filled every crevice of the gathering and meeting place. I didn't know what to do next. So I let it go on while I prayed silently seeking guidance from the Lord.

After a while, the holy chaos seemed to die down. Voluntarily, people told their stories of deliverance and healing. Many people, including some of the traditional rulers, and noted occultists believed in Jesus Christ. They confessed, "We heard and experienced the good news of Jesus Christ. We saw and experienced his power. This beat everything we have ever seen and heard. God, he is God! Thank you for leading us to him, preacher!"

How humbling! But what a joy to see spiritual freedom, peace and great joy visibly replace bondage, death and depression for many people at a single meeting. A series of follow up meetings confirmed that the conversions were genuine. People indeed converted transformationally.

I consider it a privilege that God let me in to experience the kind of experience Philip had at Samaria 2001 years ago. From two undeniable sources, I learned this.

Habitually seeing and experiencing esoteric power (superhuman power), and habitually hearing and experiencing esoteric knowledge (knowledge beyond the senses) form people. Both shape the thinking processes and behavioral patterns of victims. Esoteric power and knowledge, similar to philosophical rationalization, enslave people. Genuine conversion occurs when the latter is challenged through appropriate apologetics. That was what Paul did in Athens because Athenians were typical.

Similarly, genuine conversion only occurs when the former are challenged through appropriate biblical truth and power confrontation. These kinds of people had heard and been formed by knowledge beyond the senses. They had also seen and been formed by superhuman power (Acts 8:9-11).

The only way they could be freed from the twofold formation is to be transformed by

- a hearing (of truth) and
- a seeing (of power)

that outmatch their former "hearing" and "seeing" self-evidently. That was what and how Philip freed Simon and his townspeople from occult domination. They became genuine believers in Jesus Christ (Acts 8:5-13).

A thorough housecleaning and education about the person and role and work of the Holy Spirit should follow receiving and being filled with the Holy Spirit (Acts 8:14-17, cf. Acts 19:18-20). This prevents bitter backlashes.

Generally, spirits give in to superior spirits—superior power—in the moment of encounter. But exorcised spirits are notorious for revisiting familiar territory. Simon and the like are therefore vulnerable to devastating backlashes (cf. Acts 8:15-17, 18-24, Daniel 10:12-13 and Matthew 12:43-45).

Against that backdrop, Philip would have seen only piecemeal changes if he had stereotyped and targeted to eliminate a supposed Samaritan religion. Piecemeal changes start and end in the religion, —the religious cultural system. They lacked depth and power needed to permeate the entire culture. They also lacked appeal for non-adherents to the supposed Samaritan religion.

Similarly, Philip would have had only anthropological changes if he had targeted to bring about changes in a supposed Samaritan worldview. Those changes might go beyond the purely religious changes and might affect the entire culture.

But the best anthropological innovation lacks the power to confront and conquer bondage to superhuman power and knowledge beyond the senses—the esoteric—through the occult. Worst of all, religious changes and/or anthropological changes do not amount to spiritual—core level, transformational—conversion. Therefore they cannot replace occult domination with the presence, filling and empowerment of the Holy Spirit.

Anyone trained in anthropological skills can bring about anthropological innovations among victims of the occult, leaving them victimized by the occult. But Holy Spirit-filled people like Philip can bring about spiritual conversions among victims of the occult and lead to anthropological change among them as well.

Appropriate good news carriers

Philip impresses me as a model of childlike trust and dependence on God (Luke 18:17). Here he was. Bitter persecution had forced him to scurry out of Jerusalem. He abandoned possessions, position and all prospects for future ministry under the auspices of a mega church—the thriving church of Jerusalem. And in the middle of nowhere, unknown and without support or possible recognition and accolades, he stopped.

Philip distinguished himself from most other Jews who either avoided Samaria altogether, or raced through it, spraying flyers of the good news (Acts 8:1 and 4), and from others who ethnocentrically headed for a Jewish synagogue (Acts 11:19). He took notice of the Samaritans as people in their own rights. Like any others, they looked self-sufficient, proud and happy with their lives. And like any others, they too needed transformational encounter with Jesus Christ.

"I wish Peter or John or one of the apostles were here. But, Lord, if you want to, you can use me, even me. I am available!" He thought to himself.

I could imagine him, buried in hours of prayers, fasting, agonizing and interceding for that city.

Oh God, forgive me for taking part in Jewish ethnocentrism against Samaritans. Please, grant that they too would forgive me (cf. John 4:9). Oh God, please, help them to believe me when I tell them that it was Jesus Christ who freed me from my ethnocentrism against them. Lord, please, help them to see that he is here to free them also from any and every bondage they might have.

Lord, I know that I am not Peter. I am only plain old me, Philip. But, Lord, as I speak for you, please, stretch out your hand and work miracles as you see fit. Let these people know you as their Lord and Savior. That's all I ask, Lord. Amen!

Immediately, Philip felt a new strengthening. He felt warm and goose bumped all over. Tears of total surrender ran down his cheeks. A boulder jutting out from a heap of rocks to the edge of the townsquare invited him. He climbed and stood on it. He sang a song or two to draw and catch attention at the noon hour.

"What a voice! Who's that? He doesn't look local. What's he up to? Let's check it out. He sure has a powerful tenor voice! Listen to that!" People remarked as they turned and walked toward him, eating their lunch from brown bags.

Soon a crowd gathered. It thickened. Philip hushed. So did the crowd. Then he spoke. "I am a Jew. My name is Philip. Please, forgive us Jews for our ethnocentrism against you. And please, please, listen carefully to what I am about to tell you."

Then Philip told the story of the Messiah who had come and the difference he had made in his personal life (Acts 8:5). Did Philip use Messiah, instead of Jesus, because it was common knowledge in the region that Messiah was coming? The Samaritan woman Jesus himself had met earlier in the region seemed to indicate (John 4:25). Anyhow, a holy chaos suddenly cut Philip's sermon short.

A number of demonized persons rocketed through the crowd and headed toward Philip. Philip lacked professional know-how of preachers and exorcists. He was pretty raw at all this. Therefore he panicked and cried out to God for help. "Lord, Jesus! Please, do something!" he prayed.

And down, the demonized went, screaming and rolling on the ground before they reached Philip. Other demonized people in the crowd fell down where they stood and screamed, kicking wildly. The crippled sprang up and walked. They skipped. They danced. They held high their mats and crutches jumping and skipping and dancing around.

The Holy Spirit took over before Philip realized it. But the good thing was that, he realized it and stayed out of his way. He prayerfully watched the Holy Spirit act.

Here, there, and over here, Philip trailed behind the Holy Spirit taking note of his acts as he convicted people of their need of Jesus Christ. People wept as they repented. They sobbed. They cried. They prayed. They sang songs of joy. They praised God.

The lunch hour passed and nobody seemed to care. The thick crowd kept thickening. Latecomers rushing to the scene marveled. They asked, "What's all this? What's going on here? Somebody tell us something. What's going on?" They asked in bewilderment.

A fifty year old former crippled man showed them his crutches. He said, "Look! I am walking. I dance. I skip on my own feet. It all happened right here. Look over there. See those demoniacs who used to terrorize people near the old well. No more! They are exorcised. Incredible! Isn't it? Ever seen anything like this?" He left them. He blended in the crowd dancing and praising God!

"Incredible indeed. This is an affront to Simon! Who is responsible for all this? Where is he?" The latecomers exclaimed and muttered as they looked and listened to what was going on. Some of them said, "Simon must do something about this! Let's go fetch him!" They ran off and came back with Simon.

Meanwhile, Philip had climbed down from the boulder—his open-air pulpit. He roamed the crowd, giving assurance of salvation to those who needed it.

Simon understood the situation quicker and better than his admirers. Adept spiritists always do. As soon as he arrived, he sensed a power much sublime, greater, and awesome than him and all the powers at his disposal. He knew enough to pick up that the prevailing power stood diametrically opposed to his powers. The reality unnerved him, but it didn't floor or flog him.

He moved in closer. He saw some of his stubborn cases with the crippled and demoniacs banished. In their place, perfect wellness danced self-evidently. Some of his own devotees and novices were right there talking about Messiah and the kingdom of God. A strange sense of freedom, peace, and joy pervaded the whole place.

Everything Simon saw, heard and felt amazed him spiritually, mentally, emotionally, and physically. Here was the thriller thrilled beyond description. He pressed through the sardine-packed crowd to Philip, trembling as he neared him!

He eyeballed Philip and said. "I am Simon, an occultist. Please tell me more about Messiah. I want to know him for myself. Please help me. I need help to quit my practice!" Simon pleaded as he dropped to his knees.

The sight disgusted one of his associates. He screamed, "What are you doing, Simon? Surrendering to an unknown Jew? What has become of you? Are you mad? Up! By the gods I command you, up! Simon! Simon! Get up!" his voice faded into a whisper.

Simon wasn't out of his mind. He knew what he was doing. Therefore he ignored what his associate said. He asked Philip also to ignore him. In a moment Simon believed Jesus Christ. Off with the crowds Simon went to a nearby stream where Philip baptized them all. Holy ecstasy invaded the city momentarily (Acts 8:8, cf. verses 5-13).

The chatter about these happenings rippled to Jerusalem and fetched Peter and John. They came to minister the infilling of the Holy Spirit (verses 14-25).

In the midst of the fanfare, an angel of God (verses 26-28) and the Holy Spirit (verses 29-38) took turns in taking Philip away and leading him to convert and baptize an Ethiopian eunuch. But before the eunuch wiped the emersion water out of his eyes, the Spirit of the Lord whisked Philip away in a flash. Left alone and dripping wet, the eunuch laughed hilariously at the mystery, full of joy for knowing Jesus Christ personally.

Several rest stops down the road, among fellow travelers coming from the opposite direction, the eunuch picked up this gossip. From Azotus to Caesarea, "Government offices, stores, schools, banks and markets closed and people flocked townsquares to hear Philip the evangelist" (verses 39-40).

"I know him! Yes!" the eunuch said gratifyingly and continued his journey home—a different person.

All that gives me a multi-layer sandwich picture of Philip. One: At the base lies the first slice of bread. It declares, "Philip was filled with the Holy Spirit and wisdom" (Acts 6:3-6, compare with Philip's colleague Stephen who was full of grace and power, and wisdom and the Spirit—Acts 6:8 and 10).

The sandwich builds up, two, with a juicy slab of meat made up of repentance and vulnerability, selflessness and humility, and prayerfulness and sensitivity to the Holy Spirit. In evidence, Philip didn't ignore, stereotype or patronize the Samaritans from Jewish ethnocentric perspectives. He respected them. He told them the story of Messiah appropriately (Acts 8:4-5, cf. 11:19 and John 4:25). Isaiah 66:1-2 says God esteems such people highly. No wonder!

Then comes, three, the next slice of bread, made up of childlike trust and dependence on God (Luke 18:17). The first two layers predisposed Philip to be nothing less (cf. Acts 8:5-13).

On top of that slice, four, sits the next slab of juicy meat. It consisted of being scripturally and spiritually discerning and brave, loving and zealous, bold and courageous. Unprecedented in his experience, Philip attempted the impossible for God through reckless love for people and foolish trust in God (Acts 8:5-13, cf. 2 Corinthians 5:14, Romans 12:9-12).

Finally comes, five, the top slice of bread in the form of Christ-like obedience to God. Like Christ, Philip followed God to where he was and did what God did (Acts 8:5-8, 26-28, 29-38, 39-40, cf. John 5:19 and 30).

No wonder, even Philip's marriage didn't become an end in itself. He and his wife raised four unmarried daughters who had and used the gift of prophecy. Their home was an oasis for fellow servants of God like Paul and Luke (Acts 21: 8-9).

For me, Philip remains a challenge and comfort. He is a challenge, because he wasn't a "superlative apostle." Rather, he was as ordinary as most of us are. Yet, he attempted extraordinary things for God, through being totally available. That is exactly where Philip becomes a comfort and hope for us all. We don't have to know it all to be used by God to do the impossible.

Rather, if we would be totally available through being truly

- Holy Spirit-filled
- childlike dependent on God and
- Christ-like obedient to God

as a way of life, God would use us also mightily. We would see our counterparts of Simons and their townspeople converted transformationally. They too would transform totally in honor of the good news of Jesus Christ.

Transformational conversion requirements

How can I walk away from Acts chapter eight still in doubt about what brings transformational conversion to victims of the occult? I can't. Philip made it too clear to me what would frustrate or gladden God and occult victims.

As said earlier, see above, christianizing couched in religious and/or worldview innovations would fail to free occult victims from bondage to esoteric power. Therefore, those innovations cannot and would not convert them to Christ.

A straightforward telling of the story of Jesus by itself, as Peter did to Cornelius, would also fail, and this is why. Occult victims develop cataracts on their spiritual eyes through constant exposure and basking in the light of the esoteric. Those cataracts need removing through spiritual surgery—redemptive power confrontation.

The power confrontation here differs from the one that solicits conscious involvement of willful haters of God, like the prophets of Baal and Israel, Saul of Tarsus, and Elymas. Unlike willful haters of God, occult victims are victimized. They might even be ignorant about it. Therefore they need soft-paddled power confrontation that helps free them before they could hear and believe the good news.

Pitting the apologetics against bondage of esoteric power is like using a stethoscope to diagnose or track down the presence of an evil spirit in a demonized patient. The apologetics mismatches outlandish philosophical appeal to the mind, only, with defiant occultic way of thinking, feeling and acting, hopelessly!

But there is every hope for redemptive power confrontation. For one thing, it uses channels that occult victims are used to, that is

- seeing (superhuman power) and
- hearing (knowledge beyond the senses).

It outmatches esoteric knowledge with biblical truth—redemption in Christ. Simultaneously, it outmatches esoteric power with Holy Spirit selected and directed acts and signs.

Outmatching "seeing" and "hearing" induced by the esoteric with "seeing" and "hearing" generated by the Holy Spirit constitutes the spiritual surgery needed to free and convert victims of the occult transformationally (see Philip and my experience 2,001 years later, cited above).

In addition, Philip also made it clear that the appropriateness of carriers of the good news to this context cannot be overemphasized or assumed. In fact, inappropriate, presumptuous, self-sufficient carriers would hinder God and prospective believers through stereotyping unsaved situation and the solution for it.

Resistance and rejection would soon hit them in the face. Or short-lived cosmetic superficial changes fraught with syncretism would mock them sooner than later.

Therefore Acts 8:1-24 constitutes a model we can use, adaptively of course, to lead victims of the occult to transformational conversion.

Model

Constantly seeing superhuman power and hearing knowledge beyond the senses make esoteric power horribly real to victims of the occult. The esoteric had shaped the way they think, feel and act. The only way they can see God as truly superior to the esoteric and be changed by him is for them to see, hear and experience God as truly superior, transcendent.

Therefore, they need appropriate good news carriers who would simultaneously connect the truth and power of the good news for them to hear and see God and experience him as transcendent to anything they had ever seen, heard and experienced (Acts 8:1-24).

Principles for implementing the model

One: Be sure you have been transformationally converted. You had met Jesus Christ at the core of your being, you have fallen in love with him. Consequently, you have a heart's view, not an intellectual view, of Jesus. You are transforming totally (2 Corinthians 4:5-6).

Two: Be sure it is the love of God motivating you to lead victims of the occult to transformational conversion. And make sure it is not a misguided mission obsession to swell the statistics of heathen converts enlightened "our way" that is driving you.

Three: Be sure your every move is self-evidently childlike trust and dependence on God, and Christ-like submissive obedience to God, his word and Spirit (cf. Acts 6:3, 6; 8:1-4).

Four: Resist the temptation to impose supposed conventionalized concepts of animism as a religion or worldview on an unsaved situation that looks and "smells" animistic. Do a fresh and firsthand ethnographic study of the situation. Pay close attention to local vocabulary and conceptions of the supernatural (verses 9-11).

Five: Ethnographically and scripturally study religious figures, their status and role in the society. Again, desist stereotyping them as shamans, mediums, etc. Let internal evidence lead you to local perceptions and treatment of these public figures and reasons why.

Six: Always seek prayer support, counsel and help (if need be) from knowledgeable local or nearby believers in interpreting the data. Let the Scriptures guide you all the way.

Seven: Collect and analyze local stories of people's actual experiences of the supernatural. Prayerfully discern how these have shaped their thinking and lifestyle.

Eight: Ethnographically interview former practitioners, current practitioners, their children, suppliants, victims and critics.

Nine: Ethnographically, scripturally and prayerfully discern the extent of the influence of

- *occult vocabulary and (futuristic) messages and*
- *occult power (miraculous manifestations of occult power)*

on the thinking and life of citizenry.

Ten: Guard against relapsing into your comfort zone for interpreting, labeling and engaging the situation. Rather, recall that you are on divine appointment right where you are. God had actually hand-picked you for the hour. Let your confidence REST in him and him alone (John 15:16).

Eleven: Resort to related biblical passages for fresh insights and guidance (e.g., Matthew 10:1-42, Luke 10:1-24, Acts 1:6-8).

Twelve: Study the good news according to Jesus Christ afresh, noting his distinctives and emphasis on the author of the good news, the source of the message of the good news, the theme of the message of the good news, the messengers of the good news, the aroma of the good news (Luke 24:36-53).

Thirteen: Let the Holy Spirit lead you in presenting Jesus Christ (and eternal life in him)

- *as the message of life, peace, hope and power to challenge the esoteric messages they had heard and believed all their lives, and*
- *as freedom, security and power to outmatch all the satanic miraculous signs they had seen and believed, and the resulting unconscious bondages they had lived with all their lives.*

Fourteen: Your converts would yield to Jesus not on persuasion about Jesus, but on encounter with Jesus himself. That encounter converts them at the core of their being as nothing else could. You would be delighted to see that

- *they instantly personalize the good news of Jesus*
- *they voluntarily abandon their former human and spiritual gods to follow Jesus*
- *they spontaneously reproduce themselves (verse 12, cf. John 4:42)*
- *they transform inside out—totally.*

Fifteen: Introduce your converts quickly to the person and work of the Holy Spirit in the life of believers. Let biblical views take priority over denominational and preferred theological views of the Holy Spirit. Be faithful to the Holy Spirit, dependent on him, and let him surprise you as he equips your converts for authentic living and witness in their setting. This safeguards them against backlashes of spirits accessed through occult practice and occult victimization (verses 15-17).

Sixteen: Seek and take cues from your converts about the nature and time for baptism and public profession of their newfound faith in Jesus. Don't impose mission pressures for head counting masquerading as conventional time schedule in these matters.

Seventeen: If you have to HELP plant a church for converts from occult background, be sure it is THEIR church

- *culturally*
- *theologically*
- *liturgically*

in leadership and worship forms plus music type for worship.

Anything less, not only clones them but ill-equips them for authentic survival and authentic witness in their cultural setting and context (verses 9-13, cf. 5-8 and 14-25).

Eighteen: Be sure you are filled and are being filled—empowered and controlled—by the Holy Spirit as a way of life (Galatians 5:16, 25).

Nineteen: Remind yourself constantly that you are privileged to be co-laboring with the Holy Spirit. Therefore always discern and follow his leading. Be careful not to resist or quench him through unbelief/disbelief. Remember, disbelief is actually rationalistic belief that God can do all things, but he won't do certain things at certain times and places.

Twenty: On the scale 1-5, functionally rate 4 or 5 in being prayerful, teachable, Spirit-filled, spiritually sensitive, scripturally knowledgeable, ministerially flexible and Christ-centered in all things.

Discipleship

Wilson Awasu

8

Corresponding discipleship

Of all places, I learned at a busy port of entry checkpoint from an immigration officer that everyone knows John 3:16. He didn't recite it to welcome me to his country. Rather, he asked me to recite John 3:17 since everyone knows 3:16. I did, wondering where all this headed.

"Well done!" He said. "You're a true seminary student. Welcome!" Thud, thud! He stamped my passport.

As I located and headed to baggage claim, I thought. What is it about John 3:16 that makes it so popular? Least likely places like an immigration checkpoint scream the fact. Several thoughts came to mind. Involuntarily, I focused on "everyone who believes," "everyone!"

My mind raced to Romans 1:16. There again, "everyone who believes" occurred. Off to Romans 10:13, "everyone who believes" translated into "anyone who calls on the name of the Lord." What happens to "everyone" (John 3:16), "everyone" (Romans 1:16) and "anyone" (Romans 10:13), who believes and calls on the Lord's name?

All three texts agree that they would be saved. They would convert transformationally. Therefore, they would transform totally.

They would be free to love God as Christ did, obey God as Christ did, and trust and depend on God as Christ did. They would honor God as Christ did.

The immigration officer didn't intend it. But his intuitive customized welcome to a globetrotting seminary student got me thinking for a while.

Several years later, I had thought. If the good news of Jesus Christ is truly of God, and we know it is; and if it is God's total and final message addressed to the total human situation, then it must convert "everyone," as God intended it.

"Everyone" includes

- false starts posing as genuine conversion (chapter 3)
- unsaved conscious worshippers of God (chapter 4)
- unsaved unconscious worshippers of God (chapter 5)
- willful haters of God (chapter 6), and
- victims of the occult (chapter 7).

"Everyone" who repents and trusts only God to save them would be saved. They have to! They trusted Jesus to free them from inherited and personal rebellion against God, something that nothing, no one, else could do. He cannot but free them. He knows they are free. They know they are free. Satan knows they are free. And as they evidence their freedom through transformed lives, the world around them gets to know that they are free. Their interpersonal and interactive social contexts see and feel the effects of a humanly impossible transformation emanating them.

I think that the conversion of "everyone" who believes, plus the total life—inside out—transformation of "everyone" who converts to Jesus Christ most visibly justifies God's bitter hatred and vehement condemnation for the worship of other gods.

The worship of other gods does not and cannot

- convict, forgive and free "everyone" from human bent to be independent of God
- reconcile "everyone" who repents to God
- give eternal life to "everyone" who is reconciled to God
- give the Holy Spirit to "everyone" who has eternal life
- make "everyone" who has the Holy Spirit live as Christ did in total freedom, reckless love, childlike dependence on God, submissive obedience to God
- keep "everyone" who is Christ-like protected against Satan and the satanic, and reproductive all throughout their lifespan.

Not so the worship of God that derives from and is based on a vital personal relationship with God through Jesus Christ. It can and does abundantly generate, sustain and complete all of the above.

In view of that provision and reality, God vehemently condemns idolatry. Equally vehemently, God demands that his people should

- wholeheartedly worship God and God alone (Exodus 20:1-7, Deuteronomy 6:4-9, Mark 12:29-31)
- be totally united in diversity (John 13:34-35, 17:20-23, Revelation 7:9-12)
- selflessly love their enemies and passionately pray for their persecutors (Matthew 5:43-48)
- effectively reproduce themselves in others for onward transmission in the Holy Spirit's power until Christ returns (Matthew 28:16-20, Luke 24:36-53, John 15:16, 20:21, Acts 1:8).

Against that backdrop, two things become imperative. One, "everyone" deserves to hear nothing short of the full-kernel good news of Jesus Christ. "Everyone," needs to hear it in a way they could

- understand it and receive it, or
- understand it but reject it.

Those who reject it, on that basis, have themselves to blame.

Two, "everyone" who hears the good news, understands it and receives it must be converted transformationally. And "everyone" who converts transformationally must transform totally—inside out. God's grandest solution for the human situation can do nothing less (see chapter 2).

Therefore, in his farewell message to his disciples, Jesus spelled out all the pieces that make up the good news. Take any piece out, and you weaken the whole. More than that, dissecting the good news fragments it into competing other gospels. Each piece vies for legitimacy, and seeks to replace the good news of Jesus Christ (Galatians 1:6-9, cf. Luke 24:36-53, Acts 26:17-18, Romans 15:17-19).

But substituting another gospel for the good news amounts to open rebellion and dispensation of death instead of life. For Jesus didn't promise that any one piece of the good news would lead to transformational conversion. Rather, it is the full-orbed good news, delivered in the power of the Holy Spirit that converts people at the core of being.

At first sight, it surprised me that Jesus made "credible" and "clothed" carriers of the good news serving as its fragrance an integral part of the good news. But on reflection, I saw his wisdom in doing that. Nothing authenticates the life-giving message more than visible and tangible changes it has made in its communicators.

On the other hand, nothing abuses and violates, negates and hinders, the life-giving message of the good news more severely than much talk about it without a visible proof of it in the lives of its communicators (see 2 Corinthians 6:3-10, 7:2, cf.1 Samuel 12:1-5 and 1 Corinthians 4:1-2).

Very wisely, Jesus put it all together so succinctly (Luke 24:36-53). We could not miss it.

The good news according to Jesus (Luke 24:36-53)

36. While they were still talking about this, Jesus himself stood among them and said, "Peace be with you."

37. They were startled and frightened, thinking they saw a ghost. 38. He said to them, "Why are you troubled, and why do doubts arise in your minds? 39. Look at my hands and my feet. It is I myself! Touch me and see; a ghost does not have flesh and bones, as you see I have."

40. When he had said this, he showed them his hands and feet. 41. And while they still did not believe it because of joy and amazement, he asked them, "Do you have anything here to eat?" 42. They gave him a piece of broiled fish, 43. and he took it and ate it in their presence.

44. He said to them, "This is what I told you while I was with you; Everything must be fulfilled that is written about me in the Law of Moses, the prophets and the Psalms." 45. Then he opened their minds so they could understand the Scriptures. 46. He told them, This is what is written: The Christ will suffer and rise from the dead on the third day, 47. and repentance and forgiveness of sins will be preached in his name to all nations, beginning from Jerusalem. 48. You are witnesses to these things. 49. I am going to send you what my Father has promised; but stay in the city until you have been clothed with power from on high."

50. When he had led them out to the vicinity of Bethany, he blessed them. 51. While he was blessing them, he left them and was taken up into heaven. 52. Then they worshipped him and returned to Jerusalem with great joy. 53. And they stayed continually at the temple, praising God.

The context was the last resurrection appearance. From here Jesus ascended to heaven. Just before he ascended, he capsulated the good news for his disciples, and for us, of course.

The author and commissioner of the good news (verses 36-43)

- The crucified and bodily resurrected Jesus Christ himself (verses 36-43, cf. Hebrews 12:2).

The source of the message of the good news (verses 45-46)

- All the Scriptures (verse 44)
- Disentangled understanding of the Scriptures (verse 45).

The theme of the message of the good news (verses 46-47)

- Faith in the crucified and resurrected Jesus Christ (verse 46)
- Repentance and forgiveness to be preached in Jesus Christ's name to the nations (verse 47).

The carriers of the good news (verses 48-49)

- Credible witnesses (verse 48)
- "Clothed" witnesses (verse 49).

The aroma of the good news (verses 50-53)

- Being blessed to be a blessing to others (verses 50-51)
- Being joyful, worshipful and prayerful (verse 52-53).

That is the good news according to Jesus, in a capsule. It remains the same for all.

But, Nicodemus (John 3), Cornelius (Acts 10), Dionysius and Damaris (Acts 17), Saul of Tarsus, and Sergius Paulus (Acts 9 and Acts 13), and Simon and his townspeople (Acts 8), experienced it differently to convert at the core of being—transformationally (see chapters 3-7).

Customized good news

False starts (see chapter 3)

Accordingly, Jesus described the mystery of the good news for Nicodemus—representative of false starts—to experience the mystery and convert transformationally. Meaning, Nicodemus converted transformationally when he experienced the mystery of God in Christ and Christ as God who incarnated to redeem humanity.

Unsaved conscious worshippers of God (see chapter 4)

Peter used a straightforward telling of the story of Jesus to link up the knowledge of God and the knowledge of Jesus Christ for Cornelius—representative of unsaved conscious worshippers of God—to convert transformationally. As Cornelius experienced Jesus as God, he converted transformationally.

Unsaved unconscious worshippers of God (see chapter 5)

Paul used the apologetics consisting of God revealed in creation, conscience, folklore/poetry, Scriptures, and Jesus Christ in telling the good news to Dionysius and Damaris—representatives of unsaved unconscious worshippers of God—for them to convert transformationally. In other words, Dionysius and Damaris converted transformationally when they experienced God as permeating all creation but transcending it.

Willful haters of God (see chapter 6)

Paul used power confrontation to expose and break the occultic spell of Elymas—representative of willful haters of God—to free its direct victim, Sergius Paulus, for him to hear and receive the good news and be converted transformationally.

How tragic that ignorant disregard for Elymas' occultic spell and its effect would have prevented Sergius Paulus from experiencing the transcendent and wooing power of God. And certainly, he would have rejected the good news, he so badly wanted to hear, as a result of imposed occultic hindrance. He would have remained unsaved.

Victims of the occult (see chapter 7)

Philip combined the power of the truth and the power of signs and wonders in telling the good news to free Simon and his townspeople—representatives of victims of the occult—to convert transformationally. That means, Simon and his townspeople experienced the freeing truth and freeing power of God, both of which

179

transcend the dazzle of esoteric knowledge and esoteric power, to convert transformationally.

Without appropriate customization of the good news, the varied "everyone" cannot understand it, receive it and convert transformationally. But as it was, chapters 3-7, they converted transformationally. "Everyone" differently and uniquely experienced the same God through faith in the same Jesus Christ to convert transformationally.

It stands to reason that their growth process must match their conversion experience. Then, Nicodemus, Cornelius, Dionycious and Damaris, (Saul and), Sergius Paulus, and Simon and his townspeople would naturally continue to

- transform inside out—totally
- know, love and worship God wholeheartedly, and
- own the discipleship—maturation—process as they did the good news.

Needless to say that a one-size-fits-all discipleship program behaves like a one-size-fits-all conversion methodology, or other gospels. Both generate spurious effects through over-simplified generalizations. Consequently, they give deceptive assurance fraught with

- proselytization—cosmetic superficial changes that pose as genuine conversion and immunize against it
- syncretism—the blending of the one-size-fits-all version of the good news—a gospel—with popular cultural and religious ideas that pose as the good news and immunize against it.

Advantageously, each transformational conversion situation contains all the pieces needed for appropriate—corresponding—discipleship. Those pieces are native to the prior unsaved, but now saved, situation. The thorough, genuine, robust—transformational—conversion experience had predisposed converts for rapid growth, victorious living, and effective witness.

In other words, at conversion,

- Nicodemus (symbolic of false starts)
- Cornelius (symbolic of conscious worshippers)
- Dionycious and Damaris (symbolic of unconscious worshippers)
- (Saul), Elymas/Sergius Paulus (symbolic of willful haters of God), and
- Simon and his townspeople (symbolic of victims of the occult)

are ready to go, given the appropriate—corresponding—discipleship or maturation process. So we need a generic growth process to customize.

Growth process according to Jesus (John 8:31-32)

Again, Jesus spelled out believers' generic growth process as he did the good news. It takes believers from "belief" —saving faith—in God, through "discipleship," and "the truth," to "freedom" in Christ. Like the good news, it too needs to be customized appropriately. When it corresponds to each conversion experience, growth would be thorough, robust and reproductive.

> *"To the Jews who had believed in him," verse 31, "Jesus said, 'If you hold to my teaching, you are really my disciples.'" Verse 32, "'then you will know the truth, and the truth will set you free.'"*

Belief—saving faith—in God (verse 31a)

- means trusting only God to save, i.e., forgive and reconcile, give eternal life and the Holy Spirit, to establish a personal relationship with the repentant, forgiven and reconciled.

Discipleship—apprenticeship—under Jesus Christ (verse 31b)

- consists of learning to be Christ-like, in submissive obedience to God; in childlike trust and dependence on God; in reckless love for God, God's people, and enemies.

The truth—Jesus and his work (verse 32a)

- takes into account progressively experiencing Jesus and his victory over the power of Satan, the power of sin (as well as its guilt and punishment), the power of self (insistence on being in control), the power of anti-God social, political, religious allegiances, so that Christ's Spirit and word have the last word in all things.

Freedom—in Christ (verse 32b)

- means power, ability and decision to subject freedom of choice to conscious self-limitations to please God in all areas of life; to focus on God consistently and live joyful, peaceful and zestful, and holy and righteous in spite of circumstances and situations.

Where growth in belief, discipleship, the truth, and freedom remains robust and balanced, the Holy Spirit remains

- unresisted (Acts 7:51)
- ungrieved (Ephesians 4:30)
- unquenched (1 Thessalonians 5:19).

Therefore he uses the resulting freedom to blend his fruit of love and gifts of supernatural power for

- victorious living and
- effective self-reproduction.

That is generic growth for all believers across the board. Customized for each conversion experience, the generic becomes corresponding discipleship.

Corresponding growth process for false starts

Effective growth processes mature spiritual babies into spiritual adults. And thorough maturation accurately identifies and appropriately engages all the issues that naturally constituted the conversion experience.

For false starts, like Nicodemus, Kate, Stacie and Jeff (see chapter 3), those issues look like this:

De-mystifying their views about God

God is transcendent but he incarnated himself in Jesus Christ to redeem and relate personally with repentant people (Colossians 1:15-20). Jesus Christ embodied God. God was pleased to indwell him. Beyond speaking through the prophets, God incarnated himself in Jesus Christ so that he would be seen as well as heard in him (Hebrews 1:1-4). Subsequently, God continues to speak to people through the Holy Spirit and his word (John 16:12-15).

Unboxing their views about God

God is not a cultural, racial, tribal, denominational deity. He is the LORD God, Creator and Sustainer of all things, and all people; and he is the judge of all the world (Genesis 1-2, 12, Matthew 23:15, 28:16-20, John 17:20-23, Ephesians 1:19-23, Colossians 1:15-20).

Bridging their heads and hearts

Bridging the gap between head knowledge and experience—head and heart—to integrate them, false starts learn to have godliness to show for all the God-talk.

Ditching their doing identity

Ditching a doing-identity that derives from human-works-merits orientation to take on a being-identity that derives from God-grace-faith orientation becomes a freeing empowering comfort for false starts. They learn to substitute the spirit of the word (love, mercy, justice and righteousness) for the letter of the word (legalism) (Ephesians 2:1-10).

Dehumanizing worship

They now know experientially that the worship of God is not about us. It is all about God and God alone. That dethrones the man-made—institutionalized—religion and reinstates God as the right object, center and means of worship (Exodus 20:1-11, Deuteronomy 6:4-9, Matthew 15:1-9).

Corresponding discipleship consists of matching those areas with saving faith (belief) through apprenticeship under Jesus (discipleship), and growing experiential knowledge of Jesus and his work (the truth), to voluntary self-limitations in order to love and obey God like Christ (freedom).

That may take the form of head, heart and disciplined study of the Bible, and meditation with action plans for personal application and obedience, and with accountability to a mentor, and accountability for a mentee, etc. People like Nicodemus may have to do some rewriting to admit unbiblical views and positions they had pushed hitherto. They need to affirm paradigm shifts, landslide, total life changes they have made in terms of recent personal encounter with God himself.

When Nicodemus, Kate, Stacie and Jeff, and the like, mature thoroughly, they have a unique story to tell about God. They tell it better and more effectively than anyone else could. It would include "The grace of God found me, even me, not outside the church, but right in the church. Let me tell you how…"

That is authentic witness for Jesus. God expects it from "everyone" whom he saves. We affront God, I think, when we make Nicodemus, Kate, Stacie and Jeff tell "our" story poorly and counterproductively, through inappropriate—one-size-fits-all discipleship program, or worse, no discipleship at all.

Corresponding discipleship for unsaved conscious worshippers of God

Cornelius' conversion raised "hell" in the Jerusalem church, remember? Acts 11 recounts that the Jerusalem church criticized Peter for violating Jewish customs to take the good news of Jesus to a Roman military officer right in his home.

Momentarily, Peter faced serious socio-religious violation charges if he didn't have God to hold responsible for his actions. Providentially, however, it was God who gave Peter rooftop visions followed by unfolding interpretations, beginning with the timely arrival of messengers from Cornelius. It was God who had actually sent an angel to Cornelius, a military officer of the obnoxious Roman empire, to tell him he had recognized his prayers and gifts to needy people.

It was God the Spirit who audaciously cut Peter's sermon short and came on non-Jews in exactly the way he had come on Jews on the Day of Pentecost. And fortunately, Peter had with him Jewish colleagues. They witnessed the phenomenon firsthand. All that barely got Peter off the hook.

Now, imagine that Cornelius dropped in on the Jerusalem church to announce his conversion to Jesus Christ ahead of Peter's interrogation and defense. How would the Jerusalem church treat Cornelius? Would it believe him? Would the Jerusalem church participate in heaven's ecstasy over Cornelius' conversion?

What would the Jerusalem church build into Cornelius' church membership classes? What would have been the driving concern in all this? Remember, the Jerusalem church at that particular time was not an ordinary church. That church resulted directly from the Day of Pentecost.

And yet, "something" other than the Holy Spirit, would have dictated the way to receive and treat Cornelius after his conversion to Jesus Christ, the Lord of the Church. That "something" was and would always be "our" cultural, theological, and/or denominational, "traditions and customs."

But, as good as those traditions were/are, they would always be skeptical about, and insensitive and blind to the issues that constituted Cornelius' transformational conversion encounter with God himself. Without intending to, "our" one-size-fits-all program, because it is heavily indebted to "our traditions," it

- would discredit Cornelius' conversion experience and disregard the issues that emerged in it
- frustrate Cornelius' proper growth in his direct personal relationship with God
- affront God through "chiseling" Cornelius to fit "our" program—traditions and customs.

Cornelius might stick through it. Maybe! Then he becomes "cloned" in our image. He does as we tell him to do to be like us. But we may have to "flog" him to be like Christ for obvious reason. We didn't teach him how. And certainly, he can't tell his own story. He lost it while learning to tell "ours." Tragic!

But what does the tragedy consist of? Could it have been avoided? Of course, yes! When God continues to be God, the only one worthy of worship in the church, Jesus continues to be the only Lord and Savior in the church, the Holy Spirit and God's word continue to be final authority in the church

- we wouldn't have to interrogate Peter to believe him regarding Cornelius
- we wouldn't have to frustrate and clone Cornelius into barrenness
- we wouldn't have to resist, grieve and quench the Holy Spirit that way that often.

Fact is, Cornelius, like Nicodemus, has had a unique encounter with Jesus himself. He had converted transformationally. He deserves

God-given right and attention to mature under the guidance of Holy Spirit-filled people of God.

When he does, his growing belief in God, and on-going discipleship in Jesus, plus constant experiential knowledge of Jesus and his work, and increasing freedom from himself to become more and more like Christ in total obedience to God, he would blossom tremendously. Then he too would tell his own faith story as no one else in all the world could. It needs to be heard. But it must be cultivated appropriately.

Accordingly, and consistent with his conversion experience, the following constitute areas for continued and balanced growth—maturation.

Cornelius had known God. He had shown it through personal and family devotion, constant prayer to God and gifts to needy causes, and unquestioning obedience to God. That knowledge has now transitioned into a personal relationship to God through Jesus Christ. That relationship needs to be nurtured along these lines for it to retain its vitality.

- God in Jesus, and Jesus as God incarnated to relate personally with repentant people (John 1)

- God who works through but transcends every culture (John 4:1-42, Acts 10)

- God who works ahead of carriers of the good news (Luke 10:1-12, 17-24, Acts 8, 9, 10)

- God who intervenes in the affairs of people through dreams and visions, the Holy Spirit and angels, and other believers (Luke 1, Matthew 1:18-25, John 14-16)

- the Holy Spirit, his gifts and fruit in the life of believers (1 Corinthians 12-14, Galatians 5:16-26)

187

- the simplicity of the good news and its incredible power to convert people— "everyone" —transformationally (Luke 24:36-53, Acts 2, 3, 13, Roman 1:16-17, 15:17-21)

- the inclusiveness of the Church of Jesus Christ—Jews, Romans, Greeks, all cultures, races, tribes and languages (John 17, Revelation 7:9-12)

- the comfort and authority of God's word (Ezra 7:10, Psalm 19:7-11, John 6:63, Acts 20:32).

Corresponding growth process for unsaved unconscious worshippers of God

Paul used the apologetics, consisting of God revealed in creation, conscience, folklore/poetry, and the Scriptures and Jesus, to lead Dionysius and Damaris (and others) to transformational conversion (see chapter 5). Meaning, they converted to God transformationally, when they saw that all creation exists and functions by, through and for God (Acts 17:16-34, cf. Colossians 1:15-20).

Therefore, a discipleship program—maturation process—that correspondingly nurtures those views of God would help them grow leaps and bounds in their personal relationship with God. Then they would transform naturally, thoroughly and totally—inside out—in

- childlike trust and dependence on God
- apprenticeship under Jesus
- experiential knowledge of Jesus and his work, and
- freedom from themselves

to know, love, worship and serve God wholeheartedly.

On the other hand, a discipleship program that filters God out of and insulates him to

- obligation to use plants and animals, land and atmosphere accountably
- concern for spiritual as well as emotional, physical, and mental well-being
- delight in art and music, folklore and poetry, literature and drama
- recognition of the existence and activities of angels, evil angels, Satan, demons, and elemental forces

would truncate and derail their conversion. It would seriously impair its maturation.

Disillusioned consequently, Dionysius and Damaris, and others like them would either fall out of church or stay in it uninvolved, while looking for appropriate spiritual fulfillment wherever they find it or the closest appearance of it.

Attractive options would definitely include the New Age philosophy of life. Its emphasis on the god within who self-actualizes in

- physical, emotional, mental, psychological and spiritual integration
- religious and socio-economic, cultural, political, legal, medical integration
- elemental, environmental and religious integration, etc

would strongly appeal to them.

For a while, that philosophy and its products would hold them. But they cannot keep them for the long haul. For one thing, their conversion to Christ sank too deep to settle for shallow self-actualization drive and haven. But where would they go? The search for anchorage goes on.

Christian gossip would be quick to condemn them for poor judgment. What wouldn't come to mind so quickly is, of course, the inappropriate diet of one-size-fits-all discipleship the church fed them following their transformational conversion.

In effect, that discipleship program taught them

- to forget their comprehensive views of God, God in close involvement in all of life and creation and
- to adopt compartmentalized views of a soul-saving-hero God, totally other-worldly, unconcerned and unconscious of this world.

At once those demands nullified their conversion experience. How do you build on the nullified and tabooed?

Biblically, all this is uncalled for. Certainly, the Lord of the good news who converted Dionysius and Damaris transformationally watches over their conversion. He would complete what he began in them.

But often, he depends on Holy Spirit-filled carriers of the good news to match Dionysius and Damaris' conversion experience with an appropriate corresponding discipleship process. Then they would mature thoroughly, mastering their unique faith story. They tell it best of all and spontaneously.

Among others, Dionysius and Damaris would remind us all not to divorce God from creation. We should use natural resources responsibly not exploitively. They would also remind us not to compartmentalize life into spiritual, physical, psychological and mental components, or sacred and secular spheres.

Without that reminder or awareness, we would have a hard time making sense out of God's insistence that we love God with all our heart, soul, mind and strength integratively (Mark 12:29-30). We would disregard to our peril the interactions that occur between the seen and unseen realms of life on planet earth (Ephesians 6:10-20).

Corresponding discipleship for willful haters of God

As said earlier, we learn more about willful haters of God from Jesus himself. He describes them as willfully blind and willfully hypocritical. Their willful blindness consists of knowing, believing and saying the right things about God without grasping their full implications. Consequently, their willful hypocrisy betrays itself in decisions they make to contradict the right things they believe, know and say about God.

Therefore ignorant people or laypeople, or liberal theologians do not ordinarily qualify as willful haters of God. Rather, willful haters of God are ultraconservative hyper-evangelical theologians. Characteristically, they would kill or die, if need be, to defend the fact that God breathed the Scriptures. They are outspoken in honoring God in their verbal and written word. But by what they do, they dishonor God.

Their heads blossom with excellent knowledge about God. But their hearts wither and callous toward God. They minutely dissect the Scriptures. But they do not surrender their hearts to Jesus—the central theme and force of the Scriptures—to mold them into compassionate, tender, loving, and caring hearts. They passionately bleed over a seeming violation of doctrinal minutiae. But they fiercely outlaw or ridicule, downplay or disbelieve fasting and praying to heal people who need it (Mark 3:1-6).

They thunder, "The Scriptures are adequate for faith and life!" But, on occasion, the "traditions as handed down to us" have the final word. Not even God stands a chance before the "traditions" (Matthew 15:1-9). No wonder even silence in the "traditions" drowns deafening thunders of regular behavior of, say, the Holy Spirit, in the Scriptures. Why would the "traditions" not empower us to resist the Holy Spirit, grieve the Holy Spirit and quench the Holy Spirit at will? (Acts 7:51, Ephesians 4:30, 1 Thessalonians 5:19).

Stephen "desecrated" the "traditions" through seeing Jesus above them and "stony-hearted" ultraconservative and hyper-evangelical theologians lynched him with stones (Acts 7:51-60). Not dissimilarly, those same watchdogs of the "traditions" faulted Jesus for healing on the Sabbath. In the same breath, they justified plotting on the Sabbath to kill Jesus (Mark 3:1-6).

And that is exactly where willful haters of God split into defectors and devotees. Defectors see the traditions/institution as a terrifying mean God. They hate it and him because the total picture contradicts what they thought of God. Therefore they defect to spite the institution and God.

Devotees, on the other hand, make the traditions/institution an adorable God. They love an institution and an institutional god—deity—they could manipulate to self-serve. Therefore they become brazenly dogmatic and fanatic about the traditions/institution. Defectors end up choosing "another" god, say idolatry or the occult, outside the institution. Devotees end up choosing "another" god, the "traditions," inside the institution.

Needless to say both defectors and devotees reject God, not out of ignorance, no! They reject him and choose another god to replace him consciously and deliberately.

Elijah, Jesus and Paul (see chapter 6) knew better than condemn willful haters of God or win them over apologetically. Condemnation and/or apologetics wouldn't serve God's purpose effectively here.

But power confrontation that solicits the conscious involvement of power-drunk willful haters of God would. It always does two things that nothing else could do. One, it redemptively outmatches the power of the "god" willful haters have chosen to replace God. They experience defeat inevitably and consciously but wooingly.

Two, it redemptively compels the prodigals to accept defeat as an act of God's grace and surrender for restoration, empowerment and redirection. Rejected, it leaves them inexcusably hardened further to plunge into willful desertion of the God they had always known.

As said earlier, the latter prodigals gladden Satan and his angels as returned prodigals. The former gladden God and his angels as returned prodigals. They are deeply awed by God's love, grace, restoration, empowerment and redirection. They convert transformationally from head knowledge rebellion. They surrender their head and heart, spirit and might to God.

For them to mature thoroughly and become effective, they need to continue to know and experience the power in

- distinguishing God, God's Spirit and word from the "traditions"/institution to counter the "unholy union" of the two (Matthew 15:1-9, 23:1-39)

- God's love—the power of love—to counter self-love—the love of power (1 Corinthians 13, Galatians 5:13-26)

- God's grace to counter legalism (Ephesians 2:1-10)

- God's restoration to counter faulting and condemnation (1 Corinthians 5, 2 Corinthians 2:1-11)

- God's empowerment through the Holy Spirit to counter institutional empowerment and self-sufficiency (Luke 24:48-49, Romans 15:18-19, Ephesians 5:15-20)

- God's redirection to counter monopolized service for God with as many servants of God and as soon as possible (Acts 4:13, 6:3-7, 14:23, 20:17-38, 1 Timothy 1-6, Titus 1-3).

These are native to the conversion experience of willful haters of God. Maturing correspondingly in them, naturally customizes

- childlike trust and dependence on God alone to save (belief)
- learning to be and do from Christ himself (discipleship—apprenticeship)
- growing experiential knowledge of Christ and his work (the truth) and

193

- self-imposed limitations to obey God wholeheartedly (freedom) (John 8:31-32).

Their deeper and sometimes fuller experiential understanding of the power and grace of God, and the wisdom of God constitute a message believers and unbelievers alike need to see and hear from them. To silence it through institutional disregard or cloning affronts God. It audaciously disregards God's working in people.

Corresponding discipleship for victims of the occult

Letting unsaved situations and conversion experience determine the manner of unsheathing the good news and growth process respectively, is biblical. But it is unconventional. The difference between the biblical and conventional explains why most conversions in the Bible sunk roots transformationally, and lasted long self-reproductively.

In contrast, most conventional conversions that result from premeditated, concretized one-size-fits-all evangelistic and discipleship programs are shallow and short-lived.

Overly commitment to the conventional at the expense of the biblical makes us contemporary Pharisees, I think. Like the Pharisees of Jesus day, we hallow "our" methods, products—new gospels—and substitute them for the biblical (Matthew 15:1-9). When the results shock us with disappointment, we scapegoat stereotypically.

But in vain do we scapegoat a ferocious Satan; antagonistic Islamic fanaticism; treacherous animism; seductive pseudo-Christian or post-modern secular culture; mischievous onslaught of the New Age, naturalism, the occult, etc., for

- cosmetic superficial changes in supposed Christians
- repulsive concoctions of Christianity and other religions
- resistance and/or rejection of Christianity (see chapter 2-7).

We have no way of proving to God that we rejected biblical methods because we found them outdated and ineffective. We haven't tried them.

For core level conversions, inside out transformation, instant personalizing of the good news, spontaneous self-reproduction amaze those who try biblical methods (see chapters 1, 3-7, 10-11, cf. Roland Allen, Don Richardson, Robert Coleman, John Dekker, Tom Steffen, etc., in recommended reading).

Not surprisingly, Philip (chapter 7), Paul (chapters 5 and 6), and Peter (chapter 4) followed Jesus' model to put the emphasis where the Bible always puts it. The Bible always places the emphasis, not on programs, keys, principles, skills, but on people. They are to be

- spiritually fit and ready for the Holy Spirit's use in ways he deems fit
- spiritually and scripturally sensitive to God and the situation on hand
- childlike in trusting and depending on God and God alone to save, and
- Christ-like in self-imposed limitations to obey God wholeheartedly.

Therefore against all human reason, logic, cultural expediency, and personal comfort zone and self-preservation—security and safety—, Philip stopped in Samaria; fully knowing persecutors from Jerusalem could catch up with him anytime. Paul cursed a high ranking and respectable fellow Jew to be blind for a short time. Peter went to Cornelius, a non-Jew.

And what was I doing (see chapter 1), audaciously pretending to be like Philip, or Paul, or Peter, to toss my life out to bloodthirsty legendary spiritists to cut off just like that? No, rather, it was childlike trust in God, his promises, his nudging in the thick of it, and constraining love for woefully oppressed victims of the occult that prompted and propelled me to act "foolishly."

And in each case, transformational conversions occurred. They proved that the Holy Spirit worked while "weaklings" worked. Under his guidance, and like Jesus, without premeditation, "weaklings" matched each unsaved situation with a customized version of the good news.

When discipleship, in turn, matches—corresponds to—those conversion experiences, maturation would be thorough and effective. It would equip Nicodemus to tell his unique experience of Jesus appropriately and effectively among his peers, and others, of course. He would tell and show the joy and peace, tolerance and openness, loving and forgiving, etc. in evidence of the transformation that he never had in crash helmet—head knowledge—religion. "How refreshing to let the Holy Spirit open God's word to you!" he would celebrate.

Cornelius and Sergius Paulus would tell their respective stories similarly among fellow politicians, governors, military officers and soldiers. Churches and missions don't normally attract or reach out to these people. But now, Cornelius and Sergius Paulus are right there, among them. On-going total life transformation makes them winsome, gentle and kind, and eloquent for Jesus unintimidated.

Dionysius and Damaris, like Paul, would tell their story among philosophers without feeling intimidated by them. They understand their own kind. But they also know the aching emptiness that worshippers of the mind conceal behind ready answers for the inexplicable. They know how to customize the good news to expose that emptiness and nudge for a taste of God to see that God is indeed good (Psalm 34).

Like them, Simon and his townspeople also have a unique story to tell to glorify God and benefit the body and extend the kingdom of God. They are the ones most qualified to expose the subtle but destructive influences of the occult. For them, the superiority of God's power to the power of Satan and demons is experiential reality.

They most qualify to caution us against dichotomizing the good news into the power of truth and the power of signs and wonders. Their life long experience and conversion experience compel them to insist that victims of the occult need to hear and see both aspects of the good news to be freed and feel free from bondage to esoteric knowledge and esoteric power.

They experienced God in those ways to convert transformationally. They need to mature correspondingly before they could tell their unique story. Their maturation in Jesus would only be appropriate when it matches

- childlike trust in God alone to save
- apprenticeship under Jesus
- experiential knowledge of Jesus and his work, and
- freedom from self to love, obey and serve God wholeheartedly

to their conversion experience.

Their maturation process, then, would incorporate the following and similar concerns.

- Satan the strongman vs. Jesus the stronger man (Matthew 12:29, Luke 10:17-20)

- Mediumism vs. Holy Spirit-filledness (Acts 8:4-40, 13:1-12, 16:16-40, 19:11-20, cf. Deuteronomy 18:9-22)

- Divining future events vs. praying effectively to the God of the past, present and future (Acts 8:9-13, 2 Chronicles 7:14, Jeremiah 32:27, 33:3, Acts 4:23-31, James 5:13-18, cf. Isaiah 45-46)

- Knowledge and power that dazzle and enslave vs. knowledge and power that free and give life (Acts 8:4-13, Acts 19:11-20).

- Power to subdue and exploit vs. power to survive and overcome (Acts 8:14-24, Romans 8:12-17, Galatians 5:13-26, Ephesians 5:18, Revelation 12:11)

- Insecurity and fear vs. safety and security, trust and dependence on God (Acts 8:4-13, Romans 8:12-17, Luke 18:17, John 6:38-39)

- Quick-fixing, haphazard spurious changes and conformity vs. divulging and house-cleaning following conversion (Acts 8:4-24, 19:18-20)

- False rationalized theological assurance vs. being filled with the Holy Spirit and knowing it to prevent bitter backlashes (Acts 8:14-24, Matthew 12:43-45)

- Individualistic, competitive self-sufficiency vs. interdependent—give and take, supplementary—fellowship of believers (e.g., Philip, Peter and John in Acts 8:4-24, John 17:20-23)

When we inhibit Simon and his townspeople, and the like, in their natural growth process through a substituted unnatural one, say, "our" one-size-fits-all discipleship program, we affront God, malnourish them, clone them and impoverish them.

For even a most eloquent mastered telling of "our" story remains a poor substitute for their own story that naturally derives from their conversion experience.

Disciplers

Wilson Awasu

9

Credible carriers of the good news

Psalm 34:8 says, "Taste and see that the LORD is good." Meaning, the goodness of the LORD should not be imagined or assumed. It has to be tasted. And anyone who truly and deeply, realistically and biblically tastes the good news knows that it is indeed good. How can it not be?

Before tasting the good news personally, I was just another citizen of the world, a church-boy, though. I reciprocated resentment, and harbored bitterness in terms of it. I liked to have my own way and felt frustrated when I couldn't. I rationed love and acceptance, forgiveness and reconciliation. I went to church because my parents did and demanded that I did.

I heartlessly recited prayers I learned by rote. I read and memorized portions of the Scriptures similarly. So I was good, wasn't I? How can a 3rd generation Presbyterian not be?

But the day came when the assumed and imagined vanished. I tasted. I drank deep the good news. The eyes of my heart opened. And I saw Jesus Christ with my heart. The light of his awesomeness and wonder gripped me from within, permeated my body and enveloped me in a warm embrace. And in that moment, Jesus transformed me.

The impact and experience left me with peace I never knew; joy I couldn't explain; freedom that made me ache to be imprisoned forever by the love of God. I wept tears of joy, of absolute surrender, of newness, of deep-seated transformation. Every part of me knew I entered a personal relationship with God.

There was a lot I was yet to understand. But I knew I was no longer just a citizen of the world or just another church-boy. No! I changed citizenship. I reduced the statistics of mere church-membership. Now, I was a citizen of the kingdom of God through a personal relationship with God.

Many people identify with that experience, I know. For some, the experience occurred when they were alone with God in some quiet lonely place. Others had the experience in an auditorium, a quaint country church, or a stadium. That wasn't my experience.

God used my mom initially and later "Aunty" Florence. Seven months later, I shared the experience with my dad. He confessed he had never had the experience the way I described it. A little nudging, and he did. Three days later, he died, just like that! That was a 2nd generation Presbyterian. In three days he would have missed eternity with Christ. Thank God, he nipped the tragedy in the bud!

That incident alerted me that everybody in the church would benefit from a little nudging to ensure that they have a vital personal relationship with God. The incident birthed a consuming passion in me to nudge church people to be sure they know God and that God knows them. They live out self-evidently all they believe. God, God's word and God's Spirit have the last word in their lives self-reproductively.

I started off with nudging people at dawn from trees and rooftops. People came out in their nightwears and morning robes to check out "this tree and rooftop angel." They surrendered their lives to Christ even when they realized it was not an angel who sang and preached.

Then I organized crusades. The story at the beginning of the book is typical. Seeing others discover for themselves the joy I knew since I met Jesus makes me agree with Jesus experientially. There is indeed great joy in heaven over one sinner who repents (Luke 15:7, 10, 22-24, 31-32).

I have always wondered. God could go after that joy with or without us. After all who of us pins our chances of joy to the clumsiness or willingness, whim or caprice, convenience or expedience of reluctant others? Inexplicably, it appears, God in his wisdom does exactly that. He wants heaven to rock ecstatic over new additions to heaven. But often, he's looking for a mom, a son, a dad, a daughter; a non-pro lay person; a housemaid or housekeeper; just the ordinary, etc., to use to bring it about!

I don't seem to get over this. Why involve Philip in the conversion of the Ethiopian eunuch, Ananias in Paul's conversion, Peter in Cornelius' conversion, or me in my dad's conversion, when everything showed that God was responsible for it all?

I have not got all the answer. But I think, as of now, I have this much insight into it. God is generous across the board. He's generous with his joy over those to be forgiven and reconciled. In his generosity, he gives us the privilege to participate in the joy that he and all of heaven plus the particular repentant and reconciled feel in the moment of conversion.

No wonder Paul calls the people we help to experience that joy "our crown of rejoicing" (1 Thessalonians 2:19-20). When we help in gathering in citizens of the kingdom of God from all cultures, races, tribes and languages, we participate ahead of time in the grand finale of joy and rejoicing to come.

At that time, all the redeemed would shout at the top of their lungs, "Salvation belongs to our God who sits on the throne and to the Lamb" (Revelation 7:10). All the angels standing around the throne of God, and the elders and the four living creatures wait eagerly for that moment.

They wait to fall face down before the throne of God and worship saying, "Amen! Praise and glory and wisdom and thanks and honor and power and strength be to our God for ever and ever. Amen!" (Revelation 7:11-12).

God ensures that only people who have a vital personal relationship with him participate with him in that joy and the ministering of it. Who wouldn't? But I am amazed that he uses people as ordinary as me. I think it is because God is certain he is doing it all, he could use even people who do not feel they have anything to offer. How amazing!

But even pros like Peter and Paul, who might feel they had it all put nicely together, show that it is God who is doing it all. For truth, right from Jesus Christ our Lord and Savior, through Philip, Peter, and Paul (see above), it is clear that all of them responded spontaneously to situations that resulted in conversions, nothing premeditated, calculated, programmed. No!

Therefore, apart from the Lord Jesus Christ, I think, the outcomes though expected, surprised them. They marveled. They admitted at least to themselves that something beyond them was at work. They would agree that "that something" was the Holy Spirit. It was he who took the little nothings they said, or a song I sang, for example (see Kate in chapter 3), to touch and convert someone at the core of their being.

Closely studying instances of conversions in the Bible and the ones in my own experience, I discovered staggering realities including this. We cannot predict, program or control the moment someone converts at core of being. Neither can we prescribe what exactly converts people. But we can be proactive at being what we must be. So that the Holy Spirit would find us usable and useful when, where and how he wants.

The Scriptures agree and urge. "If you keep yourself pure, you will be a utensil God can use for his purpose. Your life will be clean, and you will be ready for the Master to use you for every good work" (2 Timothy 2:21, cf. John the Baptizer in Luke 3:2c-6, Jesus in Matthew 7:1-6, and Paul in 2 Corinthians 4:1-12).

Meaning, it is not certain anointed skills or principles to master and reproduce laidback with only a moment's notice. Rather, the focus for our readiness centers on us. It is we who must be honed, not for our comfort and confidence, but for the Holy Spirit. He is the one to feel comfortable and confident that he could use us in the moment, manner and place of his choice.

Time and time and again, our Lord seized time to get away and pray, the sinless one praying that much! (See Mark 1:35, Luke 5:16, and John 8:1.) Without that readiness and availability, even our Lord could have proselytized and sowed seeds for syncretism.

For truth, our Lord Jesus Christ would have inappropriately revealed himself to the Samaritan woman at Jacob's well if he were driven by Jewish ethnocentrism to quick fix her in Jewish prescribed ways (see above). Were he remotely self-seeking and vindictive, he would have shredded Nicodemus' flawed theology to indulge instead of leading him to convert transformationally.

Precisely, it was to help Peter rid himself of Jewish ethnocentrism before he was ready and available to lead Cornelius and his household to transformational conversion. Without that honing of himself to be spiritually fit, he would have resisted the Holy Spirit, grieved and quenched him when he cut his sermon short and came on gentiles just as he did Jews (see above).

Skills and principles are good and needful. But certainly, it wasn't honed skills that led Philip to forget that Jewish persecutors he was running away from could catch up with him any moment in Samaria. Although he lacked the skills and experience, he powerfully preached Jesus Christ and worked signs and wonders. He saw a notorious occultist and his victims convert to Jesus Christ.

All that aside, Philip could never have learned, honed and masterly used any number of skills to manipulate, or conjure, the Holy Spirit. Rather, the Holy Spirit found Philip usable and useful because he had honed himself to be

- Holy Spirit-filled
- spiritually sensitive
- childlike dependent on God and
- Christ-like obedient to God.

So the Holy Spirit whisked him away from a large crowd needing counseling after an effective crusade. He led him to convert and baptize a lone Ethiopian eunuch. Before he realized it, zoom, the Holy Spirit whisked him off again. He suddenly disappeared and reappeared many miles away preaching and converting many to Jesus Christ. Philip could never have skillfully predicted any of these or his own marriage to produce four unmarried daughters to have and use the gift of prophecy.

Unlike Philip, Paul was a pro. But he wasn't dogmatically frozen in procedures, skills, formulas, and principles. He flexed them to fit situations appropriately as they met him. And that is the point.

His confidence and effectiveness did not fixate in what he knew how to do. They fixated rather in God who did all things through him. Where he worked the hardest was himself. He honed Paul to be anything that would help bring Jews, Greek, Romans, etc., to faith in Jesus Christ. And Paul more than anybody else pushed the need and instruction to be disciplined, ready, usable and useful to God any time (1 Corinthians 9:19-27, 2 Timothy 2:1-26, 4:1-8).

I think it is in that sense—the sense of self-evident total life transformation that appropriate carriers of the good news exemplify—that the Scriptures describe their feet as beautiful. Their lives authenticate the fact. The good news of Jesus indeed brings life to death, hope to hopelessness, freedom to bondage, joy to sorrow, relief to pain, etc. (Romans 10:15, Isaiah 52:7).

This is no patching up of grosser behaviors of the downright wicked. Neither is it cosmetic retouching of self-righteous sophistry. No! Rather, the good news comes to transform life totally—inside out. And the lives of carriers of the good news evidence it winsomely. It is all right there. Prospective believers see it, and feel it. They wouldn't have to imagine "How does it look like to be converted to Christ?"

The drought

Actually, I did the study on transformational—radical, heart, core level, spiritual—conversion in response to a jolt I felt about a drought of conversions in my life. I experienced the drought at the time my head thickened with formal intellectual pursuit.

As a highly motivated M.Div. degree student, I absorbed all the knowledge that theological studies under distinguished faculty provided. The feeling, now I have under my belt, theological underpinnings of the faith I had loved and propagated as an amateur.

Th.M. Missiology degree studies added a touch of delightful color and heightened feeling. Now, in addition to theological understandings and answers, I have the missiological. Again, distinguished faculty helped shape my intellectual formation.

All that paved the way for the pursuit of a Ph.D. degree in Intercultural Studies. Lots of reading and writing, original field study and data analysis, further reading and dissertation writing, and defense, took turns.

Then graduation came and went as it came, suddenly. It left me a diversified "crash helmet" —head—pro with lots of answers, the theological, missiological and anthropological.

The jolt came in the process. It ran something like this. Do you realize that your intellectual pursuit enlarges at the expense of your passion for soul winning and the practice of it?

My first reaction was, No it hasn't! On the contrary, I am maturing and becoming sophisticated in

- my thinking and my understanding, and
- my articulation and my presentation

of the good news.

Really? The jolt queried.

Yes! Or? I said.

But a most deafening silence responded! What might this mean?

Personal inventory

I decided to take an inventory. I prayed. I fasted on and off and prayed and searched my heart, mind, spirit and will. I recounted, dissected and analyzed my habit of personal evangelism and discipleship. It was then that I discovered, or rather admitted, that I had experienced a drought of conversions. My passion and zeal and perseverance for conversions went under for the most part those years.

For some mysterious reason I had become fascinated with and confident in saying "it"

- well (sound theologically, missiologically and/or anthropologically, as the case may be)
- hard (intellectually convincing and impressive) and/or
- long (artistically repeated more for style than for emphasis)

to bring about conversion, or at least conviction.

That fascination and confidence lured me away from

- my former unqualified passion and

- my former childlike trust and dependence on God

for conversions. Though I prayed for conversions in those days, it wasn't the type of informed, agonizing and persevering prayers I knew previously.

Precisely, I now have more than enough confidence in what I knew and how I said it and what I thought it would accomplish. If the expected didn't happen, I knew exactly why. Theologically, mine was to sow the seed. Others would water... Missiologically, common knowledge consoles that products of non-Christian cultures tend to resist and reject Christianity to their peril. Too bad! Anthropologically, it has long been established that Islamic, animistic, secularistic worldviews, for example, resist the gospel. Nothing new!

At the time, I didn't see that my rationale exonerated me: I did everything right. My hearers did everything wrong. But now I realized that the jolt came from God. It was as if God told me, Look back in your personal experience!

And as I looked, I picked up a radiant thread. It glittered! It spoke for itself. Whenever I recklessly trusted God, God's word and God's Spirit; whenever I recklessly loved people, fasted and prayed for them; my focus remained on God. I sought to align my will, word, ways and works to God's will, word, ways and works. I found myself being used by God to do the impossible, and unprecedented sometimes.

In those times, it was not how well, hard, or long I said or did something. Rather, it was God using what I said and did to open the minds and hearts of people to see and receive and obey God's message. Yes, and it was his message, because I was incapable of engineering or conjuring the wisdom that shone through what I said or did, where, when and how.

I knew that God was/is always looking for people through whom

- he could speak as they speak and

- he could work as they work

to convict and convert whomever he wills and wherever and whenever he wants.

So I thanked God for the timely jolt. I also thanked him for the privilege he gave me to extend and expand my mind academically. But I fiercely committed to making all I know academically—human wisdom—serve the strictly biblical—the wisdom of God. That commitment translated into a passion right away, making me intensely desirous to seek to hear God on the issues, including conversion. Certainly he must have revealed his perfect will on conversions that lead to total life transformation! What is it?

Biblical inventory

I plunged into the Scriptures with renewed zeal, hunger and thirst. In no time, everywhere I looked, the facts stared me in the face: The Spirit of God and the temple/the Church and the nations (many cultures, many races, many tribes and many languages) always go together.

Therefore, the moment the temple/the Church or individual believers shut off—resist, grieve, quench—the Spirit of God,

- they shut themselves in
- they shut the nations out, and
- they shut God out as well.

That means the life of the temple/Church or individual believers must remain integrally, vitally connected to the source—God. Then they would remain alive and life giving (Isaiah 44, 56; Ezekiel 47, 1 Kings 8:41-43; Matthew 21:12-13; Luke 4:16-21; John 15, cf. Isaiah 61:1-2 and Acts 1:8).

Again and again, I saw it repeated. God is always looking for people he could comfortably and confidently trust and use. So that what is done, is done in the Holy Spirit (Zechariah 4:6, Isaiah 55:8). And God alone receives the glory (Isaiah 42:8, 48:11).

Such people know God intimately. They have a vital, secret, private personal knowledge of God. The effectiveness of their public witness for God depends on the authentic witness they have of God in private, secret. And consistently, they see transformational conversions. I cite a few.

Biblical illustrations

Of Levi, God had said, "True instruction was in his mouth and nothing false was found on his lips. He walked with me in peace and uprightness, and [he] turned many from sin" (Malachi 2:6).

Elijah turned the hearts of the hardened, rebellious, idolatrous nation of Israel back to God through several acts of power confrontations, all directed and led by the Spirit of God. In response, the repentant nation exclaimed, "The LORD, he is God; the LORD, he is God!" (1 Kings 17, 18).

The angel disclosed that John the Baptizer would be filled with the Holy Spirit from his mother's womb. Similar to Elijah, he would turn many Israelis to the LORD their God. He would take them from skepticism to childlike trust in God, and from rebellion to surrender to God. He would especially herald Jesus Christ (Luke 1:15-17). And he did.

Quoting from Isaiah 61:1-2, our Lord Jesus Christ announced his job description like this: "The Spirit of the LORD is on me, because he has anointed me to preach good news to the poor. He has sent me to proclaim release to the captives and recovery of sight to the blind, to set at liberty those who are oppressed, and to proclaim the acceptable year of the Lord."

Then he charged the apostles and disciples, "But you will receive power when the Holy Spirit comes on you; and you will be my witnesses in Jerusalem, and in all Judea and Samaria, and to the ends of the earth" (Acts 1:8). Accordingly, at Pentecost (Acts 2) and with Peter's initial sermon, 3,000 men, excluding women and children, turned to the Lord.

Acts 6:3, 8:1-40 say that Philip, one of the seven deacons, was well respected by all. He was full of the Holy Spirit and wisdom. And many people came to the Lord Jesus Christ through him.

Barnabas, according Acts 11:24, was a good man, full of the Holy Spirit and strong faith. Consequently, large numbers of people came to faith in Jesus through him.

Just before God sent Ananias to Saul (Paul), he disclosed to him that he had chosen Paul to take the good news to non-Jews and Jews. He would suffer a lot in the process. When Ananias found Paul, he laid his hands on him and said, "Brother Saul, the Lord Jesus, who appeared to you on the road, has sent me so that you may get your sight back and be filled with the Holy Spirit" (Acts 9:15-17).

Reporting the results, Paul said,

I will not venture to speak of anything except what Christ has accomplished through me in leading the gentiles to obey God by what I have said and done—by the power of signs and miracles, through the power of the Holy Spirit. So from Jerusalem all the way to Illyricum [Europe], I have fully proclaimed the gospel of Christ (Romans 15:18-19).

The good news and its appropriate carriers

Not surprisingly, when Jesus stated the good news (Luke 24:36-53, see chapter 8), he made the fitness of its carriers an integral part of it.

- *Verses 36-43, the crucified and bodily-resurrected Jesus is the author and commissioner of the good news.*

- *Verses 44-45, all the Scriptures and disentangled understanding of them make up the source of the message of the good news.*

- *Verses 46-47, the crucified and resurrected Christ, and repentance and forgiveness of sins in his name to be preached to all peoples constitute the theme of the message of the good news.*

- *Verses 48-49, credible and clothed witnesses are appropriate carriers of the good news.*

- *Verses 50-53, being blessed, joyful, praiseful and prayerful evidence the power of the good news to save and transform people radically.*

"Credibility," "clothing," "fragrance" marked those who saw transformational conversions in the Old and New Testaments. Their credibility derived from intimate knowledge of God. Their clothing came from the "hovering" —resting—of the Holy Spirit on them. Both their intimate knowledge of God and living in the Holy Spirit made them the fragrance of Christ

- to God
- to those who are being saved and
- to those who resist/reject the good news (2 Corinthians 2:14-17).

Model characteristics

Certain traits crystallized. They surprised me in three ways. Firstly, their ordinariness and simplicity, placing them within the reach of all of us surprised me. It also surprised me that the traits focus on who we are in Christ, not so much on our giftedness or ungiftedness in evangelism, or certain skills to master, or academic excellence.

Therefore, secondly, in being to the full who we are in Christ, we can all, to varying degrees of course, see people come to faith in Jesus Christ transformationally. It is on this basis that Jesus commands all of us to be his witnesses, telling our respective faith story. We are the most qualified to tell our faith story if we have one.

Thirdly, it shouldn't but it surprised me that I saw and see transformational conversions consistently whenever those traits characterize my life. When they don't, higher education and honed skills plus past experiences fail to generate transformational conversions.

From those perspectives, I cite, what I consider as model characteristics of effective carriers of the good news. The list is purposely inexhaustive. But it represents basic characteristics of believers who "naturally"

- thirst for
- go after and
- see

transformational conversions.

In chapters 10 and 11, I illustrate each characteristic with personal examples for encouragement and motivation. Indeed, non-pros like you and I can see transformational conversions that would gladden heaven, stun us, and keep our appetite whetted for more.

Effective carriers of the good news

1. *Have a winsome vital personal relationship with God (see Mark 1:35, John 4:31-34, Acts 4:13, cf. verses 5-14)*

2. *Have the Holy Spirit resting on them for effective and offensive witness (see Luke 1:15-17, 3:1-22, 4:16-21, Acts 1:8, 2:1-47)*

3. *Know the Scriptures and live by them (see Matthew 1:22-23, 2:5-6, 17-23, 21:1-11, etc. cf. John 15:1-11, 1 Corinthians 15:3-4)*

4. *Hear God's voice and obey him unquestioningly (see John 5:30, 10:5, 27)*

5. *Discern and follow God to do what he is doing (see John 5:19, Acts 16:6-40)*

6. *Are childlike in trusting and depending on God (see Luke 18:17, cf. Matthew 10:16 and Proverbs 3:5-8)*

7. *Love God, other believers and enemies recklessly (see Mark 12:29-31, John 13:34-35, Matthew 5:43-48)*

8. *Are prayerful and they experience instances of mysterious answers to prayer (see Luke 11:1-13, Hebrews 5:7-10, Acts 4:23-31)*

9. *Suffer intense persecution (see Matthew 5:10-12, Mark 10:28-31, 2 Timothy 3:12, 1 Peter 4:14)*

10. *Experience instances of mysterious rescue from pre-mature death (see Hebrews 5:7-10, Luke 4:14-30, Acts 12:1-17)*

11. *Encounter demons and demons recognize them (see Mark 1:21-28, Acts 16:17, 19:11-20)*

12. *Have experiences and skills but they do not box up God in them; rather, they leave God free to be God and work in fresh and new ways as he deems fit (see Mark 13:11, Acts 4:1-31, Philippians 3:1-21, 2 Corinthians 4:7, 2 Corinthians 10:18)*

13. *Are single-minded in getting the job done, no matter personal costs (see John 4:31-42, 1 Corinthians 9:19-27)*

14. Are single-minded in letting all the glory go to God, however he wants it (see John 5:19, 30, 1 Corinthians 4:1-12, Romans 15:17-19)

15. Are marked by numerous long lasting self-reproductive transformational conversions (see John 4:1-42, Luke 19:1-10, John 14:12-14, 15:8, 16, Acts 2:1-47, 8:4-40, 11:24).

All in all, humility stands out as the most distinguishing characteristic of effective carriers of the good news (John 3:30). God's wisdom shines brightest through humility. It outwits human love for power and brutish force, manipulation and intimidation.

Consistently, Jesus taught and demonstrated, and then commanded that people, who would facilitate transformational conversion, should be as defenseless as sheep, wise as snakes, and harmless as doves (Matthew 10:16). That is the surest way to outwit the "wolves" that might fight to resist the conversion of prospective believers in Christ, or fight to retrieve them when converted. It is also the surest way to desist matching the aggression of the "wolves" with any vestiges of their likeness in us (Proverbs 3:5-6, Matthew 10:16 and Luke 18:17).

In short, effective good news carriers die to themselves. They and Jesus and people around them know that Jesus lives his life through them (Galatians 2:20). Like Stephen, they are full of grace and power, and wisdom and the Holy Spirit (Acts 6:8, 10). And like Barnabas, they are known as Christ-like, and are full of the Holy Spirit and faith. The result, many people come to Christ through them (Acts 6:8, 10, 11:24, cf. Hebrews 5:7-10, John 14:21, 23-24, John 5:19, 30).

The greatest and most powerful, the loudest and clearest proof that the good news indeed transforms people totally, consists of the total life transformation that exudes from good news carriers. That way, prospective converts would not have to imagine or ask, "How does transformational conversion look like?" For a fact, when carriers of the good news truly make up its aroma, their lives do not repel or obstruct prospective believers. Rather, their lives attract them, not to themselves, but to the heavenly Father (Matthew 5:16).

10

Illustrative personal examples (A)

One: Effective carriers of the good news have a winsome vital personal relationship with God (see Mark 1:35, John 4:31-34, Acts 4:13, cf. verses 5-14).

As a freshman in university, neck-deep involvement in the normal routine of IVCF activities left me still hungry for God. I took to long hours of Bible reading, study and meditation in the woods around campus. I fasted and prayed to be filled to overflowing with God.

One evening, in usual fashion, I sat on a rock rested my head on crossed arms on my knees. I closed my eyes and prayed. When I opened my eyes, I couldn't see anything. It had turned dark and I didn't realize it. Initially, I panicked. How was I going to get out of there—no flashlight and a long way away from campus?

All of a sudden, a flash of light spotlighted me. Hmm! What might this mean? As I moved, the light around me moved as well. I walked in it all the way to streetlights a quarter of a mile away. Then the spotlight departed.

Might that be God? I wondered. I decided to test it and make sure. So I went back there three times close to nightfall. Night came. So did the spotlight. I was convinced it was God. I thanked God in my unbelief and asked. "What will you have me do, Lord?"

God directed and led me to a girls' boarding school, I never knew existed, seven miles away from campus. I started and ran for the next three years a Sunday afternoon Bible Study group in the school.

Each year, several girls surrendered their lives to Christ. Most of them went on to high school the following year. Consequently, each year, the group reconfigured itself into almost a new group. And we started all over again, hammering away conversion, assurance, growth, conduct and witness.

Remarkably, many kept the faith through high school, college and right into their professions, marriages and families, and churches.

Agnes is typical. She is a medical doctor and holds a Ph.D. degree in bio-chemical sciences. Everywhere she goes, she's literally a city set on a hill. She is an unhiddenable witness for Christ.

She often illustrates transformational conversion with two hearts and two trees. There is the sinful heart cluttered and eaten out by worms of sin. Then there is the clean heart with Christ symbolized by a cross right at the center of it (Mark 7:20-23, Matthew 12:33-37).

The one tree represents sin bearing sinful fruits, like anger, pride, selfishness, bitterness, immorality, etc. The other represents the Holy Spirit bearing the fruit of love, joy, peace, patience, kindness, goodness, faithfulness, gentleness, self-control, etc. (Galatians 5:16-26).

She had seen and continues to see many transformational conversions.

When she and I reconnected several years later, she told me that the two hearts and two trees illustration stuck with her because it was that illustration the Lord used to convert her when I used it in her school.

Two: Effective carriers of the good news have the Holy Spirit resting on them for effective and offensive witness (see Luke 1:15-17, 3:1-22, 4:16-21, Acts 1:8, 2:1-47).

Certainly, it was the Spirit of God, not the reluctant Jonah, who convicted and converted the people of Nineveh (Jonah 1-4). John the Baptizer's sermons rate poorly in terms of what qualifies as a three-points-and-a-poem evangelical sermon. But as the Scriptures predicted, he was filled with the Holy Spirit right from his mother's womb. Therefore the poor sermons he preached turned many people to God (see above).

Jeff, Stacie, and Kate (see chapter 3), experienced the working of the Holy Spirit in their lives in ways that I couldn't have consciously put together. All I knew was that in each case, before the event, I was either in the process of fasting and praying or had fasted and prayed for one thing or another.

Three: Effective carriers of the good news know the Scriptures and live by them (see Matthew 1:22-23, 2:5-6, 17-23, 21:1-11, etc. cf. John 15:1-11, 1 Corinthians 15:3-4)

The Gospels, particularly, Matthew, emphasize that our Lord Jesus Christ lived strictly according to the Scriptures. And in his own words, Jesus declared that he came to fulfill the Scriptures. Then he taught that when we live that way, our lives would touch and transform many people as his did (John 14:12-24, 15:1-11).

I discovered that people take seriously what we say about God when they see it in our lives. And they become like us accordingly.

I recall the first time 1 Thessalonians 1:1-10 strongly hit me.

- Paul presented the good news with his life and lips in the power of the Holy Spirit

- the good news convicted and converted Thessalonians transformationally
- the repentant, forgiven and reconciled Thessalonians became imitators of Paul
- they became examples of self-reproductive transformational conversion
- they literally became sounding boards of the good news.

Following my usual habit after such encounters in Scripture, I prayed that God would lead me to some place where that would happen. Right after my prayer, the high school I attended came to mind. I followed the hunch and got the pulpit at the students' Sunday evening worship service.

Sam and Emmanuel were among eight students that told me that they submitted their lives to Jesus Christ as I sang and preached. Subsequently, I discipled them.

At the time of writing, Sam who holds a Ph.D. in biological sciences and teaches college had released several musical albums. He and his wife, who is also a disciple of mine, run a diversified ministry alongside. And on regular basis, he sings and preaches just as I do.

Emmanuel is an ordained pastor in the Presbyterian Church. He preaches and teaches God's word faithfully. In addition, he prays for people to be healed as I do.

Four: Effective carriers of the good news hear God's voice and obey him unquestioningly (see John 5:30, 10:5, 27)

I was stunned the first time I heard Jesus say in Scripture that he says only what he's heard the Father say (John 5:30). Jesus is God, I thought. He could say anything he wanted. He would never go wrong. But going wrong wasn't the issue. Rather, it was deliberate self-limitations Jesus put on himself to serve God as God's servant (Philippians 2:1-11).

Then Jesus turned around to say, "My sheep hear my voice, and I know them, and they follow me" (John 10:27). His sheep don't follow strangers because they don't know the voice of strangers (verse 5). That is a thought. How does it work out? For several days I thought about that.

Before I knew it, my thoughts, and desire I think, had enrolled me in an intensive course in Jesus' discipleship school on "Learning to hear God's voice and do as told."

It was Wednesday lunch break at college. Many of us particularly liked Monday, Wednesday and Saturday lunch. So we talked about it as we walked the half-mile to the dining room from the classrooms.

About 50 feet to lunch, I seemed to hear a voice in my spirit telling me to go to my room on the 7th floor and pray instead. "Madness!" I rudely hushed the voice. No God would ask such a thing. I had skipped breakfast at seven, and snack at ten to have a big appetite at lunch. God knew I was starving!

Disregarding sound logic, the voice persisted in my spirit.

Now, the "aroma" of lunch had seized and turned us into hungry lions steadying to pounce on their prey. But I knew better than conclude that a gentle peaceful voice other than God's would invite me to prayer. So, drenched by the "aroma" of lunch, I walked past the dining room, jumped into the elevator and hit the 7th button.

Reluctantly, I dropped to my knees beside my bed to pray. Then the strangest thing happened. "Go to the rooftop and pray!" Kidding! Is this God? I asked. And he doesn't seem to make up his mind? Well! Up to the rooftop, three floors away, I went.

I crossed my arms and rested them on the chest high wall that surrounded the rooftop and started to pray. But, no! Too bad! I was in the wrong place again! "Go to the woods [a mile away] and pray there," the voice in my spirit directed. I did.

As I walked up beneath cathedral-like arches of leafy mango trees, I saw two uniformed schoolgirls approaching from the opposite direction. We greeted and passed each other by. Just as I began to focus to pray, I heard them giggle and tease. It happened a few times and continued. It became obvious that they were attempting to catch my attention.

At first I thought, I wasn't the baldheaded Elisha (2 Kings 2:23-25). But perhaps, I could invoke bears out of nowhere to eat up two "disrespectful" schoolgirls! After all I had followed God's orders to come out there to pray. And there they were trying to distract me. But, no! I felt the deepest compassion for them. It brought tears to my eyes.

So I turned around and walked back to them. We chitchatted. But suddenly, they asked, "Tell us about Jesus Christ!" Really? I thought and got to work. In no time at all, they received Jesus Christ as their personal Savior and Lord. They invited me to their school to talk to the whole school about Jesus. They gave me the principal's name and directions to the school. "We'll be expecting you!" they said and waved goodbye.

"Yes!" I said vaguely, not knowing what to think.

As soon as the nearest curve in the road hid them, I seemed to hear in my spirit, "Go back to the campus!"

By the time I got there, lunchtime had passed. Only the smell of disinfectants and wax used in cleaning and polishing the wooden tables and wood floors of the dining room remained in the air.

However as I drained a glass of iced water from a tabletop cooling tank in the dining room, I heard the chief steward call from the opposite end. "Sir, sir!" he called. When my eyes met his, he said, "I didn't see you at lunch so I reserved lunch for you. Here, take it!" Incredible!

As far as I could remember, he and I had never talked to each other. How could he notice my absence at lunch? I thanked him in amazement.

I also thanked God. In spite of initial reluctance I heard and obeyed God's voice. And I didn't miss lunch either. Wow!

Two weeks later, I located the school and met the principal. She offered to cancel the last two classes for the day and have me talk to the whole school. When I did, many students and some teachers surrendered their lives to Christ. We started a number of weekly discipleship Bible study groups for them. IVCF colleagues helped in leading them for the next several years.

That summer, I worked a study job with Ghana Television. I visited the beach weekly to read the Bible, meditate and pray. One night as I broke loose from the salty embrace of the Atlantic Ocean, I had a gentle but firm impression on my heart, mind and spirit.

It directed that I visited a Presbyterian Church twenty miles away coming Sunday. I had a vague idea about its location. So Sunday, I set off on a bus. I got off at the terminal on a hilltop. I panned and spotted a church steeple. Might it be the church I was looking for? I traced the steeple in crow-flight fashion. Delightfully, it was. I sat close to the back. Now what?

The usual proceedings began and lasted. Then the sermon started. In the second pew in front of mine, I noticed a lady read a book throughout the sermon. That was unusual for someone to do, I thought. I decided to check it out when church ended.

"Hi, my name is Wilson. What's yours?" I greeted.

"Lyn!" she responded curtly.

"Tell me, Lyn. Why did you read a book throughout the sermon?" I dared.

"Who are you? Are you a member of this church? Why do you want to know?" she protested.

"Oh, this is my first time here. But it surprised me that someone bothered to come to church and read a book during the sermon." I said evasively.

"You didn't tell me who you are. Will you, please?" Lyn insisted.

"Of course, of course! I am a student at the university in Kumasi (Ghana). I am doing a study job with Ghana Television this summer. That's all." I answered.

"So what brought you here? Why come to church twenty miles away from Accra?" she queried.

"Perhaps, to meet and be stunned by someone who reads a book during the sermon," I ventured.

"Do you have time to talk? I will like to talk to you" Lyn softened.

"Sure!" I jumped for it, still wondering…

Lyn vented for an hour. And I made mental notes. The preacher was the youth pastor of the church. He had pestered her to the point of almost driving her out of the church with a sexual affair proposition. If she knew that he was going to preach, she wouldn't have come to church that Sunday.

"I am sorry it happened to you!" I consoled. Then I asked. "What are you going to do to get him off your back?"

"Do! There's nothing I can do. Perhaps I have to change churches. Don't you think?" Lyn said and asked.

"What if you meet him in another youth pastor, what would you do then? You can't just keep running!" I pressed.

"You're right. What do you suggest I do, counselor!" Lyn teased. But I felt she meant it. After a moment of silent prayer I told her what I would do.

"I would fast and pray and ask God to take care of me while I make sure I do not secretly harbor lust."

"Are you inferring that I am to blame?" Lyn retorted, somewhat indignant.

"No! I am sorry if I hurt your feelings." I said, trying to do damage control. A disturbing silence I wished she broke took over. But when she didn't, I ventured. "Lyn, I have discovered that as young people, we can only keep our bodies, minds and hearts pure, and make them a fitting residing place for the Holy Spirit, when we see and treat ourselves like that."

"The Holy Spirit? How can he live in us?" Lyn asked in amazement.

I referred to biblical passages like 1 Corinthians 3:16-17, 6:12-20 that describe our bodies as the residence of the Holy Spirit to make the point. I emphasized that all believers in Christ, according to Romans 8:9, have the Holy Spirit. Verse 14 demands that, in addition, we surrender to his daily empowerment and leadership.

"I don't have the Holy Spirit. Teach me how," Lyn confessed.

I led her to know Jesus personally. She said a most hearty prayer, surrendering self-rule and committing to the rule of God in her life. I led her through relevant passages of Scripture to assure her of forgiveness and reconciliation to God.

Before we parted, Lyn asked, "Can you come again next week? I want you to meet some people!"

"Yes, of course." I consented.

All week I wondered as I prayed and looked forward to Sunday. Lyn introduced me to six friends and asked me to tell them about knowing and relating personally to Jesus. I did. We met a few times for follow up. By the time I returned to school, they had grasped the basics in knowing, loving and worshipping God wholeheartedly.

Needless to say, in my wildest imagination, dreaming, and strategizing, I couldn't have put all that together. But through unquestioning obedience to the leading of God, I became the privileged witness of it all.

Five: Effective carriers of the good news discern and follow God to do what he is doing (see John 5:19, Acts 16:6-40)

John 5:19, Jesus said, "I assure you, the Son can do nothing by himself. He does only what he sees the Father doing. Whatever the Father does, the Son also does." So persistent was Jesus in that commitment that he declined eating his lunch at Jacob's well in Sychar, Samaria. He told his disciples that his nourishment came from doing God's will and finishing the task (John 4:31-34).

He had just converted the Samaritan woman. Spontaneously, she abandoned her water jar at the well and ran to invite her townspeople to Jesus. In anticipation for their imminent coming, Jesus declined eating lunch.

They came. He converted them as well. They said so and asked him to spend extra time with them. He did (John 4:31-43). But at other times, when the crowds asked him to extend his stay, he wouldn't (Mark 1:35-39 and Luke 4:40-44).

The same Jesus dived into a sea of sick people. He didn't conduct mass healing. He healed only one person (John 5:1-9). But another time, he exorcised and healed people all night long (Mark 1:32-34).

Persistently, Jesus refused to let

- his mother (John 2:1-11)

227

- his siblings (John 7:1-10)
- his disciples (Matthew 16:21-24)
- the Pharisees (Matthew 12:38-45, 21:23-27, 27:41-43)
- Satan (Luke 4:1-13) or
- popular opinion of him (John 6:15)

pressurize him to do anything short of the perfect will of God.

In Christ's tenacity, I see a thin line between informed obedience and ritualized obedience to God. But strangely, even Jesus maintained that line through painful learning and agonizing prayer (Hebrews 5:7-10). So did Paul (Acts 16:6-10).

I was one of 200 delegates that listened to an associate of Billy Graham evangelistic association in a conference room at Adulfus hotel, Dallas Texas. Right after his talk, while everybody remained seated, a lady got up and walked toward the podium. A few feet to it, she dropped to the floor in the aisle. Eight guys picked her up and walked her out to the hallway. A strong inner pull urged me to invite myself, and I did.

When I got to where they'd sat her, I overheard them question her about hunger, exhaustion, insufficient sleep, drug use and so on. I prayed silently and watched and continued to listen to everything going on.

Then I said, "I don't think Kelly's problem is physical. [Kelly is my protective name for her.] It's spiritual. If you doubt me, ask her to tell you her name!" Nobody bothered. Honestly, I wouldn't have bothered either if I were one of them. What a crazy idea! Who does he think he is? Walk in here and tell us what to do... I would have thought. And perhaps they thought so too.

However, I repeated what I said three times. I did because as I prayed, the legion demoniac kept coming to my mind. When Jesus asked his name, it was the demons that spoke (Mark 5:1-20). At the time a demon is operative in a victim, it is the demon that speaks, not the victim.

Later, however, Bill, one of Kelly's helpers, took me seriously. He asked Kelly, "What is your name?" And a guttural sounding name came, stunning us all. At that, Kelly's helpers relocated to a guest room close to the lobby. I followed with much trepidation.

For two hours straight Bill and his colleagues took turns in reading out "the right" scriptural passage. Following each reading, all eight guys laid their hands on Kelly and prayed. "We command you in the name of Jesus come out!" But each time, Kelly got hold of the hands and tossed. And all of them went to the floor. But they got up and came back on as quickly as they went down.

Then Bill asked me, "Why don't you join us to pray for Kelly?"

"I want to," I started to say. "But I don't know what to say. So I am praying silently to find out from God what exactly to pray."

"Interesting!" Dave sharply retorted. Dave was Kelly's fiancé. "You were the one who got us to see that it was a demon in the first place. What else do you need?"

I felt irritated a little. I wanted to retort back. But I sensed that a distracting quarrel would result. Kelly and her helpers would be caught momentarily in a "demonic" grip. So I let go. I focused on what I had learned to date. It is one thing to discern the presence and activity of a demon. But it is quite another to know what to do to exorcise it. Presumption is sin. It could be costly (see Acts 19:13-17).

Incidentally, even until then, I didn't have the slightest clue what I should pray. The most deafening silence, lasting for fifteen minutes, invaded us. Then I felt a compassionate pain in my heart for Kelly. I sobbed and wept foolishly. I invited everybody in the room to see Kelly as a victim of the occult. "Please, enter into her pain the best you could. And let's pray together that God would free her from whatever she contracted." I pleaded. We did.

229

After a while, Bill hushed everybody and directed that I prayed alone for Kelly. Two sentences in my prayer, Kelly jumped up and praised God for her deliverance. We tested it with Scripture and we were all convinced she was indeed delivered from whatever it was.

Come and see us hug one another in celebration! Later that afternoon, at a larger meeting, 2,000 strong, in a college auditorium, Kelly gave a powerful testimony about her deliverance from the aftermath of dabbling in the occult. She warned, "Dabbling in the occult is deadly!"

Six months earlier, in a hospital in Ghana, I stood at the bedside of a college student who had claimed that she had 70 demons in her. The principal of her school, a most godly man, and others had prayed and failed to free her. Doctors had also exhausted every means to sedate her. She remained wild.

I had goose bumps all over me when I entered the room. She greeted me with a statement in German. Neither her nurses nor I understood it. So I prayed that God made her say it in a language one of us understood if it were something we needed to know. Almost immediately, she spoke in Fante. It was a contemptible threat. "We are 70 here and are comfortable here. Nobody is going to get us out of here."

How do we know for sure that there were 70 demons in a college student? So far it was her word everybody took for it. Silently I prayed that God would let us know the true truth. We waited an hour. Then I felt five pinpricks in my right palm. I took that as a hint from God. Instead of 70 demons, there were five. Next, I asked, "Lord, what do we do?"

"Tell the five demons to leave their victim" registered in my spirit.

Accordingly, I said, "Jesus orders you five demons to get out of your victim and be gone,"

An intimidating, terrorizing deep manly voice retorted in English. "How do you know we are five? There are 70 of us here. We are not going out."

That scared and confused me. I lost confidence in what I took for God's leading and direction. So back to the drawing board! "Lord, what are we up to here? Please help our faithlessness, for your name's sake," I prayed and waited.

After thirty minutes of expectant waiting, God nudged me to order the five demons out. So I did. "You, five demons, Jesus says, go!"

They screamed, twitched and went out.

Over and over again, I realize this. We would see more lasting, God honoring results—well rounded freedom and wholeness for people—if, like Jesus, we seek to know where God is working and follow after him.

Six: Effective carriers of the good news are childlike in trusting and depending on God (see Luke 18:17, cf. Matthew 10:16 and Proverbs 3:5-8)

According to Jesus, we enter the kingdom by childlike trust and dependence on God (Luke 18:17). Similarly, we effectively enter the lives of unbelievers (and hurting believers alike) only through powerlessness, wisdom and harmlessness while trusting and depending on God (Matthew 10:16).

The story I cited at the beginning of the book illustrates that type of entry into the lives of unbelievers. But I also remember an instance when I did the life a very intelligent but hurting believer schoolteacher. I call her Becky.

Becky was a single parent of four and belonged to an adult Sunday school class I once taught. She wore somber colored clothes most times. She walked as if she stepped on egg shells. She seldom spoke.

On our way to the sanctuary one of those Sundays, I dared a question. "Are you mourning?"

"Mourning! What do you mean?" she asked.

"Oh, everything about you says so; your body language, clothes, demeanor and all. Why is that?" By now we had reached the steps to the sanctuary.

"Do you have time after church? I will like to talk." She requested.

"Of course!" I consented.

After lunch at Becky's, she told me she was recovering from divorce, and adjusting to single parenthood.

"Ha-ha-ha! And you want to kill yourself for a rooster?" I teased half afraid and half unsure of what I said.

"Rooster!" she queried.

"Yes!" I affirmed.

"What do you mean?" Becky asked.

"You see, roosters don't know their children. They simply fertilize eggs."

"Ha-ha-ha!" Becky laughed. And again, "Ha-ha-ha!" she laughed until her sides hurt. Then she disclosed, "That was my former husband even when we were married."

"Well, now answer the question. Is it worth it to kill yourself after the rooster is gone?" I cautioned.

"No!" Becky said emphatically.

"Then snap out of it. Live your life. Your children need a live mom." I counseled.

"You're right! Thank you, Wilson. My 'mourning' is over!"

Indeed Becky's "mourning" ended that very moment. A breath of fresh life seemed to enter her. It transformed her instantly. Even her looks changed momentarily. Becky knew and demonstrated a new spiritual, physical and emotional zest and vitality to match her mental vitality.

At a conference in Eastbourne, England in 1999, it was easy to pick out David speaking American English three people behind me in the lunch food line. I stepped outside the line, looked back and said Hi to David.

"Hi!" David responded. "I am a student in Denver, Colorado!"

"I am Wilson. I flew in from Minneapolis, Minnesota." I leaned closer to him and whispered, teasing, I thought, "Do you have a girlfriend?"

Looking stunned, David said and asked, "I will like to talk. But I have a lunch date. Can we talk after lunch?"

"Sure!" I agreed.

Thirty minutes to our scheduled time, David found me in the hallway and said, "Several of us had discussed the topic a lot in our spare times this week. It was as if you knew. So when I mentioned your offer at lunch, some of my newfound friends here at the conference want to come and hear you talk to us. Do you mind if I invite them?"

I wondered if I had anything to say at all. Anyhow, I agreed. "Invite them!"

During the interim, my mind went to a paper I had developed on "Singlehood" several years ago. After David's group of 8, I met with two other small groups sharing ideas from that paper with them all. They were all very thankful. But I was flabbergasted.

A month later, Daniel, a Ugandan Law student, a participant in those ad hoc meetings at Eastbourne, wrote requesting a copy of my paper on singlehood and permission to make copies for circulation in his school.

What seemed so amazing and so refreshing after the event started off as a wild joke, a nonsensical naïve talk with a total stranger. But maybe it sounded like confident talk—childlike confidence—to David and Becky, but perhaps foolhardy naivety to the spiritists in the story at the beginning of the book.

Quite early in my walk with Jesus, I had learned two important lessons regarding this, though. One, I tend to sit in judgment over God's revealed will in a given situation when I pray, "Lord, teach me your will and way." I vacillate between total and partial obedience, or convenient obedience and expedient disobedience, when what God reveals or directs me to do contradicts what I think it should be. But, two, I submit my will, word, ways and works to God's when I pray, "Lord, use me in doing your will." He knows when, where and how.

The former hangs on to debilitating defiant control. The latter, on the other hand, surrenders control. No wonder it's so freeing and empowering and fruitful!

Seven: *Effective carriers of the good news, love God, other believers and enemies recklessly (see Mark 12:29-31, John 13:34-35, Matthew 5:43-48)*

God demands that his followers be marked by

- unparalleled love for God (Mark 12:29-31)

- unconditional acceptance and care for all God's people from all cultures, races, tribes and languages (John 13:34-35, Revelation 7:9-12)
- selfless love and prayer for enemies and persecutors (Matthew 5:43-48).

1 Corinthians 13:4-8 splits that love into what love is and what it is not; what it doesn't do and what it does. That love is patient and kind. Therefore it is not proud, rude, self-seeking or easily angered. Consequently, it doesn't envy, boast, keep a record of wrongs, delight in evil or fail. Rather, it always rejoices with the truth, protects, trusts, hopes and perseveres. It is altogether the fruit of the Holy Spirit (Galatians 5:22-24).

John comes along and insists that we authenticate our love for God through loving one another (1 John 4:19-20). Meaning, we walk the talk of love, particularly regarding fellow believers.

Ralph and I served on IVCF local chapter leadership committee once. That year our (self-) righteousness excelled us. We audaciously condemned cold churches and unspiritual pastors; we outlawed worldly Christian weddings; we anathemized unspiritual Christian marriages and families; and so on and so forth. The funny thing was that none of those entities needed our approval or recognition. So, what was the point?

Ralph married soon after we graduated. A year and a half later, Christian gossip circulated that Ralph had separated from his wife and stood poised to engage another Christian lady pending imminent divorce.

After some time of prayer, I looked up Ralph's wife. She confirmed the gossip. "Would you like to talk things over with Ralph, if I arranged it?" I inquired.

"No use! You can't!" she said.

"Ma'am, if you give me your permission, I can get him. Are you willing to talk things over with your husband? Please tell me." I pressed.

"Okay! If you get him to agree, I will." She consented.

"Good!" I thanked her and took off and went to look up Ralph.

When I met him, I listened empathetically to his side of the story. It looked porous.

"Ralph, will you like to talk things over with your wife? I don't see anything oddly serious in all that you've told me. Remember our pronouncements at college? Please, give yourselves a chance," I urged.

"No use, Wilson. It's too late. I am almost engaged to marry another lady." Ralph said emphatically. But he seemed pensive.

I kept quiet and let him think

Then he spoke again. "You know, my wife won't want to talk even if I want to."

"No, Ralph, she's willing to talk. She gave me her word on that." I disclosed.

"You mean, you had talked to my wife?" Ralph inquired.

"Yes!" I said.

"How?" Ralph further inquired.

"I took a trip to her hometown." I answered.

That surprised Ralph; delightfully, I hope?

We met. I prayed. I turned them loose to tell each other what they wished. I wasn't married at the time. And definitely, I wasn't pretending to be a marriage counselor.

A healthy exchange of "you are," "you did," "you said," "you were the one who…" went on and on and on. Finally, after four hours, they ran out of blame-shifting ammunition. Then silence took over. I watched them steal looks at each other, carefully avoiding each other's eyes.

Suddenly, as if cued, they burst into contagious laughter. They laughed and laughed and laughed again. I didn't know what they laughed at but I also laughed. Lung bursting laughter delightfully vacuumed the litter of blame shifting that saturated the air, and nearly choked us. Not only that, it vacuumed the separation and nipped the impending divorce in the bud. Husband and wife reconciled at no charge.

Several years later, I met Joe at a meeting I spoke at in central London. He enthusiastically made my acquaintance. He'd just come from Ghana. In his church a week earlier, Ralph and his wife talked about a ministry they ran for the newly married. They mentioned that instance when God used me to save their marriage. Joe was overjoyed to meet me in person.

Indeed, an open rebuke is better than hidden love or gossip. And wounds from a friend are better than kisses from an enemy or apathetic self-love (Proverbs 27:5-6).

Eight: Effective carriers of the good news are prayerful and they experience instances of mysterious answers to prayer (see Luke 11:1-13, Hebrews 5:7-10, Acts 4:23-31)

Surprising that the apostles saw Jesus raised the dead, calmed storms, outwitted the Pharisees, Scribes and Sadducees with unparalleled wisdom, and so on. But they never asked him to teach them to do any of those. Rather, they asked him to teach them, not how to pray, but to pray. His habit of prayer touched them deeply. They desired to be like him (Luke 11:1-13).

No wonder like him (Hebrews 5:7-10), they prayed in anticipation for Pentecost. From Pentecost they established communities for teaching God's word, fellowship and prayer (Acts 2-3). In the face of bitter persecutions, they prayed (Acts 4:23-31). They prayed and appointed deacons (Acts 6:1-15). Stephen—the first martyr—and Philip—the "apostle" to Samaritans, the Ethiopian eunuch, Azotus and Caesarea—were two of them.

For God to be the sender of the sent-out, Jesus had taught his apostles to pray to God about it (Matthew 9:35-10:8). He guarantees answered prayers to those he chooses and sends (John 15:16).

Accordingly, they would see self-reproductive transformational conversions. In that way, they glorify God and show that they are indeed Christ's disciples (John 15:8). People God sends, including Christ and like him, pray hard. They see tremendous answers to their prayers. And their fruits last self-evidently.

One afternoon on Fuller Seminary campus, Harry, a six-feet four colleague tore me from a warm conversation with six others. We isolated ourselves to talk.

I soon learned that Harry and his parents moved to the USA from Europe when he was ten in search for better medical treatment for a sickness he had. But for the past twenty years nothing had worked. He had been to a few healing churches. But they too hadn't helped. He worked with Campus Crusade briefly, but stopped because of his ill health. He came to Seminary instead. Campus gossip directed him to "Go talk to Wilson. Perhaps, he could help you!"

"Me! Help! Don't believe everything you hear." I disclaimed.

"Don't say that!" Harry said sadly.

Harry had lost much of his hair. His body retained impressions of touch like a ball of peanut butter. He needed a pillow to sit on and another for a backrest. My heart ached for him as I watched and listened to him.

Then I asked, "Can we fast and pray to ask God to reveal to us what this is all about?"

"Wilson, I am too weak to fast!" he pleaded.

"Okay, Harry, I will fast and pray for seven days. Let's see what God says." I promised.

On the 7th day, while praying at dawn, I had an impression of a jawbone on my mind. I wondered, Did it have anything to do with Harry's life-long sickness? Anyhow, when Harry and I met on campus to pray, I shared that with him. "Harry, does the jawbone remind you of anything?" I asked.

"Nope!" he said.

"Yup! That's what I thought. False prophet!" I responded, feeling somewhat disappointed.

However, we went on to pray together. I prayed that God would remind Harry about it if the jawbone had anything to do with his sickness. Harry followed. Right in the middle of a second or third sentence into his prayer, he stopped.

I stole a look. He wore a telling smile on his face with his eyes still closed. I ached to know what it meant. Then Harry disclosed.

"Wilson, now I remember. I watched a horror movie when I was five. In the movie, a mean looking guy hit people on the head with a jawbone. There was a boy about my age. When this guy hit him on the head, I felt the pain on my head. I remember vividly. That was when my sickness began. Now I know it."

"Wow! Twenty-five years! And God revealed it! What a God!" I exclaimed.

Fortunately, neither of us was overly concerned about understanding what all this meant. We focuscd on Harry's total recovery. But frankly, neither of us knew how and what to do next. Fasting and praying brought us this far, why not fast and pray more? Who knows, God might amaze us yet!

I fasted and prayed for three extra weeks. I asked God to free Harry from whatever it was and heal him totally. On the twenty-first day, the burden I had for Harry's ill health lifted. I tried hard to agonize and pray for him. But the agony wasn't there anymore. Does it mean Harry is delivered and healed? We shall see.

We met at our usual spot to pray. I thanked God for delivering Harry. Harry asked God to let him feel delivered and healed, strong and healthy.

Two weeks later, I felt two strong arms embracing me from behind as I chatted with two friends on the lawns. I wriggled to look. And there was Harry, all smiles and radiant!

"Oh Wilson!" He called, almost screaming. "For the first time in my life, I am enjoying my health. My doctors have confirmed it. Thank you, thank you!" he hugged tight. He almost crashed my rib cage!

He graduated that year. A year later, he sent me a wedding invitation card. The front cover carried a picture of him and his fiancée. His hair had started growing back. It looked like he wore a wig.

"Oops! But we didn't pray about that!" I jested in a telephone conversation with Harry while staring at the card in utter amazement.

Another story! Robert, a medical doctor, sat me down at the end of two weeks into a three-week missionary training program with Mission Training International, Colorado Springs, Colorado.

"As you know, I am going to Pakistan as a medical missionary. But I am worried that I am going out with no experience of successfully leading someone to faith in Jesus Christ. Your stories of conversion make it look so simple and easy. But I don't know." He paused. His face reddened. Then he continued. "Do you know what? I want to have one experience of conversion, at least one, before I go." He had a month to be gone.

"Are you serious about that?" I asked.

"Yes, of course I am!" Robert said declaratively.

"Let's pray that you do." I consoled and committed to pray especially for him that weekend. He walked me to the car.

All night Friday, I prayed for Robert. Saturday and Sunday, I touched the topic in my morning devotions.

Back to the training grounds at Pinecrest lodge Monday morning, Robert met my colleagues and me at the front door. He was all-smiles.

"Wilson!" he called out. "It happened! I led someone to Christ on Friday night right here at the lodge!" Robert reported ecstatically.

"You're kidding! Tell me about it" I said.

Close to midnight on Friday, Robert sat alone in the lounge catching up on the newspapers. In walked a husband and wife looking for one night bed-n-breakfast lodging. Somehow or other, after checking in, husband returned to the lounge. He and Robert chitchatted for a while. But soon, they slipped into heart issues.

By two in the morning, Robert had led him to faith in Christ. Eight hours later, the man and his wife checked out. And they were gone. "Amazing! Isn't it?" Robert exclaimed.

"Yes, indeed, Robert! This is amazing!" I agreed.

11

Illustrative personal examples (B)

Nine: Effective carriers of the good news suffer intense persecution (see Matthew 5:10-12, Mark 10:28-31, 2 Timothy 3:12, 1 Peter 4:14)

From Jesus' perspectives, persecution is a mark of discipleship (Mark 10:28-31). His own persecutions at the hands of the Pharisees speak volumes. And he taught that persecution distinguished true prophets from the false, as it does genuine disciples from the fake (Luke 6:22-23, 26).

Through experience, Paul added that anyone who desires to live a godly life consistently would be persecuted (2 Timothy 3:12). Then Peter explained. It all has to do with the presence and activity of the Holy Spirit in and through a person (1 Peter 4:14).

That reality forces shoddy and shabby worship and service of God into the open, demanding accountability, repentance and redirection. But often, open hostility results.

This hostility is fiercest where the shoddy and shabby form part of the "wolves" that keep people from knowing, worshipping and relating personally to God. But consistently, Jesus' modeled response to persecution focused on being powerless, wise and harmless as sheep, snakes and doves respectively (Matthew 10:16, cf. 20:28, 5:43-48, and Proverbs 3:5-8).

I spent part of my first year as youth worker to schools at an out station holding fort for a colleague, waiting for a delayed secondment from government employment. I thought I had enough orientation to things with the outgoing schools' youth worker a month to two earlier. So when I assumed office, I prayerfully planned and carried out weekend orientations for school chapters. What we covered looked like this,

- knowing Jesus personally
- growing in him consistently and
- witnessing about him effectively.

One weekend, I scheduled orientation for a chapter in a nearby boarding "junior" college. One hour to my departure, a high school teacher dropped in to the office. He was board member of my employer. For one and a half hours, he tried to talk me out of my impending trip.

"As a field staff," he began. "You waste precious time and resources at a nearby college with relatively older students. I spoke there recently. They're doing just fine. Devote your time to younger students in high schools in remote places. That's why you are here. Don't forget that." He scolded.

Definitely, he'd crossed boundaries. He wasn't my supervisor. Both he and I knew that. Therefore what was he doing, meddling in my work schedule and at that crucial time?

However, his lectures greatly upset me. More than that, they left me thinking and feeling God had abandoned me. My heart went from featherweight to lead-weight momentarily. I came close to canceling the trip altogether. But for some mysterious reason, I didn't.

I lost the first meeting and one hour of the second on Friday night as a direct result of all that. But the students were extremely good.

They sang and waited. I thanked them and apologized for being late, without going into details. In terribly low key, lead-weight heart fashion, I introduced what we would be covering that weekend. I asked leading questions about how other students perceived them on campus and why? Then we closed.

Saturday morning started with a prayer meeting. I talked briefly on intercession. We started to pray. To my surprise, the prayers centered on confession and repentance instead. The students sobbed, wept and cried. It went on well-passed closing time.

When we eventually closed, some of the students disclosed that deep convictions swept through and gripped hearts at the Friday night meeting in light of the questions I asked. Consequently, many of them spent the rest of the night reflecting, repenting and praying. The entire group decided to fast and pray throughout the rest of the weekend program.

Correspondingly, I decided to soft-paddle my intended program but sensitively follow the leading and direction of the Holy Spirit instead. Spontaneous prayer sessions punctuated the meetings on Saturday. By evening time, it was obvious that people wanted to talk about how they felt. I complied.

First, Charity, then Carl, Paul, Ben, Dan, and Rose, followed by Kay, Reuben, Julie, Salome, and lots of others. They confessed hypocrisy, arrogance, sexual immorality, prejudice, legalism, and unbelief. The majority admitted that they didn't know Jesus personally. KK, the leader of the group, disclosed that he had an affair with the group secretary. But both of them decided on Friday night to cut it off. And they did.

That opened the floodgates for more open confession, restitution and unrestrained wailing. They asked God to have mercy on them. It went on until three Sunday morning. We took a four-hour recess to wash down and clean up.

When we resumed, I spoke briefly on the thrice-holy God who wants to relate personally with repentant sinful humanity (Isaiah 66:1-2). I contrasted repentance that surrenders self-rule and commits to the rule of God, with remorse for "gross" acts of the flesh. In response, another long session of prayers of painful, thorough and open surrender to Christ took over.

Officially, my program ended Sunday afternoon. But demands for individual and group counseling dictated otherwise. The chapter leaders negotiated with the school chaplain and got me to preach at the school's Sunday evening worship service. Many more students received Christ as their Savior and Lord. Counseling sessions went on until Monday morning.

Students wanted to skip classes in favor of the counseling sessions. But I said, "No! We must respect school rules." I suggested that we used between and after class, lunch and supper hours for counseling sessions. As it turned out, many skipped lunch and supper. So we used those times as well for group and individual counseling sessions.

Apparent students' hunger and thirst for God and God's word, demanded that I stayed Monday night, all day Tuesday, Wednesday, Thursday and Friday, and the rest of the weekend. We used every available students' free time for counseling sessions. And we needed more.

Unknown to me, spontaneous outreach groups formed. Some of them went to the homes of teachers on campus. They sang and shared their newfound joy and peace in Jesus Christ. Others went to homes bordering the campus and did the same. Conversions happened. The chaplain let me preach that Sunday as well.

Finally, at midnight that Sunday, the students let me go on promise that I would come everyday that week to run 2-hour counseling sessions.

Three weeks later, a delegation came from the school. "We are in deep trouble!" Carl exclaimed.

"What's the trouble?" I inquired.

"One of our teachers has mounted massive persecution against us. He's sworn that he'd knock Jesus out of our hearts. And he's forcefully doing everything to achieve his goal," Charity reported.

"Tell me some of the things he's doing and their effects on new believers." I asked.

KK, passionately recounted, "This teacher is a pastor's kid himself. I just don't know what's taken hold of him. To date, he has lured two girls, new believers, into his apartment and raped them. He threatened to kill them if they told anyone about it. He also threatened to kill you if he saw you on the campus again. Some of the spies he's lined up for you confided.

"Last Saturday night, he organized an orgy on the campus. He demanded that every female student attended. Those who didn't, he has charged with breaking school rules. Accordingly, he ordered them to relocate a dunghill. He's very influential in the school. What shall we do?" KK broke down and cried like a baby. The rest of the delegation joined him. And they all wailed, "Lord, help us! Lord, help us!"

I grieved as well. The whole thing irritated me. It almost made me angry. But quickly I realized that my anger wouldn't help the students much. They needed strengthening. I needed to be strong. Then I could strengthen them.

So when they calmed down, I put the whole thing in perspective for them, using the related biblical passages on persecution. I offered to go with them to the campus and do the same for the others.

"Over our dead bodies! You aren't coming there!" They vehemently protested and threatened.

For a moment, I felt trapped, not knowing what to do tangibly to help. In a flash, I saw that there was an open option I could take, the most powerful of all. Pray! Of course! I snatched it. I promised them I would fast and pray for them and the situation. Any of them who wanted to, could join me. "And let's see what God would do!" I consoled, hardly!

A month later, another delegation came reporting this. "Our chief persecutor has accepted an invitation to direct a government crop development project 70 miles away. He starts work there in two weeks." The delegation gleefully reported.

Barely three weeks after he started work at his new station, he charred in gas flames in his kitchen. This was how. He used kerosene lanterns while his house was being wired for electricity. The night he died, he had just taken delivery of a gas cylinder out on his front yard.

He took it into the kitchen and was about to hook it up, not knowing that it leaked at the neck. He held the open flame lantern closer to be able to see. Then, boom, the marriage proved fatal.

We cannot say for sure that this was a repeat of Acts 12, particularly verse 23, which recorded that worms ate Herod to death. But verse 24 literally happened in that school following that incident. God's word continued to increase and spread for several years.

Ten: Effective carriers of the good news experience instances of mysterious rescue from pre-mature death (see Hebrews 5:7-10, Luke 4:14-30, Acts 12:1-17)

Hebrews 5:7-10, a passage cited earlier, says

> *While Jesus was here on earth, he offered prayers and pleadings, with a loud cry and tears, to the one who could deliver him out of death. And God heard his prayers because of his reverence for God. So even though Jesus was God's Son, he learned obedience from the things he suffered.*

We know that God didn't free Jesus from the death related to the atonement (Matthew 26:38-57). But certainly, he freed him from several premature deaths, sometimes mysteriously. God needed to, so that Jesus could finish his work and die appropriately and at the appropriate time and place.

Nazareth staged one of the first instances when God saved Jesus mysteriously from premature death. Jesus had just read out in the synagogue his job description as Isaiah predicted it (Luke 4:16-21, cf. Isaiah 61:1-2).

The townspeople didn't believe him. Furious, they roughly pushed him to the brow of the hill on which their town stood. They readied to toss him down the cliff headlong. But he turned and walked right through the crowd and went on his way (Luke 4:28-30, see other instances in John 7:30, 8:59, 10:39). What paralyzed the angry mob all of a sudden, if it was not God?

Similarly, in response to earnest prayers by the church, God sent an angel to rescue Peter from prison (Acts 12:1-11). At the time, Peter was under custody of four sets of four guards. In each shift that guarded him, two guards had him chained to them, and two guarded locked prison gates. Again what happened to the guards? What numbed their sense of touch, stopped their ears, and blinded them to it all?

Back in the Old Testament, God mysteriously rescued Shadrach, Meshach and Abednego from hungry flames of a fiery furnace (Daniel 3:13-30), and Daniel from famished lions in a lions' den (Daniel 6). Over all those rescues were rare. But whenever God performed them, they saved the rescued from premature death. And often, their occurrence strengthened the faith of many and caused others to believe in God.

A revival broke out and lasted four years in a girls' boarding school I visited frequently while I worked as a Set Designer for Ghana Television. The phenomenon attracted attention from all sorts of people, the seekers, skeptics, supporters, and so on. Irrespective of motive, all who came sat in the meetings with us.

However, a group of ten guys visited one time and behaved differently. They paraded the verandas during the meeting. And when we closed, they barricaded the iron gate, the only official entrance to and out of the school, in a sentry.

As I got ready to leave, the student leaders pulled me aside and disclosed. "You see those guys" pointing at them, Lucy the spokesperson said. "They are here to stab you to death. They are former boyfriends of some of the girls who got converted during the revival. They are madly mad at you because they take it that you were the one who asked their girlfriends to drop them.

"Now, listen to us. A male teacher on campus has agreed to house you overnight. Come with us. We'll take you to him."

I thought! And I prayed silently. And I felt I should decline the offer. So I said, "Thanks a lot. But I must go home!"

"Why?" "Do you want to die?" "Those guys are mean." "We saw them brandish the daggers." "Please, stay!" They pleaded in popcorn popping fashion. And they started to weep.

Their weeping touched me deeply. Momentarily, it almost confused me. But I knew I must go. I said so again. As I wriggled out of the grip of their love, the tune to a favorite hymn came to mind.

> *My Jesus I love Thee, I know Thou art mine*
> *For Thee all the follies of sin I resign.*
> *My gracious Redeemer, my Savior art Thou;*
> *If ever I loved Thee, my Jesus 'tis now.*

I sang it audibly as I walked toward the gate and right past my intended assassins in broad daylight without a stir from them. I waited by the street, 20 feet from the gate, visible and still singing audibly, and picked up a taxi 15 minutes later. I was gone, safe and secure. How do you explain that, if not in terms of God?

In the story at the beginning of the book, I was the one who invited legendary spiritists to an open contest of sudden death. In this other instance, I simply bumped into a death plot engineered by embittered wounded lovers seeking revenge. But in each case, God mysteriously protected and rescued me from premature death.

Both cases strengthened the faith of believers, including my own, and caused numerous others to believe in God. Yes!

Eleven: Effective carriers of the good news encounter demons and demons recognize them (see Mark 1:21-28, Acts 16:17, 19:11-20)

Unlike people, Satan and demons quickly recognize Jesus as the Son of God, and as their conqueror and destroyer respectively (Genesis 3:15). That was why Satan met Jesus face to face and tried to get him to defect from God and God's purpose (Luke 4:7-13). When Jesus refused, Satan tried pushing the deal through Peter. But that also failed (Matthew 16:13-23). Eventually, Satan entered Judas just before he betrayed Jesus to the Sanhedrin (Luke 22:3-6).

Demons for their part, disclosed their recognition of Jesus as the Son of God and their destroyer through self-appointed proclamation of the Messiah (Mark 1:21-28, 5:9-15). But each time, Jesus ordered them to shut up. And they did (Mark 5:7-8), before he exorcised them (Mark 1:32-34).

Satan and demons would always wriggle to get out of the grip of the grandeur of Jesus Christ's presence. Therefore, whenever and wherever, through whomever and whatever Christ's presence shines, Satan and demons cannot help but betray discomfort in one way or another (Matthew 8:29).

Not surprisingly, a demon in a slave girl, publicized self-appointed that Paul and his teammates were servants of the Most High

God. They had come to Philippi "to tell you how to be saved" (Acts 16:16-17).

On the contrary, a demon defied the seven sons of high priest Sceva when they presumed to exorcise it. Resisting them, it said, "I know Jesus, and I know Paul. But who are you?" At that, the demonized person leaped on them and attacked them with such violence that they fled from the house, naked and badly injured (Acts 19:13-16). Next morning, the incident made front-page news in the local newspapers (verse 17).

Once upon a time, my usual dawn devotion took over, extended and could have continued well past 10 were it not for a knock on the door. I answered the door. And there was Tim, the principal of an engineering school attached to Ghana Television.

Instead of the usual exchange of greetings, he ordered. "Quick, quick! Dress up. We're in trouble. Come with me quickly. Elsie slapped Jones and left the rest of us, six in number, totally powerless to continue exorcising her. Hurry, hurry, we must be going, now!" Tim sounded and seemed desperate.

Both Elsie and Jones belonged to our workplace lunch hour Bible study group. For all I knew, both believed and loved Jesus. Jones pastored a charismatic church. And Elsie belonged to a charismatic church. What might this mean? What hope was there for me if Elsie, or the demon oppressing her, slapped Jones and pinned six godly men to the wall? Too many perplexing thoughts raced through my mind like free traffic on an unpatrolled freeway.

In much trepidation, I jumped in the car with Tim. Silence escorted and ushered us into a tense, terrifying and intimidating situation. Elsie stood restless in the center of a large empty room in a house. Her helpers stood petrified in a loose circle along the four walls. Tim and I joined the circle.

Elsie's eyes flashed, rolled and scanned. Rhythmically, she panned the room from left to right and right to left, then clockwise and counterclockwise. But each time she did, she stopped short of me on either side. Was that a clue? I thought vaguely. Let's wait and see.

Suddenly, deep compassion for Elsie gripped me. Tears ran down my cheeks shamefully. What is this? I fruitlessly protested inside me. A moment later, Elsie started to weep as well. I took that as a cry for help.

Quite uncertain of what I was doing, I drew near her. I shied away from laying my hands on her. But I prayed, asking Christ to do for her what he had said in John 8:36. "If the Son makes you free, you will be free indeed." And he did. Elsie prayed, describing Jesus as Christ and calling him her personal Savior and Lord (1 John 4:1-3, 5:1).

Similarly and dissimilarly, another incidence occurred two years later 800 miles away at a youth camp. Some camp officers gathered to exorcise a demonized camper. As they prayed, the demon cried out, "Stop praying Wilson Awasu's type of prayers!" I wasn't at the camp. Neither did the victim and I know each other. But apparently, the victimizing demon knew something about me. I got the story from one of the exorcists some time later.

1985, while conducting field research into folk religion in Ghana, Togo and Benin, I bumped into a legendary spiritist through referral. He had spent 15 straight years acquiring spiritual power and medicine, and had practiced spiritism for the past 75 years. Though he was old and blind, he looked strong. His white-haired hairy legs, arms and hands, and white-haired bushy hair, eyebrows and lashes made him look like he was caught in a blizzard without snow gear. I went to see him with someone he had exorcised six months earlier.

Right after we exchanged greetings, before I introduced myself to him, he said, "I am going to a meeting right away. Come back to see me in two hours."

A blind old man, going to a meeting, where? I thought, thinking I could walk him there and use the walking time advantageously. So I asked, "Where's your meeting? I could walk you there!"

"Thanks! But that wouldn't be necessary. My meeting is midair. All I have to do is lie down in my bed and I'll be gone." He said.

Hmm! That was something I'd never heard before or thought possible. He must be kidding, I concluded. Skeptically, I complied.

Two hours later, my referral and I reentered. The aged spiritist called me by my name and said. "So you are a student in the United States. You're returning in a week. You must be hard pressed with time. How can I help you?"

Exactly a week from then, I was scheduled to return to school in Pasadena, California. Needless to say I was dumfounded momentarily. I managed to ask, "How did you know that?"

"Ha! I told you I was going to a meeting midair?" He said and paused for a response.

"Yes!" I said.

"Well, I learned about you there. I needed to know whom I am talking to. You see that?" He disclosed.

I didn't see that, but I said, "Okay, okay!"

Honestly, I would have been intimidated if, instead of recalling relevant Scripture, my imagination took the better of me. But in recalling Scripture, I realized with renewed confidence in God that it had nothing to do with me. It all had to do with Christ and the grandeur of his gripping presence (Mark 1:23-24, Acts 16:16-17).

We never stop learning, do we?

Twelve: Effective carriers of the good news have experiences and skills but they do not box up God in them; rather, they leave God free to be God, to work in fresh and new ways as he deems fit (see

Mark 13:11, Acts 4:1-31, Philippians 3:1-21, 2 Corinthians 4:7, 2 Corinthians 10:18).

Jesus more than anyone else, could settle for a one-size-fits-all methodology and he would be right and effective. After all, before his incarnation, he was God's creative word. In the creation, God didn't repeat any command for creating existence out of non-existence. One command sufficed in each case (Genesis 1-2, John 1:1-3, Colossians 1:15-20).

When a military officer believed and confessed that, Jesus highly commended him (Matthew 8:5-13). The officer did not have the privilege of seeing Jesus

- exorcise demons and heal the sick
- calm the storms and raise the dead
- forgive sins and convert people

with a single command. That was the remarkable thing about the military officer's faith.

But Jesus didn't stereotype methodology in healing, teaching, or converting people. Rather, he flexed methods. For example, he healed people based on their own faith, the faith of others, or purely out of compassion for them.

He exorcised Mary Magdalene, a social outcast, to convert her (Mark 16:9). He dined with another social outcast, Zacchaeus, to convert him (Luke 19:1-10). He unconditionally accepted and freely conversed with yet another social outcast, the Samaritan woman, to covert her (John 4:1-42). Then he reasoned with Nicodemus, a seasoned elite theologian, to convert him (John 3:1-21). And characteristically, Jesus more than anyone else taught through many varied simple stories in everyday life—the parables. Matthew 13 is typical.

Jesus stood poised, to use any and every situation to impart life transforming glimpses of the incomprehensible God. How audacious to reduce that God to fruitless quick-fix formulas! As we know, Paul didn't.

Rather, he patterned himself after Jesus to win all sorts of people for Christ. In his own words, he said,

> *Though I am free and belong to no man, I make myself a slave to everyone, to win as many as possible. To the Jews I became like a Jew, to win Jews. To those under the law I became like one under the law (though I myself am not under the law), so as to win those under the law. To those not having the law I became like one not having the law (though I am not free from God's law but am under Christ's law), so as to win those not having the law. To the weak I became weak, to win the weak. I have become all things to all men so that by all possible means I might save some. I do all this for the sake of the gospel, that I may share in its blessings (1 Corinthians 9:19-23).*

Churches in Corinth, Galatia, Ephesus, Philippi, Colosse, Thessalonica, etc., evidenced the fact that he indeed won many varied people for Christ through flexing methodologies.

Paul eagerly showed that Jesus was focus (2 Corinthians 4:5). He did everything possible to let his converts derive and base their faith on the wisdom of God, not the wisdom of people (1 Corinthians 2:3-5). Similarly, he let his life make it plain that the power working in and through him exclusively belonged to God (2 Corinthians 4:7).

Paul healed and taught effectively. He converted many people. But like Christ, he didn't box God up in quick-fix one-size-fits-all formulas, keys, principles, or certain "hallowed" how-tos, etc. No rather, he said,

> *Since God in his mercy has given us this wonderful ministry, we never give up. We reject all shameful and underhanded methods. We do not try to trick anyone, and we*

*do not distort the word of God. We tell the truth before God,
and all who are honest know that (2 Corinthians 4:1-2).*

Paul's life, and his teaching ministry and writing to churches and
individuals show that he placed the emphasis where it belongs—
people who are ready and fit for the Holy Spirit and useful and usable
by him whether they are conscious or unconscious about it (2
Timothy 4:1-2).

On the contrary, a quick-fix propensity can mint out one-size-fits-
all how-to bestseller without prior experience or effectiveness.
Therefore it comes as no surprise when repercussions cancerously
ravage in three directions.

One, the genius of the quick-fix stands condemned for violating
Scripture and teaching others to do so. "Anyone who breaks one of
the least of these commandments" says Jesus, "and teaches others to
do the same will be called least in the kingdom of heaven, but
whoever practices and teaches these commands will be called great in
the kingdom of heaven" (Matthew 5:19).

Two, the "apostle" of the quick-fix solution stands guilty of
shoddy and shabby work. It burns up like wood, hay and stubble
before God. It robs the "apostle" of eternal rewards (1 Corinthians
3:10-15).

Three, the quick-fix solution backfires, making the quick-fixed
worse than the original situation (Matthew 12:43-45, cf. Matthew
23:15).

As I said earlier, I learned through bitter experience, not by quick-
fixing, but by policing for God. By default, I realized that sometimes,
when I fasted and prayed for medically incurable sicknesses, people
got healed. And "people" meant anybody—believers and unbelievers
alike.

Somehow or other, I realized that some healed unbelievers ran off
with the healing. They didn't go on to receive Christ as Savior and

Lord, on my time schedule. I became frugal. No, worse than that! I made becoming a believer in Jesus Christ the condition for fasting and praying for unbelievers to be healed. How noble! How God honoring! How faithful, I thought. Here was God's policeman!

But I was tragically mistaken. God doesn't need people to police his mercy and grace. And certainly, he didn't need me as a policeman. The healings stopped for unbelievers as well as for believers.

I took time off for reflection and self-searching. And there it stood in bold relief. I had become "Jonah." I knew who deserved and didn't deserve God's mercy and grace. How audacious! To nail down the point, the Lord led me to his word of comfort.

"Heal the sick, raise the dead, cure those with leprosy, and cast out demons. Give as freely as you have received!" (Matthew 10:8). Jesus had said this to the apostles when he sent them on a short-term mission trip. And now in the thick of personal evangelism and discipleship, he said it to me to de-robe me of my police uniform and re-robe me with compassion instead. What a God!

Guess what? Back in those robes, the healings started all over again across the board (Luke 17:11-19). No wonder Colossians 3:12-17 says

Therefore, as God's chosen people, holy and dearly loved, clothe yourselves with compassion, kindness, humility, gentleness and patience. Bear with each other and forgive whatever grievances you may have against one another. Forgive as the Lord forgave you. And over all these virtues put on love, which binds them all together in perfect unity.

Let the peace of Christ rule in your hearts, since as members of one body you were called to peace. And be thankful. Let the word of Christ dwell in you richly as you teach and admonish one another with all wisdom, as you sing psalms, hymns and spiritual songs with gratitude in your hearts to God. And whatever you do, whether in word or deed, do it all in the name of the Lord Jesus, giving thanks to God the Father through him.

I learned and I continue to learn to let God be God in everything and everyway all the time.

Thirteen: *Effective carriers of the good news are single-minded in getting the job done, no matter personal cost (see John 4:31-42, 1 Corinthians 9:19-27)*

The record of Jesus' conversion of the Samaritan woman opened with Jesus asking her for a drink of water. But the record didn't say she actually gave him the drink of water. Later, when the disciples returned with lunch and urged him to eat, he declined. They wondered whether he had had lunch from another source.

Quickly, he resolved their dilemma. "My food is to do the will of him who sent me and finish his work" he said (John 4:32, 34). Now, that is extremely remarkable, coming from someone who arrived at Jacob's well exhausted from a long journey (verses 4-8).

But in terms of sacrifices Jesus had made much earlier, skipping lunch compared poorly. Here was God who decided to become human and serve God the Father as his servant. Once incarnated, he imposed stringent self-limitations on himself to obey God submissively and impeccably. To the extent, he was willing to experience being severed from the oneness of God for a horrible moment (Philippians 2:5-11). That was the moment God made him human sinfulness and punished him with the punishment it deserves (2 Corinthians 5:21, cf. Isaiah 53:1-12).

Just before it happened, Jesus had dreaded it so much so that he agonized in prayer and sweated blood. After the event, he cried out, "My God, my God, why have you forsaken me?" (see Matthew 26:36-46, 27:45-46.)

Though he was God, the Scriptures insist that he learned submissive obedience to God the Father through what he suffered

(Hebrews 5:7-10). Triumphing victorious through resurrection and ascension, God gave him unparalleled authority. He enthroned him "far above all rule and authority, power and dominion, and every title that can be given" in this and the next age. God made him the head of the Church, which is his body. Accordingly, Jesus fills everything in everyway (Ephesians 1:21-23).

Through his incarnation and life, ministry and teaching, atonement and resurrection, Jesus modeled that

- we become true disciples of his through dying to ourselves (Luke 14:25-35, cf., Galatians 2:20)
- we bear much fruit through dying to ourselves (John 12:24-26) and
- we triumph through dying to ourselves (Revelation 12:11).

Everything Jesus stood for, modeled and taught regarding knowing, loving and serving God acceptably stands diametrically opposed to do-as-you-please, pampering, laidback, feeble and flabby following of Jesus (Luke 9:57-62).

Again, Paul evidenced a perfect grasp and commitment to that vision and message. He declared

> *We put no stumbling block in anyone's path, so that our ministry would not be discredited. Rather, as servants of God we commend ourselves in every way: in great endurance; in troubles, hardships and distresses; in beatings, imprisonments and riots; in hard work, sleepless nights and hunger; in purity, understanding, patience and kindness; in the Holy Spirit and sincere love; in truthful speech and in the power of God; with weapons of righteousness in the right hand and in the left; through glory and dishonor, bad report and good report; genuine, yet regarded as imposters; known, yet regarded as unknown; dying, and yet we live on; beaten, and yet not killed; sorrowful, yet always rejoicing; poor, yet making many rich; having nothing, yet possessing everything (2 Corinthians 6:3-10).*

The student revival I cited in #9 above constitutes a closest personal experience. Recall the lead-weight heart that resulted from my reaction to the schoolteacher's scolding. A moment earlier I had felt confident that God was with me. A featherweight heart and spirit convinced me about that. All of a sudden, it disappeared. I felt abandoned by God himself. "There goes my seven-day fast to get ready for the Master's use!" I sulked and asked, "Where is God? Why did he allow this to happen?"

But through it all, I learned a very important lesson. Unlike me, of course, God doesn't have to eliminate obstacles before he works. They don't hinder him. In fact, they glorify him when he finds someone who would unjustly endure and faithfully persevere within them.

That weekend, and the following weeks and months, I learned more than I taught. For example, I learned to discern and follow the movement of the Holy Spirit. I learned to ditch puny schedules rather than resist, grieve or quench the Holy Spirit with them (Acts 7:51, Ephesians 4:30, 1 Thessalonians 5:19).

Similarly, see Harry's story cited in #8 above, I learned that Christ's life in us doesn't know holding back. It knows only giving out. It is used to giving out God's life and glory, Christ's peace and joy (John 15:15, 17:4, 8, 14, 22, 24; John 6:33; John 15:11, 17:13). But we have a genius for getting in the way.

This perspective would always frown at seven days, and twenty-one days of fasting. But the perspective of Christ's life, on the other hand, sees it as eternal investment. It gladly commits to seeing Harry liberated and healed, strong and healthy, to the glory of God and thanksgiving to God.

All this reminds and keeps me reminded of the sustained self discipline that our Lord Jesus Christ modeled and Paul exemplified (John 17:19, 1 Corinthians 9:24-27, 2 Timothy 2:20-26, 4:7).

Fourteen: Effective carriers of the good news are single-minded in letting all the glory go to God, however he wants it (see John 5:19, 30, 1 Corinthians 4:1-12, Romans 15:17-19)

Let's assume that it is possible to get the nations to do as we tell them in worshipping God. So they

- believe as we do, e.g., accept that with a few exceptions, God is all-powerful
- worship as we do, e.g., use our songs and worship forms and styles, and
- read and interpret God's word as we do, e.g., insist that God's word is errorless and authoritative until it meets human reason, medical science, psychological reality, etc.

The carving of the nations in our image proves so effective. It robs them of all self-initiative and self-expression. Their knowing, worshipping and serving God totally derives from us and depends on us.

When all that is said and done, two eternal problems confront us. One, we have no kingdom—after death existence in bliss—to reward their faithfulness. Two, we have no way of convincing God to welcome them to his kingdom though we had carved them in our image, not his. Then what?

That is a daunting thought, to say the least. Effective carriers of the good news remind us that anyone can engineer those tragedies. Therefore from the word "go," they show self-evidently that "we do not preach ourselves, but Jesus Christ as LORD (YHWH), and ourselves as your servants for Jesus' sake" (2 Corinthians 4:5).

Paul, who penned those words, had once tried to carve all worshippers of God in the image of the Sanhedrin (Acts 8:1, 9:1-31). Then he learned that "chiseling people in our image," masquerading as discipling them in the name of God, amounts to an audacious attempt to chisel God in our image.

It must have shocked Paul when he heard divine screaming, "Saul, Saul, why are you chiseling me?" He identified the wailing as God's. But to make sure, he asked, "Who are you, Lord?" And the chilling answer came, "I am Jesus, whom you are chiseling. But rise and enter the city. I have work for you to do for me." The chiseled consoled the chiseller, and entered into partnership with him (Acts 9:1-6).

The shock and wonder continued when Ananias visited Paul shortly. But for the gracious encounter with Jesus on the Damascus road, Ananias would have been "marble" in Paul's hands. Now, it wasn't Paul's chiseling hands, but Ananias' comforting and empowering hands. Paul felt them rest on him. And he heard Ananias call him "brother." Yes!

"Brother Saul," Ananias called affectionately. "The Lord Jesus, who appeared to you on the road, has sent me so that you may get your sight back and be filled with the Holy Spirit" (Acts 9:17).

Swiftly, Paul's eyesight returned from a three-day blindness. The Holy Spirit filled him. I could imagine Ananias and Paul hug each other—the-would-have-been chiseled and chiseler momentarily "drunk" with the Holy Spirit and love. In hallowed silence, their spirits communed with each other, "It's all about the grace of God! It's all about the grace of God! Yes, grace, grace, God's grace. That's all there is to it. It's all about God, not us…"

And this is the first lesson that authentic carriers of the good news learn experientially. Before Ananias left home to go look for Paul, Jesus taught him that only God could transform a persecutor of the Church into the Church's greatest apostle (Acts 9:10-16).

But sheer weight of that reality overwhelmed Paul himself. He confessed that he was unworthy to be seen and treated as an apostle of Christ, because he had once persecuted the Church (1 Corinthians 15:8-11).

And it is hard for me to think that unlike Paul, Peter attributed the conversion of the 3,000+ people on the day of Pentecost, or that of Cornelius and his household to himself (Acts 2:1-42, 10:1-48). For Peter often pointed to Jesus as the worthy one to receive all the glory (Acts 3:11-16, 4:5-12, 19-20). The disclaimer had an obvious ring of truth to it, even the Sanhedrin saw it and admitted it. They attributed Peter and John's boldness to Jesus (Acts 4:13).

When the Scriptures attributed many conversions to Barnabas, they did so in terms of the presence and work of the Holy Spirit in and through his life (Acts 11:24). And John the Baptizer had the Holy Spirit from his mother's womb to be able to prepare Israel effectively for Christ's coming (Luke 1:8-17, cf. 3:1-22).

Amazing that even our Lord Jesus Christ had to have the Holy Spirit rest on him before he served God acceptably (Luke 3:21-22, 4:16-21). And repeatedly, he emphasized that he did everything, including submission to dying as a criminal, to glorify God the Father who sent him (John 5:30, 8:28-30, 12:49-50, 14:30-31).

But Jesus is the one God had appointed to mirror the glory of God most perfectly to the world (Isaiah 42:1-9). Conversion occurs at core of being only when people see with their hearts the glory of God as it is manifested in Jesus Christ—i.e., seeing, believing and trusting Jesus as God (2 Corinthians 4:5-6, cf. John 14:8-11). And there's coming a day when every human who had ever lived would confess that Jesus Christ is Lord, to the glory of God the Father (Philippians 2:11).

Not surprising, in the city of God, when time surrenders to eternity, the sun and moon would surrender their respective light to the glory of God and the glory of the Lamb—Jesus Christ our Lord (Revelation 21:22-27).

At least two things happen to anyone who has ever stood, walked or glimpsed God's glory. One, it transforms them inside out visibly (e.g., Moses—Exodus 3:1-4:17; Isaiah—chapter 6:1-13; the Samaritan woman—John 4:1-30, 39-42; Paul—Acts 9:1-31, etc.).

Two, they stay off tampering with God's glory. They fiercely know that God trades his glory with no one and for nothing (Isaiah 42:8, 48:11).

Consequently, they stay out of the way so that

- people hear God and God alone
- people convert at the core of their being
- people have the life of the Christ and relate personally to God (2 Corinthians 4:1-12).

They maintain a contagious vital personal relationship with God (John 17:19).

I hope that the conversion and healing stories I cite in this book self-evidently declare God as the sole doer. That is what I know and am trying to communicate. In view of that conviction, I am convinced that anybody, any believer in Jesus Christ could and should see transformational conversions.

Then it comes naturally for us to say "we have this treasure in jars of clay to show that this all-surpassing power is from God and not from us" (2 Corinthians 4:7).

Fifteen: Effective carriers of the good news are marked by numerous long lasting self-reproductive transformational conversions (see John 4:1-42, Luke 19:1-10, John 14:12-14, 15:8, 16, Acts 2:1-47, 8:4-40, 11:24)

Moments before our Lord Jesus Christ ascended to heaven, his disciples asked him to give them his timeline for freeing Israel from colonial rule to restore Israel to self-rule (Acts 1:6). What a disappointment if that was how they had seen Jesus and what they had expected of him all along! Jesus' response showed that, whatever it was, it didn't disappoint him.

He zeroed in on the empowerment that the coming Holy Spirit would give them. When he comes with power, he would help them straighten out their priorities. Then they would be witnesses of Jesus, beginning from Jerusalem, rippling through Judea and Samaria, and to the farthest corner of the earth (Acts 1:7-8).

I wondered why Jesus left it at that. But as I thought about the whole scenario, several realities came to mind. One, Jesus had etched his life, vision, message and burden, and his manner of commitment, empowerment, protection, tenacity and effectiveness on the hearts, minds and spirits of the 500, 120, 72, but particularly the 12 (Mark 3:14-15, Matthew 10, Luke 10:1-24, cf. Acts 1:12-15, 1 Corinthians 15:6). The etching was too deep for easy corrosion.

Two, at least the 12 and 72 could not quickly forget that they had personally and effectively participated in Jesus' ministry (Matthew 10 and Luke 10:1-24). Three, Jesus knew that it was his Father who gave the disciples to him. In turn, he had given them God's word. They had assimilated it. It had transformed them irreversibly. Nothing could undo that (John 17).

And now, four, he orders them to wait for the coming of the Holy Spirit. He comes to empower them. He would also remind them of all that they had become through seeing, simulating and personalizing in Christ (John 13-16). How could the Holy Spirit fail?

Five, Jesus had prayed, asking the Father to keep and protect them from Satan and the satanic (John 17). How could the Father fail? Six, Jesus had promised that he would be with them always as they evangelize and disciple the world (Matthew 28:16-20). Jesus wasn't tantalizing them.

Seven, Jesus knew that he had met and conquered Satan, and human rebellion and self-love incisively and decisively. He had planted the kingdom of God in people to form the invincible Church in the visible world. And soon he was going to be enthroned invincibly in the invisible world (Matthew 16:13-19, John 17, Ephesians 1:15-23, Colossians 1:15-20, 2 Thessalonians 2:5-7).

In view of that reality, eight, he anticipates a bride made up of many cultures, races, tribes and languages (Revelation 7:9-12).

From those perspectives, nine, he awaits the consummation of all things in his crowning and cohabiting with his people, and everlasting rule of all things—a new world order—in peace, righteousness and justice (Revelation 21-22).

Meaning Jesus had left behind, not a latest strategy, program, or a set of techniques or skills, but

- his conquest of Satan and all anti-God forces, and had opened the door to forgiveness and reconciliation to having the life of Christ and relating personally to God
- people stamped mentally, spiritually and emotionally with the transmittable life of Christ, and
- God's word, name and glory that transform, guide, separate and protect people who have and transmit the life of Christ reproducibly.

Anticipatorily, he had left behind

- the Holy Spirit who perfectly represents Christ to empower, teach, guide and use people who have the life of Christ to disciple others similarly, and
- the invincible body of Christ consisting of "little-Christs" in perfect agreement with the Holy Spirit and God's eternal plan to resist anti-God forces and ways through extending the victory and life of Christ in and through the transformed.

The day of Pentecost (Acts 2) launched that combination and thrust. And within 30 years, the 12, 72, 120 and 500 had indeed become churches in most cities of the world. The impact rocked the foundations of the pagan world of the day.

Effective carriers of the good news in any generation come from the same fabric as the 12, 72, 120 and 500 and Pentecost. Inevitably, but not automatically, transformational conversions mark successors as they did predecessors. Leading people to meet Christ and convert at core of being and discipling them self-reproductively constitute transmitted family resemblance (cf. Acts 13:1-3, 18:7-11, 18, 19:8-20, 20:31).

Memories I treasure the most include times that my mom and I had strengthened each other's faith, sometimes until two in the morning, whenever I visited her. We compared notes on, say, strengthening and growth through instances and/or acts of mysterious answers to prayer, forgiving unrepentant offenders, backbreaking tolerance, reckless love, etc.

Our closing prayers usually centered on this. I thanked God for the way my mom had modeled Christ for me, and how her godly life had tremendously influenced mine. She always thanked God for the privilege she had to have lived to see me fear God, love his word, and talk about Jesus Christ our Lord so passionately.

Consistently, her parting words to me were, "Remember to fear God always!" I miss those times. But I am happy for her to have gone on to be with Christ.

I recall, I was guest speaker at a pastors' conference in New York City. Sam, whom I had discipled and Peter whom he had discipled spoke there as well. It amazed and thrilled all three of us to be speaking side-by-side each other at the same conference. But it also humbled us with a deep sense of gratitude to God who made it happen.

Sam and I don't ever get tired of sharing stories of conversions, and continued opportunities and expectations we have for more of those stories.

I can sit all day all night listening to Emmanuel's latest stories of conversions, healings, deliverances and reproductive discipleships. But I am amazed that he's more eager to hear my latest insights into

God's word, comfort and challenges of prayer, surprises from God, etc.

"Yesterday," I had discipled Sam and Emmanuel. "Today," we pour into each other's life blessings of things the Holy Spirit continues to do in and through our lives to glorify Christ.

Ben is my nephew. Once, when he was 13, he helped me to dust off a spiky sisal houseplant. To provoke his thinking, I likened our prickly painful experience to the frustration the Spirit of Christ meets in his attempts to keep us pure. Unknown to me, Ben agonized under the resulting conviction for a day and a half. Then he came to ask, "Uncle, how can I be pure consistently in Christ?"

I led him to faith in Jesus Christ. He prayed a most heartfelt prayer surrendering self-rule to God. And he committed to the rule of God in his life. His instant devotion to God's word and understanding and use of it amazed me. In a month, he had memorized many portions of the Scriptures. He had written verses like Psalm 91:14 on the jacket of his Bible: "Because he cleaves to me I will deliver him. I will protect him, because he knows my name."

Two months later, he challenged two powerful spiritists, much older than his grandfather, and led them to Christ. Their conversion rippled into hundreds of conversions among their suppliants and followers.

Betty and I first met on a bus then in her church by default (see chapter 2). I led her and four others through her to Christ. While I discipled them, death took two of her sons, age 5 and 7. She led her surviving son, age 9, to Christ. Today, she's an ordained pastor in the Church of Nazarene. And her son is an evangelist.

I can go on to talk about Mary, a missionary to Gambia; Michael, a quiet witness for Christ in Virgin Islands; Agnes, an insatiable soul-winner in Philadelphia, Pennsylvania; Stacie, a discipler in St Louis, Missouri; Charity, a minister to unwed teenage mothers in Ghana; and

Akos, an avid intercessor and discipler in Scotland, United Kingdom, and numerous others. But that is not the point.

Rather, the point is to show how all this confirms Christ's plan for gathering in kingdom citizens. It's all about Christ's life in people touching and connecting other people directly to Christ to convert them transformationally and transmittably at the core of being. Nurtured in

- modeled vital personal relationship with God
- modeled rounded knowledge of God's word
- modeled Christ-like submissive obedience to God's word
- modeled childlike trust and dependence on God through pristine habit of prayer and fasting
- modeled submission to the empowerment and direction of the Holy Spirit, and
- modeled reckless love toward God, other believers and enemies,

the discipled cannot help reproducing themselves for onward transmission.

That's how God's kingdom in people expands and extends itself until Christ returns.

Recommended reading

Roland Allen, Missionary methods (1962). Grand Rapids: Wm Eerdman's printing company.

Gary Althen, American ways (1988). Yarmouth: Intercultural Press, Inc.

J. Sidlow Baxter, Divine healing of the body (1979). Grand Rapids: Zondervan

Don Bierle, Surprised by faith (1992). Lynwood: Emerald books.

Henry T. Blackaby & Claude V. King, Experiencing God (1994). Nashville: Broadman & Holman Publishers.

Gregory Boyd, Letters from a skeptic (1994). Colorado Springs: Charior victor publishing.

Jerry Bridges, The pursuit of holiness (1996). Colorado Springs: Navpress.

Jerry Bridges, The practice of Godliness (1996). Colorado Springs: Navpress.

Mark Buchanan, Your God is too safe (2001). Sisters: Multnomah Publishers Inc

Robert E. Coleman, The Master's way of personal evangelism (1997). Wheaton: Crossway Books.

Charles Colson and Nancy Pearcey, How now shall we live (1999). Wheaton: Tyndale House Publishers, Inc.

Lawrence J. Crabb Jr., Effective biblical counseling (1979). Grand Rapids: Zondervan Publishing House.

Max de Pree, Leading without power (1997). San Francisco: Jossey-Bass.

John Dekker, Torches of joy (1988). Westchester: Crossway Books

James F. Engel & William A. Dyrness, Changing the mind of missions (1984). Downers Grove: IVP.

Gordon D. Fee, New Testament exegesis (1993). Philadelphia: The Westminster Press.

Michael Griffiths, The example of Jesus (1985). Downers Grove: IVP.

Nicky Gumbel, Questions of life (1997). Eastbourne: Kingsway Publications.

Jan David Hettinga, Follow me (1996). Colorado Springs: Navpress.

Paul Hiebert and Eloise Hiebert Meneses, Incarnational Ministry (1995).Grand Rapids: Baker Books

Paul Hiebert, R. Dan Shaw, Tite Tienou, Understanding Folk Religion (1999). Grand Rapids: Baker Books

Paul G. and Frances Hiebert, Case studies in missions (1987). Grand Rapids: Baker Book House.

Geert Hofstede, Culture and organizations (1997). New York: McGraw-Hill.

Holy Trinity Brompton, Alpha Manual (1995). London: HTB Publications.

Holy Trinity Brompton, Alpha Training Manual (1994). London: HTB Publications.

Michael Kearney, World View (1984). Novato: Chandler & Sharp Publishers.

Jay Kesler, Being holy being human (1988). Minneapolis: Bethany House Publishers.

Sherwood Lingenfelter, Agents of Transfromation (1986). Grand Rapids: Baker Books.

Rebecca Manley Pippert, Out of the saltshaker (1979). Downers Grove: IVP.

Hannah More, Religion of the heart (1993). Orleans: Paraclete Press.

Henri J.M. Nouwen, In the name of Jesus (1989). New York: Crossroad.

John Piper, A Godward life (1997). Sisters: Multnomah Publishers.

Donald C. Posterski, Reinventing evangelism (1989). Downers Grove: IVP

David Prior, Jesus and power (1987). London: Hodder and Stoughton.

Don Richardson, Eternity in their hearts (1984). Ventura: Regal Books.

Don Richardson, Peace child (1981). Ventura: Regal Books

Christian Schwarz, Natural church development (1996). Barcelona: MCE Horeb Viladecavall.

James Spradley, Participant observation (1980). New York: Holt, Rinehart and Winston.

Tom Steffen, Passing the Baton (1995). La Habra: Center for Organizational & Ministry Development.

John R.W. Stott, The message of Ephesians (1979). Leicester: IVP

Joseph Stowell, Following Christ (1996), Grand Rapids: Zondervan Publishing House.

Douglas Stuart, Old Testament exegesis (1984). Philadelphia: The Westminster Press.

Dallas Willard, The Divine Conspiracy (1998). San Francisco: Harper & Row.

John Wimber, Power evangelism (1986). San Francisco: Harper & Row.

Walter Wink, Naming the powers (1984). Philadelphia: Fortress Press Publishers.

Phil Yancey, The Jesus I never knew (1995). Grand Rapids: Zondervan Publishing House.

K.P. Yohannan, Revolution in world missions (1989). Lake Mary: Creation House Strag Communications Company.

About the Author

Wilson Awasu (Ph.D., Fuller Theological Seminary) is a missiologist, researcher and missionary training consultant. He is the author of *Unmasked Conflict*. He and his wife Anna live in Lakeville, Minnesota.

Printed in the United States
6360